# READING THE PRESENT IN THE QUMRAN LIBRARY

## Society of Biblical Literature

Symposium Series

Christopher R. Matthews,
Editor

Number 30

READING THE PRESENT IN THE QUMRAN LIBRARY
The Perception of the Contemporary by
Means of Scriptural Interpretations

# READING THE PRESENT IN THE QUMRAN LIBRARY

The Perception of the Contemporary by Means of Scriptural Interpretations

Edited by

Kristin De Troyer and Armin Lange

with the assistance of Katie M. Goetz and Susan Bond

Society of Biblical Literature
Atlanta

# READING THE PRESENT IN THE QUMRAN LIBRARY

Copyright © 2005 by the Society of Biblical Literature

All rights reserved. No part of this work may be reproduced or transmitted in any form or by any means, electronic or mechanical, including photocopying and recording, or by means of any information storage or retrieval system, except as may be expressly permitted by the 1976 Copyright Act or in writing from the publisher. Requests for permission should be addressed in writing to the Rights and Permissions Office, Society of Biblical Literature, 825 Houston Mill Road, Atlanta, GA 30329 USA.

Library of Congress Cataloging-in-Publication Data

Reading the present in the Qumran library : the perception of the contemporary by means of scriptural interpretations / edited by Kristin De Troyer and Armin Lange.
     p. cm. — (Society of biblical literature symposium series ; no. 30)
Includes bibliographical references.
ISBN-13: 978-1-58983-150-6 (paper binding : alk. paper)
ISBN-10: 1-58983-150-0 (paper binding : alk. paper)
    1. Dead Sea scrolls. 2. Bible. O.T.—Criticism, interpretation, etc., Jewish. 3. Bible. O.T.—Influence. 4. Bible. O.T.—Criticism, interpretation, etc. 5. Contemporary, The. I. De Troyer, Kristin. II. Lange, Armin, 1961– III. Series: Symposium series (Society of Biblical Literature) ; no. 30.
BM487.R35 2005
221.6'09'01—dc22
                                                                                            2005016896

13 12 11 10 09 08 07 06 05    5 4 3 2 1
Printed in the United States of America on acid-free, recycled paper
conforming to ANSI/NISO Z39.48-1992 (R1997) and ISO 9706:1994
standards for paper permanence.

# Contents

Abbreviations .................................................................................. vii

### Introduction

Is It True? Hermeneutical Reading of the Present
   *Christine Helmer* ........................................................................ 3

### Part 1: Dead Sea Scrolls

Pesharim: A Mirror of Self-Understanding
   *Jutta Jokiranta* ........................................................................ 23

Contemporizing Halakic Exegesis in the Dead Sea Scrolls
   *Lawrence H. Schiffman* ............................................................ 35

Jeremiah and the "Diaspora Letters" in Ancient Judaism:
   Epistolary Communication with the Golah as Medium
   for Dealing with the Present
   *Lutz Doering* .......................................................................... 43

Justifying Deviance: The Place of Scripture in Converting to a
   Qumran Self-Understanding
   *George J. Brooke* ..................................................................... 73

### Part 2: Ancient Judaism

"Reading the Present" in the Animal Apocalypse (*1 Enoch* 85–90)
   *Loren T. Stuckenbruck* ............................................................ 91

Why Has Daniel's Prophecy Not Been Fulfilled? The Question of
   Political Peace and Independence in the Additions to Daniel?
   *Ulrike Mittmann-Richert* ....................................................... 103

## Part 3: The Textual Tradition of the Hebrew and Greek Bible

Reading Deuteronomy in the Second Temple Period
*Sidnie White Crawford* .................................................................................127

Building the Altar and Reading the Law: The Journeys of
Joshua 8:30–35
*Kristin De Troyer* .........................................................................................141

## Part 4: Authoritative Literature in Ancient Israel and Judah

Interpreting the Exile: The Experience of the Destruction of the
Temple and Devastation of the Land as Reflected within the
Nonpentateuchal Biblical Abraham Tradition
*Beate Ego* ...................................................................................................165

Reading the Decline of Prophecy
*Armin Lange* ...............................................................................................181

## Conclusions

Linking the Past, the Present, and the Future in the Hebrew
Bible and the Dead Sea Scrolls
*Kristin De Troyer* .........................................................................................195

Bibliography.........................................................................................................203

Contributors .......................................................................................................219

Index of Biblical and Related Literature...........................................................221
    Masoretic Text    221
    Septuagint    226
    Pseudepigrapha    227
    Dead Sea Scrolls    228
    Ancient Jewish and Rabbinic Literature    230
    New Testament    231
    Classical Literature    231

Index of Authors .................................................................................................233

# Abbreviations

| | |
|---|---|
| AB | Anchor Bible |
| AOAT | Alter Orient und Altes Testament |
| ASOR | American Society of Oriental Research |
| BDR | Blass, Friedrich, Albert Debrunner, and Friedrich Rehkopf. *Grammatik des neutestamentlichen Griechisch.* 17th ed. Göttingen: Vandenhoeck & Ruprecht, 1990. |
| BJS | Brown Judaic Studies |
| BKAT | Biblischer Kommentar. Altes Testament |
| BZAW | Beihefte zur Zeitschift für die alttestamentliche Wissenschaft |
| CBQMS | Catholic Biblical Quarterly. Monograph Series |
| CRINT | Compendia Rerum Iudaicarum ad Novum Testamentum |
| *CurBS* | *Currents in Biblical Studies* |
| DJD | Discoveries in the Judaean Desert (of Jordan) |
| *DSD* | *Dead Sea Discoveries* |
| FAT | Forschungen zum Alten Testament |
| FRLANT | Forschungen zur Religion und Literatur des Alten und Neuen Testaments |
| *HAR* | *Hebrew Annual Review* |
| HAT | Handbuch zum Alten Testament |
| *JBL* | *Journal of Biblical Studies* |
| *JJS* | *Journal for Jewish Studies* |
| *JQR* | *Jewish Quarterly Review* |
| JSHRZ | Jüdische Schriften aus hellenistisch-römischer Zeit |
| *JSJ* | *Journal for the Study of Judaism* |
| JSJSup | Journal for the Study of Judaism Supplement Series |
| *JSOT* | *Journal for the Study of the Old Testament* |
| JSOTSup | Journal for the Study of the Old Testament Supplement Series |
| JSPSup | Journal for the Study of the Pseudepigrapha Supplement Series |
| KHC | Kurzer Hand-Commentar zum Alten Testament |
| *NRTh* | *Nouvelle Revue Théologique* |
| NTS | New Testament Studies |
| OBO | Orbis Biblicus et Orientalis |
| *PAAJR* | *Proceedings of the American Academy for Jewish* Research |

| | |
|---|---|
| *RevQ* | *Revue de Qumran* |
| SBLEJL | Society of Biblical Literature Early Judaism and Its Literature |
| SBLMS | Society of Biblical Literature Monograph Series |
| SBLSBS | Society of Biblical Literature Sources for Biblical Studies |
| SCS | Septuagint and Cognate Studies |
| SJLA | Studies in Judaism in Late Antiquity |
| STDJ | Studies on the Texts of the Desert of Judah |
| TBT | Theologische Bibliothek Töpelmann |
| TSAJ | Texte und Studien zum antiken Judentum |
| WMANT | Wissenschaftliche Monographien zum Alten und Neuen Testament |
| WUNT | Wissenschaftliche Untersuchungen zum Neuen Testament |
| *ZAW* | *Zeitschift für die alttestamentliche Wissenschaft* |
| ZBK.AT | Zürcher Bibelkommentare. Alten Testament |

# INTRODUCTION

# Is It True? Hermeneutical Reading of the Present*

*Christine Helmer*

## 1. Introduction

The ascription of truth to a sacred text seems on the surface to be a tautology. Are sacred scriptures not by definition true and hence both authoritative and normative for the faith and morals articulated on this foundational axiom? But questions begin to surface when the truth of scripture is held as the object of scrutiny. The question of scripture's truth in an Enlightenment context is measured according to specific criteria of truth determining all texts, not exempting texts set apart as sacred by a religious tradition. The biblical text according to the Enlightenment paradigm is not to be treated with a special reverence unexamined by reason. Indeed the Bible is to be regarded as any other book might be; it is to be held up to the same type of rational and hermeneutical scrutiny determining the academic engagement with any text.

It was this critical conceptual paradigm that led to the eighteenth and nineteenth-century erosion of one of Protestant Christianity's pillar doctrines. The doctrine of scripture was based on a theory of the personal, verbal, and real inspiration of the Bible and its authors, and on the attributes predicated of the text as such; its function was to guarantee the holiness of scripture—both Old and New Testaments in the Protestant canon—as an infallible source for theological knowledge that functioned as practical knowledge necessary for salvation. Such a doctrine did not fare well against the Enlightenment public inquiry into the features claimed for the Bible. Its truth as asserted was shaken by the storms of historical criticism that required proof and demonstration according to the criteria determined by scholarly consensus. The truth of scripture was contested

---

\* I thank Stephen T. Davis and Armin Lange for feisty conversations on this topic. I am grateful to the Alexander von Humboldt-Stiftung for generously funding my stay in 2004 as a Humboldt Research Fellow at the Eberhard Karls Universität Tübingen. This opportunity facilitated the writing of this paper.

by truths of history and science. Protestant theologians found themselves in increasingly uncomfortable positions. The stand-off position meant inevitable entrenchment against the rising hegemony of the real sciences. The accommodation stance varied by the degree to which scripture could be rendered acceptable to scientific (*wissenschaftlich*) criteria of knowledge. The resulting gap between scripture as privileged by intra-religious criteria and scripture as determined by the public truths of the Enlightenment was one that theology had no choice but to negotiate.

Some lamented the loss of doctrinal innocence, others welcomed the mature opportunity to engage the new sciences. The important question set in the dialogical context of modern public discourse, however, does not inevitably lead down the slippery slope of accommodation. If the Enlightenment paradigm presents theology with inevitable challenges of conceding to modernity, then the converse should also be entertained: how can theology explain the truth of the religious texts deemed significant in the history of a respective religious tradition?[1] Rather than viewing the developments of modernity as a threat to doctrines safeguarding the privileged status of the Bible, the theological guild is challenged to raise the question of why the Bible has continued to exert the power of its truth throughout the life of a religious tradition. The truth question would address the reasons for scripture's enduring power. Rather than hiding behind a checklist of doctrinal technical terms, such as authority and normativity, theology would tease out the rational, doctrinal, and pious ways in which scripture is regarded by faithful adherents as a text to which the truth predicate is applied.

If scripture's truth is to be a starting-point for inquiry, then the conceptual problem can be stated in the following terms. The truth of the Bible has oscillated since the Enlightenment between two claims. One claim is represented by the Enlightenment view captured by Benjamin Jowett in the nineteenth century: scripture is to be interpreted like any other book.[2] The other claim is represented by a reverential paradigm that regards the Bible as the "book of all books" (*Buch der Bücher*), the special instrument used by the Holy Spirit to convey the same spiritual truths to generations of believers. It is the aim of this chapter to show that this latter claim concerning biblical texts as constitutive in a significant way

---

1. This question might also be designed to include the question concerning the cultural impact of the Bible, for example, its constitutive role in Western art, literature, and science. I am restricting the paper's range to solely the way in which theology might consider the truth of scripture in the historical and hermeneutical terms that can be recognized by those who reverentially adhere to its truth.

2. Benjamin Jowett, "On the Interpretation of Scripture," in *Essays and Reviews* (ed. F. Temple et al.; London: Parker & Son, 1860), 377.

for religious faith and morals can be rendered according to various ascriptions of truth; as religious texts, they make certain claims that can be examined by scholarly and public scrutiny. Furthermore, the texts have a certain transhistorical persistence that can be explained by investigating the ways in which they articulate a unique understanding of specific dimensions of life. Sacred scripture has the status of a truth bearer in a maximal sense: it conveys the truth of a God who is faithful to a chosen and beloved people throughout the history of its wandering. As bearing the truth to new generations, the texts hermeneutically situate the truth question. "Is it true?" is related to the question, "Is it true for me and for us?"

This chapter's study of scriptural truth proceeds in three steps, each focusing on a specific arrangement of the two perspectives of scripture highlighted above: the Bible is to be regarded as any other book and the Bible is to be esteemed as the paragon of books. The steps are organized according to different types of truth ascriptions. By focusing on these different ascriptions, I show that the Bible's truth can be determined by both perspectives from a substantive thesis proposed from the "Bible as paragon" perspective. The argument is structured in this way in order to demonstrate the contribution of this perspective to public inquiry, rather than its withdrawal from the judgment of reason. I begin with (1) the ascription to the Bible its historical truth value as the foundational document of particular religious traditions. Because my area of study is the Christian tradition, I will make my argument in terms of the Christian Bible composed of two testaments. Then I turn to (2) the ascription to the Bible, as text, its transparency both to an objective reality "behind" it that constitutes the religious tradition as such, and to subjective construals of that reality from diverse perspectives "in front of" the text. I conclude with (3) the ascription to the Bible its spiritual value that might best be described as the "mystical engagement with the spirit of the text."

## 2. Ascription as Foundational Document

Protestantism at its Reformation origins upheld a particular canon of the biblical text as its critical tool against doctrinal consensus. The ensuing history of Protestantism grows from this ground. Whether in its Lutheran or Calvinist forms, the Protestant spirit highlights the normative function of scripture in theology. Seventeenth and eighteenth-century Protestant Orthodox doctrinal claims and the historical-critical approaches to scripture emerging in the eighteenth century, while critical of each other, showed an equally similar view of scripture. Both esteemed, from different perspectives, the foundational documents of (Protestant) Christianity as constitutive in a decisive way for the history and theology of the ensuing religious trajectory. In this section I answer the question, "Is it true?" by studying the ascription of foundational power to scripture from both a reverential and a critical position.

Protestant Orthodox theological and historical-critical approaches differ on the surface regarding their respective views of scripture. Orthodox dogmatic treatises articulated theologies of scripture that ascribed certain properties to the biblical text. The text, or, more precisely, the canon, had specific attributes that constituted its infallible capacity to guide believers to salvation.[3] The Bible as the book of all books was venerated because of its soteriological infallibility and theological normativity. Historical approaches to the Bible, as Hans Frei argued in *The Eclipse of Biblical Narrative*, established historical referentiality as the text's truth, thereby eroding the conceptual force of scripture to absorb phenomena into its frame of reference.[4] The texts were to be regarded as documents of historical events and, as such, could be correlated with those historical events unearthed by historical and archaeological research. Historical study acquired the capacity to determine the referential truth or falsity of the text.

The difference between a theological and a historical understanding of the canon betrays an uncomfortable antithesis. Although the object seems to be the same, the two approaches to it are wildly disparate. What does the Jerusalem of soteriological necessity have to do with the Athens of empirical verifiability? And in this battle, history wins: according to scientific consensus, history is given the power to trump theological ascriptions of truth. It is this losing battle that Friedrich Schleiermacher laments in a letter to his friend Friedrich Lücke. Schleiermacher reveals his fear that the truth of scripture might be discredited by developments in historical and natural sciences.[5] If natural science proves that creation did not take place over six days and if the canon is shown to be the result of historical authorship rather than divine inspiration, then the consensus of reasoned inquiry trumps the alleged historical and scientific assertions of the Bible. Once its scientific trustworthiness is undermined, its theological content

---

3. For the Protestant Orthodox doctrine of Scripture, see Heinrich Schmid, ed., *Doctrinal Theology of the Evangelical Lutheran Church* (trans. C. A. Hay and H. E. Jacobs; 3rd ed.; Minneapolis: Augsburg, 1961), 38–91 (= §§6–12) and Heinrich Heppe, *Reformed Dogmatics: Set Out and Illustrated from the Sources* (rev. ed.; ed. Ernst Bizer; trans. G. T. Thomson; London: Allen & Unwin, 1950; repr., Grand Rapids: Baker, 1978), loci II–III. Lutheran Orthodoxy numbers four attributes that account for why the Bible is the "only source of truth" and "as the Word of God, the only means by which we can attain unto faith" (Heppe, *Reformed Dogmatics*, §7 [50]): authority, perfection (or sufficiency), perspicuity, and efficacy (§§7–11 [50–80]).

4. Hans W. Frei, *The Eclipse of Biblical Narrative: A Study in Eighteenth and Nineteenth Century Hermeneutics* (New Haven: Yale University Press, 1974).

5. Friedrich D. E. Schleiermacher, "The Second Letter," in *On The Glaubenslehre: Two Letters to Dr. Lücke* (trans. J. Duke and F. Fiorenza; American Academy of Religion Texts and Translations Series 3; Atlanta: Scholars Press, 1981), 60–62, 65–68.

is also rendered suspect. The Enlightenment privileging of claims established by scientific consensus falsifies the text's claims. The burden is left to theology to accommodate its understanding of biblical claims to acceptable methods of inquiry or to risk antiquation in a rational age. Theology once the queen of the sciences now flees the very scientific discussion she bore.

This view represents, however, one early Enlightenment model of the relation between theology and history, formulated by Lessing and premised on the incommensurability between historical truths of fact and eternal truths of reason. Lessing presupposed the conceptual antithesis between time and eternity as well as the epistemological dualism of empirical and speculative reason.[6] If an epistemological continuum is posited between the two sources of knowledge, however, and if a metaphysical paradigm is proposed that unites history and eternity in an essential way, then the gulf is not only bridged, but rendered moot. This monistic framing of the conceptualizing of epistemological and metaphysical issues in biblical interpretation characterizes the post-Kantian search for system. Its novel solution is proposed by the theologian and philosopher, Friedrich Schleiermacher.

Schleiermacher advocates a theological position that is radically historical in its understanding of its subject matter. Theology studies religion, and religion is an empirical, historical phenomenon.[7] Although it is a phenomenon distinct from other human activities, such as political organization and academic study, religion represents a necessary element of what it is to be human. The same historicity characterizing human existence constitutes religion, moreover. Religion is essentially historical, suspended between an original and identifiable *terminus a quo* and an eschatological *terminus ad quem*. According to Schleiermacher's theory of history, the origin of a historical sequence is of decisive significance to what ensues; history's final cause is subordinate to its efficient cause. The determinative "inner" unity at the origin is simultaneously set with a crucial "outer" event.[8] The appearance of such an original point cannot be explained from the preceding; its novelty is identified with the new appearance of an inner unifying perspective and an outer historical event. This new appearance is determined by a unique set of properties that sets the historical and conceptual parameters for

---

6. The "accidental truths of history can never become the proof of necessary truths of reason" (Gotthold Ephraim Lessing, "On the Proof of the Spirit and of Power," in *Lessing's Theological Writings* [ed. H. Chadwick; Library of Modern Religious Thought; Stanford, Calif.: Stanford University Press, 1967], 53).

7. See the famous "introduction" to Schleiermacher's dogmatic *magnum opus* in Friedrich D. E. Schleiermacher, *The Christian Faith (1830/31)* (ed. H. M. Mackintosh and J. S. Stewart; trans. D. M. Baillie et al.; Edinburgh: T&T Clark, 1999), §§1–31 (1–128).

8. Schleiermacher, *Christian Faith*, §10 (44–52).

the ensuing series.⁹ The origin of a historical trajectory is constitutive for what follows in a way that any other moment continuous with it does not. Hence the questions regarding the founder of a movement, the foundational religious idea and how it took shape, and the early context of its reception become key historiographical questions.

This historical claim concerning religion implies a specific understanding of the religion's foundational texts. The canon—in Schleiermacher's case, the Christian canon—is privileged as the literary fixing of ideas generated by a foundational experience.¹⁰ The canon is seen as a historical (in a nontechnical sense) document that fixes, in literary form, an experience that is foundational to the respective religion it funds. The text thus captures the identity between the religion's original outer moment and its inner unity. The New Testament articulates the experience of Jesus Christ as a unique person from many authorial perspectives, yet those perspectives agree as to the transformative effect that Christ has on individual persons.¹¹ The Old Testament as contained within the Christian Bible identifies Yhwh's covenant as the object of Israel's witness, thereby establishing the New Testament witness to Christ as one of its possible historical and theological outcomes.¹² The identifiable appearance of Jesus on the religious stage and the transformative effect of his person that continues to shape Christian identity through history are the religion's distinct outer and inner traits textually fixed in historical proximity to their historical source. The Christian canonical criterion of apostolicity can be understood both to make the historical point that the foundational experience of the Christian religion is tied to the real presence of Christ and to make the theological point that the experience of redemption is attributed solely to this one source. The canon

---

9. For a detailed exposition of Schleiermacher's theory of history in relation to the historical origin of a religion, see Christine Helmer, "Transhistorical Unity of the New Testament Canon from Philosophical, Exegetical, and Systematic-Theological Perspectives," in *One Scripture or Many? Canon from Biblical, Theological, and Philosophical Perspectives* (ed. C. Helmer and C. Landmesser; Oxford: Oxford University Press, 2004), 13–50.

10. Friedrich Schleiermacher, *Brief Outline of Theology as a Field of Study* (trans. T. N. Tice; Schleiermacher Studies and Translations 1; Lewiston, N.Y.: Mellen, 1990), §47 (28).

11. Schleiermacher's remark concerning the unity of the New Testament canon in his *Hermeneutics and Criticism* (Friedrich D. E. Schleiermacher, *Hermeneutics and Criticism and Other Writings* [trans. A. Bowie; Cambridge Texts in the History of Philosophy; Cambridge: Cambridge University Press, 1998], 54) dovetails with his determination of the theological unity of Christian dogmatics (cf. Schleiermacher, *Christian Faith*, §11, proposition [52]).

12. The Hebrew Bible/Old Testament has rabbinic Judaism and Christianity as its two possible outcomes. On the "double outcome" of this text, see Bernd Janowski, "The One God of the Two Testaments: Basic Questions of a Biblical Theology" (trans. C. Helmer), *ThTo* 57 (2000): 297–324.

is not privileged in the sense that it contains infallible knowledge concerning Christ's person and work. Rather as a historical record of early individual experiences of Christ, the Christian canon establishes the christological and soteriological parameters concerning the historical significance of the foundational moment in the Christian religion.

The ascription of foundational historical and conceptual-theological status to the Bible does not imply a diminution or rejection of a reverential attitude towards this text. Rather, the example from Schleiermacher's thought shows the delightful fit between the inquiry into historical and religious knowledge, on the one hand, and the privileged, unique place that Christianity assigns to the Bible, on the other hand. Categorical knowledge concerning the constituent elements of history in general and historical religion in particular is used to tease out features embedded in the Bible's own records of its subject matter. Scripture's truth as a historical document rests on the understanding of its historical origin as religiously significant for the rest of the historical series. The Bible can be read in this sense as "the first member in the series"[13] on both its own terms and in the terms of methodologically controlled and critical inquiry. Schleiermacher is a paradigmatic thinker who conceptualized the complementarity of different accesses to scripture on the basis of a historical theory of religion. The historical embeddedness of religion is worked into the New Testament's claim concerning an original relation between experiences essential to Christianity's transhistorical character and the texts expressing those experiences.[14] So a text's religious significance is taken seriously on its own terms as well as on the terms of categorical knowledge explaining the historical significance of origins for religion. The truth of these historically foundational texts is established for today by the fact that they set the historical-experiential and conceptual-metaphysical parameters for the rest of the religious tradition.

The possibility of agreement between historical experience and metaphysics will now be shown in a second ascription to the Bible: the Bible's transparency to an objective truth that is constituted at diverse points along the religion's historical trajectory by many subjective perspectives.

### 3. Ascription as Objective and Subjective Truth

The Bible is a collection of texts that at one level of ascription sets the parameters for a respective religious tradition by historical proximity to foun-

---

13. This is Schleiermacher's term in *Christian Faith*, §129, proposition (594).

14. On the experience-expression correlation, see my account of Schleiermacher's text theory in Christine Helmer, "Biblical Theology: Bridge Over Many Waters," *Currents in Biblical Research* 3 (2005): 169–96.

dational events. The texts render events significant for the ensuing history of the religion through interpretation. But interpretative access to the past as one ascription of truth requires another ascription in order to provide criteria for testing the truth of these records. Such a testing is already constitutive of religious experience as such: if a religion is to be truly living, the experiences "of something" invite reflection on the intentionality (content and referent) of that experience as well as on the unique ways in which it is experienced. In this section, I address a second ascription to the Bible in terms of its "objective and subjective truth."[15] A determination of the Bible's objective truth gives reasons for why this book's articulation of particular experiences remains transhistorically powerful. An exploration of the Bible's "subjective truth" conversely shows why these experiences are only available as interpreted through different individual and communal lens.

The Bible is said to be true in a transhistorical sense. It not only records the past but is open to future experiences that are deemed to be in some type of continuity with the past. It is this transhistorical potential for experience that a reduction of the Bible to mere text cannot explain. If the text is only a record of the past, then why is it consistently used as a document for testing and confirming extrabiblical experiences "of something"? The Bible discloses transhistorical potential for experiencing the self/world/God relations precisely in its intentionality in order that these experiences can be tested as to how they dovetail with, conform to, or agree with some description of those relations as set in the Bible. As text, the Bible is itself the product of human engagement with reality. And its use throughout a religious tradition witnesses to the faithful endurance of specific ways of engaging reality and the contours of that reality. The text witnesses to something beyond itself.

At this juncture, the distinction between text and subject matter, as Brevard S. Childs has noted, is helpful.[16] The biblical texts offer a particular grasp of the world to be experienced and known. As religious texts, they give something of the self/world/God relations to be known, and by this, they open up a range of experiences that is contextually translatable. The ascriptions of particular experiences to a deity, for example, the Trinity in Christianity, and the subsequent walk of life in relation to this God, point beyond the text to a subject "behind it." This is not a metaphysical reification "of something" that can be construed independently of the text; the text is itself composed in view of prior experiences of this reality. What is prior continues to be the source of inspira-

---

15. For a detailed account of the New Testament's objective referent and subjective interpretations, see Helmer, "Transhistorical Unity," 13–50.

16. Brevard S. Childs, *Biblical Theology of the Old and New Testaments: Reflections on the Christian Bible* (Minneapolis: Fortress, 1997), 23–29.

tion for composition. Furthermore, the text continues to serve as the original identifier for the same reality that is subsequently experienced. Truth in this transhistorical sense refers to the endurance of similar experiences of God in different historical contexts. It is the reason for the continuity of various experiences of God amid historical diversity.

The biblical text enters into dialogical engagement with other individuals who, in their respective communities, read the text in light of their own experiences of its subject matter. The text becomes the basis of dialogue by virtue of its intentional expressions. The self-understanding of the biblical text in virtue of its transhistorical potential to enter into dialogue regarding its referent is already available in specific passages. The book of Ezekiel punctuates its prophecies with the phrase "that you shall know…" (e.g., Ezek 37:13) in order to open up future attribution of majestic acts to Yhwh.[17] Similarly, the New Testament writers stress the verb "to see" (e.g., Luke 24:31) in order to point to possible future experiences of seeing Christ and being transformed by him. Clues in the text point out the text's intention: to open up possibilities for knowing, seeing, and experiencing the one whose mercies are new every morning. These clues express the confidence that this very reality of which the text speaks will be faithful in the future. On the basis of literary clues, it seems that the text admits its own transparency to a referent "behind" it. As interpretations of this referent, biblical texts render it transparent for subsequent generations to interpret.

The capacity to shape or even create novel experiences of a transhistorically continuous reality is ascribed to these texts. Theologians in the Christian tradition appeal to the *ad fontes* motto when sifting away interpretative sediments of the tradition in order to *get back to* the Bible's foundational layer (although this is not a hermeneutically tenable position). They do so with the desire to experience anew the reality witnessed by it. Specific texts evoke new experiences with the freshness of its original recording. Western Christianity, for example, can be narrated as a history of experiences with Paul's Letter to the Romans. Of all the texts in the New Testament corpus, Romans is acknowledged to possess a privileged status in the New Testament. Reading this letter has often recapitulated the foundational experience of the Christian religion: the experience of a life whose sinful existence inevitably ends in death, and the death of one whose gift of life is extended to all (Rom 7:24–25). In their commentaries on Romans, theologians such as Augustine, Lombard, Luther, Calvin, and Barth rehearse their experiences of sin and grace with a liveliness that echoes the newness of Paul's experience of the risen Christ.

---

17. On a similar point in the book of Isaiah, see Armin Lange's essay, "Reading the Decline of Prophecy," in this volume.

The fact that fresh experiences of a subject matter behind the text perpetually arise in the history of the Christian church requires a metaphysics that accounts for God's continued action in history. Divine faithfulness is a biblical-theological theme that is addressed theologically in terms of a metaphysics of being and becoming. A strict appropriation of the Greek apathy axiom will render God's involvement with historical messiness in a nonliteral way, whereas a view more keenly attuned to the biblical God who changes with and in history will not have difficulty in attributing anthropomorphisms to the deity. Christian theology, furthermore, has tended to conceptualize the God behind the text in metaphysical-trinitarian terms. Hegel appealed to a trinitarian metaphysics in terms of an objective theory of self-consciousness, for example, in order to determine the historical working of the God of Israel through priest and cult, through Christ and cross, through the Holy Spirit and the church, in the speculative-trinitarian concept of divine self-alienation and return.[18] Nevertheless, metaphysics is not "the thing itself" (*die Sache selbst*) but an explanation concerning the reality to which the Bible attests. The metaphysical concern with the reality behind the text that has the potential for continued experiences of precisely this reality explains why a religious trajectory constantly refers back to its original texts. The Bible's objective truth lies precisely in this metaphysical explanation. The Bible is objectively true, not by virtue of some property that the text might have, but by virtue of its capacity to refer to a subject matter that continues to be accessible to the immediacy of experience regardless at which historical point, or in which language, or in which culture that text is read.

Although accessible in the immediacy of experience, the objective truth, however, is not exhausted by expression. If such was the case, then subsequent generations would cling to literal formulas as the embodiment of that objective truth without seeking the immediacy of its experience for themselves. Objective truth is metaphysically "incarnate" in expressions of experience without ever fully being exhausted by them. Subjective truth is the interpretative construal of experiences of a distinct reality. That truth is not exhausted by one expression. It is expressed in the thoughts and actions of one individual life, in the thoughts and actions of individual believers throughout the history of a religion, and in the thoughts and actions of various communities constituting the religious community as a whole. Objective truth as transhistorical faithfulness is related to subjective truth as the diversity of interpretations capturing glimpses and facets of an objective truth that continuously lures towards novelty.

---

18. See Cyril O'Regan's masterful book on Hegel's trinitarian metaphysics, *The Heterodox Hegel* (SUNY Series in Hegelian Studies; Albany: State University of New York Press, 1994).

If metaphysics studies the reality witnessed by the text, then hermeneutics investigates the textual records of experiences of that reality. The experience "of something" is already interpreted experience. In order to relate metaphysics to hermeneutics, however, an account must be given of how experience can consist precisely in its interpretative schematization. Such a philosophical account of the categorization of reality goes beyond the scope of this paper.[19] Nevertheless, a brief outline of this modern principle can be mentioned in connection with Kant. It was Kant who, in epistemological terms, defined the objects of possible experience as those objects to which the categories of the understanding in conjunction with the schema are applied; experience is experience solely by virtue of its categorization. Kant's epistemology has decisive hermeneutical consequences. He restricted his epistemological study to pure reason, thereby eliminating the linguistic or cultural determination of the categories. His dialogue partners, Johann Georg Hamann and Johann Gottfried Herder, however, advocated the linguistic constitution of reason, thereby setting the philosophical stage for modern views concerning interpretative accesses to the world. The world appears as it does because it is already interpreted. This insight has been deepened by contemporary critical theorists who have refined hermeneutical tools to slice deftly through the infinite complexity of linguistic, social, historical, political, and cultural factors constituting places of being in the world as sites of interpretation. Language, concepts, and interpretative coefficients arise from culture and become tools of experiential expression.

The potential for interpretation is already established by the cultural milieu from which expression arises. By using common linguistic terms, syntax, and concepts, an author appeals to transindividual mechanisms that make communication and understanding possible in the first place. Even by individuating common grammar and concepts according to her own individual semantic field, experience, and linguistic competence, an author grounds her expressions on a common terrain that facilitates intersubjective communicability. The testing of the truth of any subjective expression presupposes such intersubjectivity. If an individuated expression could not be related to a common cultural-linguistic milieu, there would be no way of testing whether that expression were an anomalous standpoint or one perspective among many of a subject matter held in common by others.

Subjective truth, although it must be tested, is the significant guarantor of the continuity of a specific religion through time. A particular religion is

---

19. Schleiermacher provides such an account in the *Dialektik*, especially in the second or "formal" part that discusses the relation between perception and linguistic categorization. See Friedrich D. E. Schleiermacher, *Vorlesungen über die Dialektik* (vols. 2.10/1-2 of Kritische Gesamtausgabe; ed. A. Arndt; 2 vols.; Berlin: de Gruyter, 2000).

not only established at a foundational moment; its longevity requires that a common experience unite those generations rising up long after the original protagonists have died. In the christological terms of the Christian canon, this is known as the equivalence in redemptive efficacy between Jesus' bodily presence and his spiritual presence in the community.[20] According to Schleiermacher who argued this claim, there is no soteriological difference in the effect of Christ's person before and after his (alleged, for Schleiermacher) resurrection. The same person is experienced as effecting redemption by those who saw him in the flesh and by those to whom he is "circulated" in the Christian church. The subjective schematization of this experience ascribes soteriological efficacy to Christ in individuated ways. Expressions of experience are contextualized and individuated in the particular languages, concepts, and cultural coefficients of those articulating these experiences. Beautiful, infinite variety characterizes the life of a religion, not flattened, uniform conformity. Both the formation of the New Testament and its transhistorical power can be explained by Schleiermacher's understanding of the relation between experience and expression. Diverse sightings of Christ are individually schematized in the Gospels and in post–New Testament history, yet there is one Christ to which all schematizations point.

The relation between the objective and subjective truth of the Bible explains why the Bible continues to be revered for its transhistorical power and why it is "open" to critical reflection of its truth claims. Lovers of scripture are not necrophiliacs. Lovers of scripture are captured by its living truth. What Protestant Orthodox theologians explained in terms of the text's properties can be understood as the text's being caught up by the action of the spirit in order to permeate the life of the religion. The text is inert; yet as a document endowing life to the tradition, it is to be conceived as the literary witness to a transhistorical reality that is experienced subjectively in "many and various ways" (Heb 1:1). The love of knowledge, furthermore, has its own methods, criteria, and concepts that are applied to the testing of truth. Both the objective and subjective truth of the biblical texts is available for critical study precisely because these texts continue to be hermeneutically relevant in the present. Historical reflection presupposes, at least at a minimal level, the relevance "for us" of the documents it studies. Reading the past in light of the present assumes a hermeneutically minimal requirement that initial concepts and questions be used to "open" the text for dialogue with its authors about its subject matter. Study of the text then applies a refined interpretative apparatus to investigate the truth of its claims, to compare expressions with other accounts of the same reality, and to give a complex picture of the subject. Critical biblical interpretation can read the pres-

---

20. Schleiermacher, *Christian Faith*, §14,1 (68–69).

ent precisely by investigating the past with hermeneutical seriousness and moral accountability. The critical study of the Bible's objective and subjective truth can correct present views, add diverse perspectives to present topics of discussion, and improve the sophistication of biblical arguments. By its contributions to the study of the past, biblical interpretation actually participates in the liveliness of reflective engagement with the Bible's truth.

The second claim, as discussed in this section, ascribes objective and subjective truth to the Bible. This ascription intends to overcome a reduction of the Bible to a mere text by expanding an understanding of it in terms of its subject matter. The transhistorical faithfulness of a God "behind" the text and the multifarious experiences of this reality "in front of" the text capture the text in its transparency to reality. The metaphysical and hermeneutical determinations of the text's transhistorical power open up the text to its truth that is to be both enjoyed and studied. The Bible's truth is not eternal, captured in one formula once and for all. Rather, its transhistorical power opens up possibilities of exploring its truth from experience of and reflection on its objective and subjective dimensions.

### 4. Ascription of Transformation by Oral Embodiment

The Bible as a written text is a document caught at the living intersections of those who read it in light of their own experiences of its referent. The experience of a subject "behind" the text conveys to the respective religion its status as a living tradition. Yet the Hebrew Bible and New Testament report another way of experiencing "the text." It is this unusual and distinct experience that discloses the way the Bible accounts for a unique understanding of its reality. This is the experience of "eating the scroll." The third ascription to the Bible is the truth of transformation that occurs when the written word is physically ingested and digested. The physical intimacy experienced by eating the scroll discloses something about scripture's truth. A theological reflection on the physically embodied relation to the Bible will explain this relation in terms of its transformative effect on the present.

The predication of life to the divine word's agency is inscribed into the many layers of the biblical text.[21] The Psalter, for example, places pivotal emphasis on a life lived in taking delight in God's law (Ps 1:4, 6). At the beginning of this book, at a key introductory place, the life enjoyed by this life-time preoccupation is likened to a tree, whose leaves never wither (Ps 1:3). The book of

---

21. The questions concerning the precise meaning of the term "word of God" with all of its differentiations is a vast theological question that cannot be answered here. For the purpose of this chapter, I appeal to the term only to draw the connection between the spoken and written word in view of its determination as life-giving power.

Jeremiah proclaims the prophetic word of God, the life-giving promise of a new covenant (Jer 31:31), while Deutero-Isaiah issues words of comfort and good tidings (Isa 40:1). In John's Gospel, Peter exclaims when Christ asks his disciples if they too will abandon him, "Lord, to whom can we go? You have the words of eternal life" (John 6:68).[22] The word as the power of God is determined by those features characterizing God's faithful identity through time. The word is the instrumental cause of creation (Ps 33:9; John 1:3) and the promise of life continuing in times of exile (Jer 29:5–7). By relating the word to God, whether the law in Ps 119, the prophetic word in the prophets, wisdom in Sir 24:1–34, or the word that has become incarnate (John 1:14), the life-creating power that is constitutive of the divine essence is ascribed to it.

An important theological task is to recover this biblical connection between the word and God in terms of its determination as the commitment to "abundant life" (cf. Ps 23). The biblical connection between word and its particular agency as life-giving power has tended to be understood in a neo-Kantian paradigm in exclusively epistemological terms. In *Canon and Criterion in Christian Theology*, William Abraham criticizes the post-Enlightenment epistemologization of scripture as a collection of the self-evident axioms of faith, guaranteeing (Protestant Orthodox) theology's truth.[23] The literal identification of the word with the text and the resulting reduction of spiritual power to text play into a type of sacramentality that privileges the cognitive apparatus in receiving and understanding the word. If a religion limits its understanding of the Bible in this way, it results in an identification of experience with a cognitive understanding of the text. By reducing the dynamic biblical concept of the word to the written text, scripture becomes a source of knowledge rather than a source of life.

In order to break open this epistemological interpretative restriction, biblical theology and systematic theology require a new conceptual paradigm for determining the relation between the word and life. An idiosyncratic resource for such a conceptualization is the account of "eating the scroll." The command to consume the written word is a rare occurrence in the Bible. Ezekiel is told to eat the scroll inscribed on the front and back with "words of lamentations and mourning and woe" (Ezek 2:10), and its taste is sweet as honey (Ezek 3:3). John is commanded by the angel to eat a little scroll that tastes sweet as honey at first, but then turns bitter in the stomach (Rev 10:10). Other biblical passages allude to the nourishing function of the word. Jeremiah, for example, exclaims that the word he ate "became a joy and the delight of my heart" (Jer 15:16). These

---

22. All scripture quotations are from the New Revised Standard Version.
23. William J. Abraham, *Canon and Criterion in Christian Theology: From the Fathers to Feminism* (Oxford: Clarendon, 1998).

descriptions of command to physically ingest the written word of God offer a unique and unexpected glimpse into the way in which the word as text is related to a particular form of prophetic life.

Rather than being read or heard, the text is eaten. Analogous to physical sustenance by food, it is ascribed a nourishing quality of a distinct kind. Just as physical eating and drinking sustain life, so too the physical ingestion of the word conveys life to its recipient. That the transfer of this power occurs through physical unity with the consumed material points to a truth about the relation between word, text, and flesh. The communication of spiritual power through the physical text and its inscription into the flesh disclose the reality that the word seeks its substantialization in the flesh. Spirit seeks its embodiment in the physical realm. It was Friedrich Christoph Oetinger, the eighteenth-century Swabian mystic, who made this truth his life's quest: "The telos of divinity is corporeality."[24] "Eating the scroll" discloses a fundamental inseparability between spirit and flesh, as the apostle Paul or the Absolute Idealist philosophers admitted. The latter built metaphysical systems on the basis of the principle of identity between nature and spirit; both poles were understood to be strung out on a continuum with a point of indifference at the center at which the one pole of nature merged with its opposite, spirit, and vice versa.[25] As inseparable from the body, spirit is disclosed to have reality only when substantialized as a physical reality. Spirit seeks out corporeality in order to inscribe it with its life; by doing so, it conveys the truth of embodied life.

The life of the spirit has its telos in the transformation of physical reality. Yet this transformation achieves special significance in those biblical characters who are asked to eat the scroll. By becoming embodied in a reality not uniquely its own, the scroll inscribes its own content onto it: when Ezekiel eats the scroll, the written word becomes united with his own body. Its content is united with the body, determining the prophet's identity and mission. The scroll tastes sweet to him, in spite of the warning concerning the nature of his addressees (Ezek 3:7) and he is subsequently equipped with the protection of a fearless forehead "harder than flint" (Ezek 3:9). The body is caught at the intersection of the text's intentionality and its individual reception so that it becomes the place at which the text's reality is substantialized. Special persons, such as Ezekiel, become key signifiers of the text by their own witness in the body to an intentional sub-

---

24. Cited in Oswald Bayer, *Das Leibliche Wort: Reformation und Neuzeit im Konflikt* (Tübingen: Mohr Siebeck, 1992), 184.

25. On the requirement of a spirit/nature continuum for the notion of "open" system, see Christine Helmer, "Novelty and System in Schleiermacher's Thought," in *Schleiermacher and Whitehead: Open Systems in Dialogue* (ed. C. Helmer, with M. Suchocki et al.; TBT 125; Berlin: de Gruyter, 2004), 126–27.

ject "behind" it and by their own individual incarnation of the text "in front of" it. These are the "ambassadors of God," as Schleiermacher proclaims in the *Speeches,* chosen to mediate the infinite to the finite.[26] These are the "seers" who keep open experiences of transcendent mystery because their own reality has been transformed by the object of their witness.

The ascription of life-transforming capacity to the oral ingestion of the text takes into account the marginal accounts in the Bible of unusual text handling. While marginal, these accounts offer a powerful dimension to the text's truth. Such accounts interpret the "hermeneutical reading of the present" to be an experience incarnate in the body. The location of the body in the present tense at a particular spatial point is a unique property of the body. Only in the flesh is there a present tense. Where the reality of the text is substantialized in embodied reality, there the body represents this reality in the present. The truth of the body rests on its spatio-temporal existence as that place where experience of the text is rendered in the present. The hermeneutical reading of the present is turned into the bodily presentation in the present of the reality that has transformed it. By eating, the present is read in such a way that to it is given the life-sustaining property of the text's spirit. The truth of the text consists precisely in its transformation of the present by bringing the present to its living explication in the body.

## 5. Conclusion

The book called the Bible has been read, over and over again for a few millennia, in many languages and cultures. For what purpose? Is it to appease curiosity in a quaint monument of the past? Is it to justify current ethical, social, or political practices by historical texts? I have focused this chapter on a dissimilar pair of attitudes toward the Bible in order to show how both can help in working out three different ascriptions of the Bible's truth. By these ascriptions, I attempted to describe the Bible's unique and privileged role it enjoys in the Christian religion as well as its hermeneutical openness for methodologically controlled historical-critical and theological inquiry. The reverential attitude towards scripture can be opened to rational investigation in such a way that it presents its own transformation of rational categories. The testing, applica-

---

26. Friedrich Schleiermacher, *On Religion: Speeches to its Cultured Despisers* (trans. R. Crouter; Cambridge Texts in the History of Philosophy; Cambridge: Cambridge University Press, 2000), 7 (speech 1). Also: "Such people are true priests of the Most High, for they bring deity closer to those who normally grasp only the finite and the trivial; they place the heavenly and eternal before them as an object of enjoyment and unification, as the sole inexhaustible source of that toward which their creative endeavors are directed" (ibid.).

tion, and honing of these categories can, in turn, deepen knowledge concerning that which has traditionally been ascribed to sacred texts. (1) The Bible, as the historically original and foundational document for the particular religion of Christianity, is valorized for the reason that it sets the conceptual parameters for subsequent experience in the religion. This capacity is related to its literary fixing of an experience (or set of experiences) that is foundational to a particular religion at a historical site as proximate as possible to the original experience(s). Hence as foundational document, the Bible's truth consists in its relevance for funding experiences that reflect unity among diversity. (2) I then discussed the Bible in terms of the objective truth of a transhistorical metaphysical reality behind the text and of the subjective truth of hermeneutical diversity in front of the text. By this twofold truth, scripture's uniqueness as a text was deemed in terms of its transparency to a reality that continues to be experienced, while a metaphysical and hermeneutical analysis attempted to explain why the subject of the text could be experienced as continuous through time, yet in many individual ways. (3) The Bible as written scroll showed the ascription of transformative truth to the movement of spirit's desire to be substantialized in the body. The "eating of the scroll" transforms the prophet's present reality by making the scroll's content its own reality. By its inscription onto the body, the prophet renders the text in a present tense that only the body can re-present. The word's truth, in these cases, is an incarnate truth. The body reads the present by presenting its truth in order to transform life.

# Part 1:
# Dead Sea Scrolls

# Pesharim: A Mirror of Self-Understanding*

*Jutta Jokiranta*

## 1. The Task

The theme of this volume was first formulated as "reading the present: the perception of the contemporary by means of scriptural interpretation." The question may be formulated: How did the ancients interpret their contemporary reality by means of scriptural exegesis? One "common" exegetical question when studying ancient texts is: How did the contemporary of an ancient author color his or her work? Ancient authors, who were often interpreters of Scripture, were influenced by their present reality, historical situation, and social circumstances—modern scholars, then, desire to reconstruct that reality on the basis of their texts. But in this volume, as I understand it, we are going further. We are looking, not so much at "the reality behind the texts," but at the ancient interpreters' *perception* of that reality, their *assessment* of experiences. What kind of reality is *created* by their scriptural interpretation? How does reading the Scriptures color their picture of reality?

The two phenomena are, of course, intertwined. There is no scriptural interpretation without a context; it never takes place in a vacuum. On the other hand, a person's reality is interpreted on several levels and by several means, only one of which may be scriptural interpretation. Therefore, defining a methodology to answer our question is a separate task, and will not be undertaken in this essay. Here I can only make two statements. First, I understand that the theme of this volume concerns finding a certain kind of *Sitz im Leben* of the texts. Every text has a social context and functions in a specific way in its context. When we examine the texts that contain scriptural interpretation, we look for the ways in which scriptural interpretations functioned in a community

---

* This article was prepared under the auspices of the Academy of Finland and its Research Unit on the Formation of Early Jewish and Christian Ideology (University of Helsinki). I should like to express my gratitude to Prof. Raija Sollamo for her helpful comments and to the Intertestamental Literature project for our stimulating discussions.

and shaped its self-understanding and identity and its place in life. Secondly, the danger of circular reasoning exists if we first reconstruct the reality of the authors, on the basis of their texts, and then ask how these authors viewed this reality through their scriptural interpretation. This problem is real in the case of the pesharim, and I shall address it in the following.[1]

## 2. Pesharim and the Historical Reality

The pesharim are a group of texts within the Qumran library that explicitly cite the Scriptures and interpret them with the technical term "pesher" introducing the interpretation.[2] Prophetic texts receive an actualizing interpretation, an application with regard to the life and theology of the community. This is especially true for the "enemy readings" of the community. The authors of the pesharim found their enemies described in several descriptions of enemies in the Scriptures. Their enemies correspond to the oppressors of Hab 2 (1QpHab), to Nineveh, the city of bloodshed of Nah 3 (4QpNah), to the wine drinkers of Isa 5 (4QpIsa[b]), to the conspiring nations of Ps 2 (4QFlor), and to the successful wicked of Ps 37 (4QpPs[a]).[3]

I see at least two possible functions in this kind of enemy reading. Imagine a religious group that has opponents or that opposes others. What could be more powerful in labeling outsiders than to use a shared tradition and to label the outsiders as the wicked of this shared tradition? This is "propaganda" by its very nature. The reader of the pesharim gains the impression that the Scrip-

---

1. The danger of circular reasoning decreases or increases according to the amount and relevance of evidence from independent sources. If we can reconstruct a probable picture of the historical setting from other sources, then this danger is small. In the case of the pesharim, this is very difficult, as the whole enterprise of reconstructing the history of the Qumran community shows. Who was the Righteous Teacher? Who was (were) the Wicked Priest(s)? The pesharim have been used to reconstruct the community history, and we have to be aware of these theoretical presumptions when we proceed to other questions concerning their interpretation.

2. For a general introduction and literature, see Maurya P. Horgan, *Pesharim: Qumran Interpretations of Biblical Books* (CBQMS 8; Washington, D.C.: Catholic Biblical Association of America, 1979); Devorah Dimant, "Pesharim, Qumran," *ABD* 5:244–51; Shani L. Berrin, "Pesharim," in *Encyclopedia of the Dead Sea Scrolls* (ed. L. H. Schiffman and J. C. VanderKam; 2 vols.; Oxford: Oxford University Press, 2000), 2:644–47.

3. The original edition of the Cave 4 pesharim was published by John M. Allegro, *Qumran Cave 4.I (4Q158–4Q186)* (DJD 5; Oxford: Oxford University Press, 1968); and Pesher Habakkuk by Millar Burrows, ed., with the assistance of John C. Trever and William H. Brownlee, *Isaiah Manuscript and the Habakkuk Commentary* (vol. 1 of *The Dead Sea Scrolls of St. Mark's Monastery;* New Haven: American Schools of Oriental Research, 1950). See further the texts in Horgan, *Pesharim,* or the texts with translations by Florentino García Martínez and Eibert J. C. Tigchelaar, eds., *The Dead Sea Scrolls Study Edition* (Leiden: Brill, 1997).

tures were all about the community and its adversaries—Scripture is dualistic in its sharp division between the two groups, and the world is manifested as a place of struggle and dichotomy. A group facing adversity also attempts to find an explanation to its present experiences. Searching for this in the Scriptures is natural for a group which defines itself in scriptural terms and sees itself preserving and continuing that tradition. Scripture contains the right way of life, so it also speaks to the fate of contemporary people. The prophets of old are to be studied afresh, and studied in the light of the Scriptures themselves.[4] It is the "theological quality assigned" to the experiences of the ancient authors that we are looking at in this volume, not the experiences themselves.

Some of the pesher interpretations commence with the words פשר הדבר לאחרית הימים "the interpretation of the matter concerns the latter times," implying that these authors and their group believed themselves to be living at a turning point. God was about to act.[5] The very term "pesher," used by the authors of these works as a technical term, points toward understanding revelation as *judgments* that are to be pronounced on persons and groups, a model for which is found in the book of Daniel.[6] God's visitation was at hand, and the pesharim showed which persons and groups were doomed.

But what is the reality with which the pesharim are concerned? Do we have access to the specific circumstances of the authors of the pesharim?

Modern historical reconstructions are many. Scholars once attained a kind of a consensus that since the pesharim speak about the Teacher of Righteousness,

---

4. This is similar to what Ulrike Mittmann-Richert finds in the Additions to Daniel: prophets of old (Jeremiah, Habakkuk, Hosea) help the author(s) of the Additions to gain a new understanding of the book of Daniel; see the contribution of Ulrike Mittmann-Richert in this volume.

5. 4QpIsa[b] II,1; 4QpIsa[c] 23 II,10. Annette Steudel, "אחרית הימים in the Texts from Qumran," RevQ 11 (1993): 225–46, defines the expression אחרית הימים as "a limited period of time, that is the last of series of divinely pre-planned periods into which history is divided." This period covers aspects of past, present and future. The expression does not describe the eschatological end-time in the sense of the end of history, but rather the "transition to another period of time," the future time of God's visitation, a *change* of act, see Géza G. Xeravits, *King, Priest, Prophet: Positive Eschatological Protagonists of the Qumran Library* (STDJ 47; Leiden: Brill, 2003), 6–7. In the Scriptures the expression is used in connection with the distress that the people encounter, with an explanation of this distress, and with the change that God brings about. On this basis, the expression may be understood as time of turning to God and God's significant acts. See also George J. Brooke, *Exegesis at Qumran: 4QFlorilegium in Its Jewish Context* (JSOTSup 29; Sheffield: JSOT Press, 1985), 177, and Shemaryahu Talmon, "The Signification of אחרית and אחרית הימים in the Hebrew Bible," in *Studies in the Hebrew Bible, Septuagint, and the Dead Sea Scrolls in Honor of Emanuel Tov* (ed. S. M. Paul et al.; Leiden: Brill, 2003), 795–810.

6. The dreams and visions that Daniel interpreted were not about any future events, but specifically the future fate and judgment of King Nebuchadnezzar and King Belshazzar. See the suggested etymology of the term "pesher" in Horgan, *Pesharim*, 230–37.

they provide us with information about the early history of the community, the formation of the group, and the reasons that led to the emergence of a separate group, usually set in the second century B.C.E. In a recent book, James Charlesworth argues that the pesharim pass on traditions of the group's beginnings. The reason for writing the pesharim was to explain why the Righteous Teacher and his followers suffered and lived in exile in the wilderness. "History, especially of the origins of the Qumran group, is primarily preserved in the pesharim."[7] Maurya Horgan, in a central collection of the pesharim, thinks that the pesharim "moved freely from one period of time to another," from the early times of the community, up to the times of Hyrcanus II and Aristobulus II, the coming of Romans, and the end of times.[8]

Taking this idea further, Bilhah Nitzan proposes that the pesharim present an overall view of the final historical events, continuing the tradition of Daniel. The redemption seemed to tarry, and the coming of Rome needed to be explained.[9] The belief in divinely planned history needed strengthening. Pesher "was intended to show that ... all that occurs in the reality of history ... does not deviate or contradict the words of the ancient prophets and visionaries."[10] Each prophetic book was interpreted to cover a different period in Second Temple history.

Furthermore, the pesharim have been seen as a late phenomenon, viewing and reviewing the community traditions. George J. Brooke writes, "Any history they (the pesharim) represent is in the first instance the history of the period of their composition; say at the turn of the era, or even later. We have no reason to suppose that their author or authors had actually lived through the earlier events they may purport to describe."[11]

---

7. Charlesworth, *The Pesharim and Qumran History: Chaos or Consensus?* (Grand Rapids: Eerdmans, 2002), 3, 15, 70. According to Charlesworth, the tradition of the community history may have been in oral form before it was written down in the pesharim.

8. Horgan, *Pesharim*, 6–8.

9. Bilhah Nitzan, "The *Pesher* and Other Methods of Instruction," in *Mogilany 1989: Papers on the Dead Sea Scrolls Offered in Memory of Jean Carmignac, Part II: The Teacher of Righteousness* (ed. Z .J. Kapera; Kraków: Enigma, 1991), 212: "It became clear that the hope for redemption in the coming downfall of the fourth power—the Greco-Syrian—was an increasing illusion." "This disillusionment ... was accompanied by a domestic disappointment, namely in the leadership during the Hasmonean period."

10. Ibid., 212–13, 215.

11. George J. Brooke, "The Kittim in the Qumran Pesharim," in *Images of Empire* (ed. L. Alexander; Sheffield: Sheffield Academic Press, 1991), 137. According to Brooke, the authors of the pesharim may not have been direct heirs of the earlier inhabitants of the Qumran site. See also Philip R. Davies, *Behind the Essenes: History and Ideology in the Dead Sea Scrolls* (BJS 94; Atlanta: Scholars Press, 1987), 104.

Yet another, rather different, suggestion, presented by Gregory Doudna, is that the events reflected in the pesharim are about a particular situation of the community in the first century B.C.E. By identifying the wicked figure as Aristobulos II and the righteous teacher as Hyrcanus II in the Nahum Pesher, Doudna takes the history of the pesharim to a specific religious-political level.[12]

It is widely acknowledged that the pesharim are not history in the normal sense of the word.[13] The historical reading of the pesharim is difficult for several reasons.[14] First of all, the pesharim provide us with the religious point of view of the community, not an objective account of the emergence of the community and its conflicts. It is rather the community's identity and self-understanding that come forward as interesting subjects for study, not the conflicts themselves.[15] Secondly, the pesharim use scriptural, stereotypical language. Brooke has demonstrated how the information concerning the Kittim in Pesher *Habakkuk* is so fully saturated with Scripture that ultimately the historical information we learn about the Kittim-Romans is very little.[16] The stereotypical names, for

---

12. Gregory L. Doudna, *4Q Pesher Nahum: A Critical Edition* (JSPSup 35; London: Sheffield Academic Press, 2001). In this view, a pesher becomes a political document that views the major dramatic events from a religious perspective and the whole Qumran library is the library of a high priest. On the other hand, Michael O. Wise, "Dating the Teacher of Righteousness and the *Floruit* of His Movement," *JBL* 122 (2003): 71–72, 80, sees Hyrcanus II as a good candidate for the "Wicked Priest." Wise collected all the historical references in the Scrolls, many of which come from the pesharim. While these references may be of interest in the overall dating of the Scrolls, the problem lies in handling the symbolic names in the pesharim in a similar way to the explicit historical names.

13. E.g., Phillip R. Callaway, *The History of the Qumran Community: An Investigation* (JSPSup 3; Sheffield: JSOT Press, 1988), 140–42, 68–71. Horgan, *Pesharim*, 6: "The history recounted in the pesharim, like the history recounted in the biblical books, is an interpreted history." The pesharim have, however, an extra factor compared to many biblical books: they are bound to interpreting Scripture. Their interpretation of history thus occurs at least in a different form, tied to scriptural interpretation.

14. Compare these to the list given in Charlesworth, *Pesharim and Qumran History*, 81–82, of the considerations that a scholar needs to bear in mind when assessing Second Temple sources.

15. A useful distinction in research is also between *emic* and *etic* descriptions: *emic* descriptions are given by the "natives" themselves, concerning *what* and *how* they thought, whereas etic descriptions seek to explain *why* the natives thought and behaved in a particular way; see John H. Elliott, *What Is Social-Scientific Criticism?* (Minneapolis: Fortress, 1993), 38–39.

16. The pesher has been studied for information on the specific historical battles and for the war strategies of the Romans, but according to George J. Brooke ("Kittim in the Qumran Pesharim," 159), "we can learn little or nothing of the history of the Qumran community from these texts, and little enough about the Romans." Yet study of the scriptural allusions in the pesher reveals that the pesherist viewed the Kittim as part of a larger eschatological scheme, similar, for example, to the end-time Gog of Ezek 38, and that they were seen to pose a cultic threat to the Jews.

example the "liar" or "Ephraim," function as theological evaluations of individuals and groups, rather than as secret code names for them. It is possible that these nicknames were applied to different opponents in the course of history.[17] In addition, intertextuality plays a significant role in the pesharim. They share terminology with many other Scrolls, such as the Damascus Document, the War Scroll, and the Hymns. These connections may define the context and meaning of certain expressions.

### 3. Multiple Historical Readings

Although the above mentioned historical reconstructions share many aspects, they identify the historical setting behind the texts differently and they see *the role of history* in the texts in a different way. Let us look at one example of different ways of viewing the reality behind the text. According to 1QpHab XI,2–8, the Wicked Priest pursued after the Righteous Teacher and even tried to have the community of the Teacher stumble on the Day of Atonement. The traditional identification of the wicked priest is Jonathan. We may agree or disagree with this, but many scholars agree that this passage includes historical information: the Wicked Priest actually visited the Teacher; the conflict was intensified by a different calendar followed by them and possibly differences in the nature of the fast day.[18] We do not know, of course, exactly what they experienced as we do not have direct evidence of this incident in other sources.[19] But pesher is always a "two-way mirror": it portrays history and spirituality.[20] If we acknowl-

---

17. Håkan Bengtsson, *What's in A Name? A Study of Sobriquets in the Pesharim* (Uppsala: Uppsala University Press, 2000), 297. Compare also the audience-reception point of view applied in the *Damascus Document* by Maxine L. Grossman, *Reading for History in the Damascus Document: A Methodological Study* (STDJ 45; Leiden: Brill, 2002), 4–5, 17–21.

18. The calendar controversy was first observed by S. Talmon, "Yom Kippurim in the Habakkuk Scroll," *Bib* 32 (1951): 549–63. Joseph M. Baumgarten, "Yom Kippur in the Qumran Scrolls and Second Temple Sources," *DSD* 6 (1999): 184–91, suggests that Yom Kippur was considered to be a day of fasting and self-affliction for the Qumranites, in contrast to the joyous celebration reflected in the rabbinic tradition. As Baumgarten himself remarks, however, we have little evidence of any particular ascetic forms of self-affliction practiced in the Qumran community.

19. Cf. similar themes in 1 Macc 2:29–38; 2 Macc 4:32–35; 6:11.

20. Charlesworth, *Pesharim and Qumran History*, 14. Doubt has been cast on the historical reliability of the passage: Davies, *Behind the Essenes*, 93–97, suggests that the passage was constructed by borrowing language from the Scriptures and from the Hodayot (1QH XII, formerly IV); but see qualification of this methodology in Timothy H. Lim, *Pesharim* (Companion to the Qumran Scrolls 3; London: Sheffield Academic Press, 2002), 67–69. If the passage is open to historical doubts, it is also possible to take it as a late label given to a (neutral?) confrontation between an important figure of the community (the Righteous Teacher) and a high priest (now understood as a wicked priest).

edge the basic historical reliability of this passage,[21] there still remain two possibilities. First, this is understood as a *crucial* event in community's history. Shemaryahu Talmon suggests that Yom Kippur was charged with special historical significance due to the persecution of the Teacher on this day.[22] Recently, Noah Hacham has studied references to communal fasts and argued that the only public fast in the Scrolls is Yom Kippur. He thinks that the observance of Yom Kippur is understandable "because the sudden trauma of the persecution on Yom Kippur is a fresh memory in the consciousness of the sect."[23]

Another way of reading the passage is to see it as telling only a *part* of history. This event was presented as an example of the wicked acts of a wicked priest, an example that ideally fits with the quotation of Hab 2:15: "Woe to anyone making his companion drunk, spilling out his anger, or even making him drunk to look at their festivals!" The passage may speak of the wrong calendar and practices of the opponent, but most of all it speaks about his arrogance, daring to fight against their teacher. The wicked priest is wicked as he not only breaks the Sabbath, but he tries to make *them* stumble—the wickedness of one leader is demonstrated in contrast to the role of the other as a victim.

There have been attempts to define methods to distinguish between scripturally loaded information, and information not derived from Scripture, which would be more transparent and thus more feasible in historical reconstruction.[24] These approaches acknowledge the real difficulty and uncertainty of discerning reliable historical information and interpreting it. The thesis of this paper is that the pesharim are more a mirror of the community's identity than an exact report of community events. This is not to deny that a historical reality is present behind the stereotypical language, but to highlight that it also serves ideologi-

---

21. It has been suggested that this passage was constructed by borrowing language from the Scriptures and from the Hodayot (1QH XII, formerly IV); see Davies, *Behind the Essenes*, 93–97. But see qualification of this methodology in Lim, *Pesharim*, 67–69. As the passage is open to historical doubts, it is also possible to see it as a late *label* given to the (neutral?) confrontation of a high priest (*now* understood as a wicked priest) and an important figure of the community (the Righteous Teacher).

22. Shemaryahu Talmon, *The World of Qumran from Within* (Jerusalem: Magnes, 1989), 186–99.

23. Noah Hacham, "Communal Fasts in the Judean Desert Scrolls," in *Historical Perspectives: From the Hashmoneans to Bar Kokhba in Light of the Dead Sea Scrolls: Proceedings of the Fourth International Symposium of the Orion Center, 27–31 January 1999* (ed. D. Goodblatt et al.; Leiden: Brill, 2001), 137. See also Joseph M. Baumgarten, "Theological Elements in the Formulation of Qumran Law," in *Emanuel: Studies in the Hebrew Bible, Septuagint, and Dead Sea Scrolls in Honor of Emanuel Tov* (ed. S. M. Paul et al.; VTSup 94; Leiden: Brill, 2003), 38–39, for the meaning of this incident for the community.

24. Davies, *Behind the Essenes*, 92; Charlesworth, *Pesharim and Qumran History*, 70–77.

cal functions of the community.[25] For the purposes of this paper, two general views of the presumed reality of the pesherists will suffice: the community of the authors of the pesharim was an organized community, comparable to "voluntary associations,"[26] but in tension with outsiders, experiencing (real or imagined) distress and persecution. For some (but not all) authors of the pesharim, the coming or presence of the Romans was a real issue.

### 4. Reading the Present in Pesher Habakkuk

I shall take one pesher, the Habakkuk pesher, and study its basic outline from the perspective of social identity. Habakkuk is only one of the many scriptural books depicting a foreign enemy sent to punish the people of Israel that the pesharim quote. At the beginning of the book of Habakkuk, the prophet complains about the violence in the land and the well-being of the wicked (1:2–4). God's answer is the Chaldeans, a frightening and cruel nation (1:5–11). But the prophet is not entirely satisfied with God's way of dealing with wickedness by means of more wickedness (1:12–17). He laments about the silence when the wicked swallows a person more righteous than he is. In chapter 2, God promises a vision that will come true in time. The faithful shall live. The violent and greedy actions of the conqueror are then condemned in five woes (2:5–19); the conqueror himself will be destroyed because of his deeds.[27]

---

25. By studying the scriptural allusions we may learn more about the assessments. For example, according to George J. Brooke, "Isaiah in the Pesharim and Other Qumran Texts," in *Writing and Reading the Scroll of Isaiah: Studies of an Interpretive Tradition* (ed. C. C. Broyles and C. A. Evans; Leiden: Brill, 1997), 625, the expression "scoffers in Jerusalem" in 4QpIsa$^b$ is an abbreviated citation of Isa 28:14, and thus the pesherist assesses these scoffers as leaders who "have made covenant with death and agreement with Sheol."

26. The definition by Sandra Walker-Ramisch, "Graeco-Roman Voluntary Associations and the Damascus Document: A Sociological Analysis," in *Voluntary Associations in the Graeco-Roman World* (ed. J. S. Kloppenborg and S. G. Wilson; London: Routledge, 1996), 131: "an organized association of persons who come together on a voluntary, contractual basis in the pursuit of common interests, both manifest and latent. To the association each member contributes, by contractual agreement, a part of his/her time and resources." To what degree the membership in the Qumran community can be considered as "part-time," with individual interests, occupations, and property, remains uncertain; the form of membership probably varied in the course of time and from place to place. See the discussion of the usefulness of this category in John J. Collins, "Forms of Community in the Dead Sea Scrolls," in Paul, *Emanuel*, 98–104.

27. The woes do not explicitly mention Chaldeans but are understood to refer to them in the present form of the book. The woes may include material that was originally social criticism against the rulers of Judea; see Klaus Seybold, *Nahum, Habakuk, Zephanja* (ZBK; Zurich: Theologischer Verlag, 1991), 45, 70.

The main scheme of the scriptural text is thus: (1) the wickedness among the people; (2) the foreign nation that comes to punish the people; and (3) the oppressing nation is accused and will be punished itself. This is more or less the text that the pesherist knew. What was his choice and emphasis? How did he deal with the scheme and entity of the scriptural text?

The pesherist ignores the genres of prayer and lament in the scriptural text. He seeks identifications. In doing so, he paints a picture in which the enemies surround the righteous. We find that the enemy of the scriptural text is identified not only as a foreign power, the Kittim, but the five woes against the oppressor are applied to the (wicked) priest/liar, and to the Gentiles in general. As in the case of the biblical text of Habakkuk, the pesher has several actors, and the Kittim are not the (only) target in the pesher. Furthermore, the pesher creatively raises a third enemy besides the wicked and the Kittim: the traitors.

What is striking is that the pesherist does not explicitly state that the Kittim are sent by God to punish the wicked—on the contrary, he seems to deny it in IV,16–V,8. This passage is difficult to interpret and includes variants compared with the Masoretic Text, but the basic idea of punishment through the hand of the nations seems to be denied.[28] In interpreting the woes of the oppressor, the pesherist does see the Kittim as bringing doom upon the wicked priests (IX,3–7, perhaps in IX,8–9;[29] X,2–5). But the punishment of the wicked priests is not really executed by the Kittim exclusively: they will take the wealth of the last priests (IX,3–7), but otherwise the pesher refers to disease brought upon the wicked priest (IX,1–2, 10–11),[30] to fire (X,5,13), to the anger of God (XI,14), and simply to destruction by God (X,2–5;[31] XII,5; XIII,3–4), without any clear reference to a foreign power. Thus, the Kittim are vividly described and—at the most—are exercising the limited task of being part of divine punishment. The scheme of the pesher is: (1) wickedness of the people: traitors; (2) a foreign power is coming (but not as punishment?); and (3) both the wicked and the nations are punished by God.

The power of the pesher is to place the wicked enemies of its own nation on the same line as the Gentile enemies and oppressors. The foreign enemy functions as a prototype of wickedness to which other types are paralleled. As

---

28. The next passage (V,8–12) focuses on the traitors again, and therefore this preceding passage could be seen to stress the faithfulness of the elect, not the issue of punishment at all.

29. However, these enemies may be Jewish enemies; see William H. Brownlee, *The Midrash Pesher of Habakkuk* (SBLMS 24; Missoula, Mont.: Scholars Press, 1979), 156.

30. Brownlee (ibid., 145) fills in the lacuna so that the these diseases come from pain-inflicting angels, according to 1QS IV,12.

31. The Kittim may be included in the nations of X,4, yet God does not give his judgment *by* the nations but *among* the nations.

a theological statement, this could sound like "yes, we are threatened by the enemy, those who are ordained by God to come (Kittim) *and* those who are as violent and far away from God as the Gentiles (the wicked), but those who remain faithful shall live."[32] The prophet Habakkuk received a surprisingly close answer: the faithful shall live.

This phenomenon is what social identity theorists would call social creativity. When members of a group are not satisfied with its present status but cannot leave the group, they have to create a positive reevaluation of the in-group. This is done by means of several strategies: groups may find new dimensions with which to compare themselves; they may redefine the value of an existing comparison so that what was regarded as weakness is seen as a strength; or groups may also select new out-groups for intergroup comparisons. These strategies, if successful, will bring the group a positive social identity, even if its status has not changed.[33]

Social identity is of central importance in a voluntary group such as the Qumran group. Identity needed to be continuously protected and defined. Selecting new dimensions for intergroup comparisons may be represented when the community draws the line harshly. It is no longer a question of breaking God's covenant and the right halakah but of being faithful to the community and belonging to the elect ones. The Habakkuk pesher recurrently refers to the traitors or presumes their presence.[34] The traitors are the closest enemies. "Since they are not with us, they are against us." The traitors are placed in the enemy camp together with the wicked, and the wickedness of the enemy is paralleled with that of the pagans. The righteous will judge all of them in the final act by God.

Ancient Israel survived its crisis of exile with the understanding that the exile did not come as a random attack by its enemies but it came as deserved punishment for its sins, sent by God. In a similar way, the community survived its unstable and frequently threatened existence[35] by redefining its afflictions as

---

32. Yet it is not always quite clear whether the pesherist places the Kittim and the wicked of his people in parallel (both are equally wicked; both will be punished by God, as in the *War Scroll*), or the wicked of his people and the nations in general in parallel (both are equally wicked and both will be punished by Kittim)? Either way, the wicked are paralleled with the Gentiles. If the Kittim are seen in a punishing role, it seems to me that they have come or are seen to have come, and their coming therefore requires an explanation, rather than that the pesherist *expects* them to come for the vindication of the righteous. The Kittim are not the final word in the scenario.

33. Michael A. Hogg and Dominic Abrams, *Social Identifications: A Social Psychology of Intergroup Relations and Group Processes* (London: Routledge, 1988), 56–59.

34. At least in II,1–9; V,7–12; VIII,1–2; possibly in I,11; II,14–15; X,9–13.

35. Or, its experience as being threatened. We may assume many possible causes for these threats. In a "voluntary association" a group had to recruit new members in order to survive; a group in "exile" had to defend itself against accusations, possible renegades had to be dealt with,

true markers of the faithful ones. The presence of foreigners—the sword—is one curse of breaking the covenant, as are other afflictions, for example famine and plague, which form the time of distress. In this, the community had the Scriptures to facilitate understanding. The Scriptures picture the righteous as tested and applaud those who will stand the test of refinement (Dan 11:32–35; Mal 3:3; Zech 13:9; Ezra 9; Sir 2:1–5). The Scriptures also view the growing distress as a mark of the closeness of redemption.[36] The theology of the time of testing is well developed in many Qumran texts (e.g.,4QpPs[a] II,9–12; 4QMidrEschat IV,1ff.; IX,9ff.).[37] In the Habakkuk pesher, the traitors in particular are the black background against which one can see light. Those who suffer voluntarily now are shown to be on the right side.

## 5. Conclusions

Although actualizing in intent, the pesharim do not strictly follow a fulfillment pattern in the sense that they match a particular scriptural passage with a particular event or person, and claim that this is the way that the passage has been fulfilled. For this purpose, many of the pesher sections seem all too faithful to Scripture. Some of them are even close to literal simple-sense interpretation, a continuation of biblical exegesis.[38] As a whole, the pesharim contain more events that are expected to occur than those that have occurred and are fulfilled, and the interpretations are not fixed.

The pesharim do not wish to present historical facts as such, but rather point out boundaries. They herald the future fulfillment, and the focus is primarily on group relations and judgments, not on events and timings. The revealing of the prophetic mysteries not only includes revealing the *process* of history but also the *result* of history, as well as promoting this specific view of history.[39] Only *Pesher*

---

etc. In addition to these social issues, the group had to respond to theological and religious challenges, such as: How is God dealing with his people? How are his promises going to be fulfilled? What is our role in God's history?

36. E.g. Isa 2:10ff.; Joel 2–4; Zeph 1–2.

37. The idea of the time of distress and testing may even be present where we would not expect to find it: at first glance, the quotation of Hab 1:12–13a in 1QpHab IV,16–V,8 does not mention distress, yet the pesherist probably understood the word צור not (only) as the noun "rock" but also as referring to verb צור, "to bind/to harm, damage," since he includes in the pesher a noun with a similar meaning: בצר למו "in their distress;" see Brownlee, *Midrash Pesher*, 88–89.

38. For example, 4QpHos[a] II,1–7 has hardly any sectarian terminology, and 4QpPs[a] III,11–13 states in scriptural terminology the destiny of the wicked.

39. George J. Brooke, "The Pesharim and the Origins of the Dead Sea Scrolls," in *Methods of Investigation of the Dead Sea Scrolls and the Khirbet Qumran Site: Present Realities and Future Prospects* (ed. M. O. Wise et al.; New York: New York Academy of Sciences, 1994), 340, stresses how much the citations actually determine the way the commentary runs. Scripture, citations and allusions,

*Nahum* (4QpNah) includes explicit historical names (I,2–3)—and even here the names are used to define a period of time in which Jerusalem was not occupied by foreign powers, rather than showing specific interest in these individuals. In my opinion, we have little evidence to show that the primary purpose of the pesharim was to present the major historical events, in which the group emerged and lived and which it thought it had fulfilled.[40]

By reading their present in the light of the Scriptures, the pesher authors contributed to constructing the identity of the community. In *Pesher Habakkuk* this includes such things as the dichotomy between the righteous and the wicked, the depiction of archenemies on the same line as pagan enemies, the stress on the time of testing as the mark of chosen ones, and selecting certain individuals as stereotypical of community and noncommunity members. Faithfulness to the community is promoted by the application of the prophet Habakkuk's message to the community's reality, while still remaining faithful to the key message of Habakkuk himself: "Wait and be faithful." Even though filled with sobriquets that can be identified as historical persons and groups, the pesher is most of all a mirror of the self-understanding of the group. It is the values of the community that the readers of the pesharim learn in order to perceive and understand their contemporary reality correctly.

---

have the controlling place, and the language remains stereotypical. Timothy H. Lim, *Holy Scripture in the Qumran Commentaries and Pauline Letters* (Oxford: Clarendon, 1997), 132–34, notes how a pesher may vary in its way of interpreting—from inspired revelation to mere interpretation, from a pattern of fulfillment to mere glosses on words in the citation.

40. Contrary to Charlesworth, Pesharim and Qumran History, 115, "Each (biblical) book was chosen for select passages or chapters that can be used to prove that prophecy pointed to the historical events that had already occurred or were transpiring," and Xeravits, King, Priest, Prophet, 51, "the aim of the interpretation is to tell things about the past, present and future history of the Community," I would say that the pesharim tell things about the past, present, and future but that this is not their real aim. I do not see the pesharim as such a unified collection that one could see a deliberate constructing of different phases of community history between the different pesharim. Cf. Brooke, "Kittim in the Qumran Pesharim," 158, "The commentaries are written to demonstrate that the period in which the author and his readership live has indeed an eschatological character." The eschatological character is the starting point in the pesharim, which of course defines their nature but perhaps does not exhaust their function.

# CONTEMPORIZING HALAKIC EXEGESIS IN THE DEAD SEA SCROLLS

*Lawrence H. Schiffman*

Scholars of the Dead Sea Scrolls and related literature have become accustomed to the notion that the Qumran sectarians practiced a form of contemporizing exegesis for prophetic books and the Psalms known as pesher.[1] This form of exegesis involves the understanding of ancient—First Temple period—texts of prophecy as if they related to the present-day times of the authors of the pesher texts. Further, the pesher literature makes the claim that the inspired interpreter—the pesherist, in our case the priestly Teacher of Righteousness[2]—was the only one to know the true meaning of the passage in question. The pesher form of exegesis, and the texts that flowed from it, were understood to provide an accurate interpretation of an ancient prophet, claiming that his words actually applied not to his long-ancient past but to the present Greco-Roman period. This approach was in turn founded on certain specific methods of hermeneutical manipulation, yielding a newly relevant prophetic message.

From the early days of Qumran research, scholars have observed the relationship of this kind of interpretation to certain New Testament passages in which the main point is to show that Jesus' life, career, and death had been foretold by the Israelite prophets.[3] Despite the tendentiousness of this hermeneutic, it shared with the equally tendentious and presentist pesher literature the claim

---

1. Lawrence H. Schiffman, *Reclaiming the Dead Sea Scrolls: The History of Judaism, the Background of Christianity, the Lost Library of Qumran* (Philadelphia: Jewish Publication Society, 1994), 223–41; Maurya P. Horgan, *Pesharim: Qumran Interpretations of Biblical Books* (CBQMS 8; Washington, D.C.: Catholic Biblical Association of America, 1979), 229–59; William H. Brownlee, *The Midrash Pesher of Habakkuk* (SBLMS 24; Missoula, Mont.: Scholars Press, 1979), 23–36.

2. 1QpHab 2:5–10; 7:1–5.

3. Cf. E. Earle Ellis, "Biblical Interpretation in the New Testament Church," in *Mikra: Text, Translation, Reading and Interpretation of the Hebrew Bible in Ancient Judaism and Early Christianity* (ed. M. J. Mulder; CRINT 1; Minneapolis: Fortress, 1990), 691–725.

that the words of the Hebrew biblical prophets were of direct relevance to the period of the exegete.

This paper seeks to call attention to some examples in the Dead Sea Scrolls of a similar phenomenon in legal, halakic exegesis. We have in mind the transference of material from its original scriptural relevance to a new, present Second Temple period context. In these cases, the original historical context of the legislation gives way to a reality that is thrust upon it by the historical circumstances and the reigning interpretation. These passages now assume a meaning perhaps not intended but now dominant in sectarian halakic textual tradition.

We begin with what may be seen as a macro version of this phenomenon, the composition and redaction of the *Temple Scroll*.[4] In the finished scroll, we effectively see a translation of law from the desert period—that of the Levitical code for the most part—from tabernacle to temple setting. This process has numerous ramifications, but the clearest is the temple plan itself. The author of the temple source—the architectural plan of the expanded temple—sought to take the tabernacle and desert camp (see below) and use it as a scriptural model to create a "modern" (i.e., Hellenistic period) ideal plan for a Jewish temple. He therefore had to translate, with the help of material from Kings, Ezekiel, and Chronicles, the details of the tabernacle into specific architectural requirements. This was based on a combination of biblical interpretations of the relevant passages and the architectural norms of his day. But the final product of his temple plan created an up-to-date way of realizing the halakic requirements of the Bible in his own age.[5]

Because this was an ideological plan, the author expected that he could establish the contours of the demographics of the country, even to the point of expecting people to dwell in cities in houses of stones (11QT 50:12).[6] This represented his derivation from the Torah's laws of stone homes that had contracted mildew (*ṣaraʿat*) of a chronic type (Lev 14:33–57) and other such material in the Bible.

---

4. See the editions of Yigael Yadin, *The Temple Scroll* (3 vols.; Jerusalem: Israel Exploration Society and the Shrine of the Book, 1983); and Elisha Qimron, *The Temple Scroll: A Critical Edition with Extensive Reconstructions* (Beersheva: Ben-Gurion University of the Negev; Jerusalem: Israel Exploration Society, 1996).

5. Lawrence H. Schiffman, "Architecture and Law: The Temple and Its Courtyards in the *Temple Scroll*," in *From Ancient Israel to Modern Judaism: Intellect in Quest of Understanding: Essays in Honor of Marvin Fox* (ed. J. Neusner et al.; 4 vols.; BJS 159; Atlanta: Scholars Press, 1989), 1:267–84.

6. Lawrence H. Schiffman, "Sacred Space: The Land of Israel in the *Temple Scroll*," in *Biblical Archaeology Today, 1990: Proceedings of the Second International Congress on Biblical Archaeology* (ed. A. Biran and J. Aviram; Jerusalem: Israel Exploration Society, 1993), 398–410.

Another good example of this overall hermeneutic of transformation to the author's own time is that of the bringing up to date of the Torah's law of the king that takes place in the so-called Law of the King in the *Temple Scroll*.[7] Here an entire section of Deuteronomy dealing with the appointment of a king, his duties, obligations, the laws of war, and other such matters has been transmogrified by this form of contemporizing exegesis into a proposed ideal political order for Hasmonean period Judea. This is essentially a call for governmental reform, that was actually never heard, but the author intended this as a full-fledged "interpretation" of the commands of the Torah on this matter.

These examples will suffice for us to remark on how this phenomenon encompassed for the author/redactor the entirety of the Torah. Often gathering together various sections on one topic, based as they are on versions of what biblical criticism considers to be the sources of the Torah, the scroll fuses them together into a sort of companion Torah to the original, canonical text.[8] The very shape of this final product, starting at the end of Leviticus with the tabernacle description, and summarizing the law on all kinds of matters relating to temple, sacrifice, political affairs, marital law, etc., points to the whole document as a statement on how God's original Torah calls on a Jew to live in the troubled times in which the author/redactor lived.[9] He uses halakic pseudepigraphy—placing his own ideas and those of the sources effectively in the mouth of God—in order to present his own views for the present—an update for contemporary times of God's own words.[10]

---

7. Yadin, *Temple Scroll*, 1:344–62; Lawrence H. Schiffman, "The King, His Guard, and the Royal Council in the Temple Scroll," *PAAJR* 54 (1987): 237–59; Moshe Weinfeld, "'Megillat Miqdash' 'o 'Torah la-Melekh,'" *Shnaton* 7 (1987/9): 214–37.

8. Yadin, Temple Scroll, 1:73–77; Jacob Milgrom, "The Scriptural Foundations and Deviations in the Laws of Purity of the Temple Scroll," *Archaeology and History in the Dead Sea Scrolls: The New York University Conference in Memory of Yigael Yadin* (ed. L. H. Schiffman; JSOTSup 8; JSOT/ASOR Monographs 2; Sheffield: JSOT Press, 1990), 83–99; idem, "The Qumran Cult: Its Exegetical Principles," in *Temple Scroll Studies* (ed. G. J. Brooke; JSPSup 7; Sheffield: Sheffield Academic Press, 1989), 165–80.

9. Hindy Najman, *Seconding Sinai: The Development of Mosaic Discourse in Second Temple Judaism* (JSJSup 77; Leiden: Brill, 2003), notes that the author did not intend to replace the original Torah, only to supplement it.

10. Lawrence H. Schiffman, "The Temple Scroll and the Halakhic Pseudepigrapha of the Second Temple Period," in *Pseudepigraphic Perspectives: The Apocrypha and Pseudepigrapha in Light of the Dead Sea Scrolls: Proceedings of the International Symposium of the Orion Center for the Study of the Dead Sea Scrolls and Associated Literature, 12–14 January, 1997* (ed. E. G. Chazon et al.; STDJ 31; Leiden: Brill, 1999), 121–31. Cf. Moshe J. Bernstein, "Pseudepigraphy in the Qumran Scrolls: Categories and Functions," in Chazon et al., *Pseudepigraphic Perspectives*, 1–26.

The Sadducean/Zadokite halakic trend, like the Pharisaic-rabbinic,[11] faced a major challenge because of the transfer of Jewish life from the desert to the land of Israel. Both trends had to explain how the Torah's laws for the desert camp and tabernacle could be observed in an environment in which Jews now lived in the city of Jerusalem and the surrounding hinterland of the land of Israel. Yet the Torah contained legislation primarily assuming the desert camp. Much of this legislation seemed to contradict itself regarding the sanctity of the camp, and it seems that both trends found a similar, if not actually common solution. This solution, expressed in similar terms in the *Temple Scroll*, 4QMMT, and tannaitic sources, essentially explains the Bible's laws in a contemporizing fashion. This interpretation has two steps: differentiation followed by contemporization.

The first stage, that of differentiation, was accomplished by dividing the "camp" references into three types. These included, if we may use the admittedly anachronistic tannaitic terminology, the camp of the divine presence, the camp of the Levites, and the camp of Israel.[12] These, in turn, refer to the tabernacle itself, the area surrounding it that was inhabited by the Levites in the desert, and the camp of Israel, that is, of the rest of the tribes that surrounded the tabernacle and tribe of Levi. This complex exegesis, of which I have given here the briefest of sketches, is what I have termed differentiation, that is, differentiating the various usages of "camp" one from the other. Whether this exegesis accords with the plain meaning of the text is not our concern here.

The next stage was that of contemporization. Here the map of camps was transferred from the Sinai Desert to the city of Jerusalem and the surrounding land of Israel. In this case, it was decided that the temple, whatever its architectural plan, was equivalent in sanctity to the tabernacle, the camp of God's presence; the *temenos* (or Temple Mount) was equivalent to the camp of the Levites; and the city of Jerusalem was equivalent to the camp of Israel. At least so it was for the tannaim and the author(s) of MMT. But the *Temple Scroll* went further, with its plan of a three-court temple instead of the two-court tabernacle and Solomonic structures. It placed the camp of Israel inside its outer court, so that the *temenos* became a model of the desert camp, and created named gates

---

11. Cf. Y. Sussman, "Ḥeqer Toldedot ha-Halakhah u-Megillot Midbar Yehudah: Hirhurim Talmudiyim Rishonim le-'Or Megillat Miqṣat Maʿaśe ha-Torah," *Tarbiz* 59 (1989/90): 11–77. A shortened English version is available as "The History of the Halakha and the Dead Sea Scrolls: Preliminary Talmudic Observations on Miqṣat Maʿaśe ha-Torah (4QMMT)," in Elisha Qimron and John Strugnell, *Qumran Cave 4.V: Miqṣat Maʿaśe ha-Torah* (DJD 10; Oxford: Clarendon, 1994), 179–200.

12. *T. Kelim B. Qam.* 1:12; *Sifre Num. Naso* 1; *Num. Rab.* 7:8; *b. Zev.* 116b; cf. Maimonides, *H. Bet ha-Beḥirah*, 7:14.

for the various tribes in accord with the patterns of the original (or imagined) desert camp.[13]

In either case, after the first process of differentiating the camps, these exegetes updated and so contemporized the Scriptures by means of interpretation, applying in this way biblical law to the circumstances of their own day.

A somewhat different form of contemporizing halakic exegesis occurs in polemical context, as exemplified by the Admonition of the Zadokite Fragments (*Damascus Document*).[14] In this text several halakic rulings are delivered in the context of an attack on others, most notably the Pharisees who are seen as going astray from the true path of the Torah (CD 4:17–5:11). What is interesting here is that these legal interpretations come in close proximity to pesher interpretations that are similarly polemical (4:12–17). In this case, the contemporizing aspect consists not in any outright allusions to the author's own period. Rather, it is in the selection of the halakic points of dispute and the claim, true or false, by the Qumran text that the author's interpretation of the law is necessarily correct. These subjects are clearly sectarian markers—better, hot-button issues—that set the sectarians off from their opponents. This is why they fulfill a polemical purpose. The halakic exegesis is therefore employed to support a ruling that itself is of highly contemporary importance, especially to the community that assembled the Qumran scrolls.

Two examples of this phenomenon, quite well known as they are, will suffice. The sectarians cite the biblical accounts of creation and the flood to justify the claim that polygamy is forbidden (CD 5:1). We all know that there is dispute about the meaning of the word *be-ḥayehem*, "in their (masc.) lifetimes." I take it to mean that divorce is permitted but remarriage forbidden unless the spouse dies. Once marriage takes place, the spouses are connected until death (as the Protestants say at weddings, "until death do us part"). Whether one agrees with this view of *be-ḥayehem* or not, there is no question that the simultaneous marriage of one man to more than one woman is seen as forbidden. This view is, of course, totally at variance with the explicit statement of the Torah and its narratives. This prohibition was later accepted by early Christianity, but was

---

13. L. H. Schiffman, "Exclusion from the Sanctuary and the City of the Sanctuary in the Temple Scroll," *HAR* 9 (1985): 301–20. Cf. Talmon, "The 'Desert Motif' in the Bible and in Qumran Literature," in *Biblical Motifs: Origins and Transformations* (ed. A. Altmann; Studies and Texts 3; Cambridge: Harvard University Press, 1966), 55–63. Repr. in Shemaryahu Talmon, *Literary Studies in the Hebrew Bible: Form and Content: Collected Studies* (Leiden: Brill, 1993), 216–54.

14. E. Qimron, "The Text of CDC," in *The Damascus Document Reconsidered* (ed. M. Broshi; Jerusalem: Israel Exploration Society and the Shrine of the Book, Israel Museum, 1992), 9–49; Joseph M. Baumgarten, *Qumran Cave 4.XIII: The Damascus Document (4Q266–273)* (DJD 18; Oxford: Clarendon, 1996). See Baumgarten (3) for a table of correspondences of the Qumran manuscripts of the Admonition to the genizah text.

actually really new in Second Temple period Judaism. The exegesis put forward here is intended to justify a new, that is, contemporary, halakic ruling.

The second example I wish to put forward is also in the area of marriage law. The sectarians, again like Christians after them,[15] forbade marriage to one's niece (CD 5:8; 11QT 66:16–17 = 4Q524 15–22 4;[16] 4Q251[17] 2–317), a practice that one later rabbi particularly praised.[18] This prohibition was said to have been derived from a biblical law, namely that a woman may not marry her nephew (= a man may not marry his aunt). We are told by the Zadokite Fragments (CD 5:9–10) that the biblical laws of consanguineous marriage are stated from the point of view of the male, with the reverse prohibition assumed. This statement is in fact false, as can be seen from the examination of the two lists of prohibited consanguineous marriages in Lev 18 and 20 and their Qumran versions and adaptations. In other words, this again is an exegesis designed to support a new, sectarian prohibition. This is true of this and our previous example, even if other sects, such as Christianity, accepted the same views.

These examples need to be seen in light of what we know of the overall theory of "revealed" and "hidden" law, *nigleh* and *nistar*, in Qumran sectarian documents. The sect divided the law into two categories—the *nigleh*, "revealed," and the *nistar*, "hidden." The revealed laws were known to all Israel, for they were manifest in Scripture, but the hidden laws were known only to the sect and were revealed solely through sectarian exegesis. The notion of revealed and hidden laws discloses to us a system of sectarian legal theology. The revealed law—that is, the Torah and the words of the Prophets—was known by all of Israel, who, nonetheless, violated it. The hidden law, on the other hand, was known only to the sect. These hidden laws constituted the very points of disagreement around which the sect coalesced. The written Torah, originally revealed by God, had been modified later by His prophets through their divine visions. The hidden law, the *nistar*, had also developed over time and would continue to change, but it did not originate at the same time as the revealed Torah. Rather, it represented God's constant, ongoing revelation of Torah interpretation disclosed to the sectarians during and through their study sessions. These two types of

---

15. Chaim Rabin, *Qumran Studies* (Scripta Judaica 2; London: Oxford University Press, 1957), 91–93.

16. Émile Puech, *Qumrân Grotte 4.XVIII: Textes hébreux (4Q521–4Q528, 4Q576–4Q579)* (DJD 25; Oxford: Clarendon, 1998), 103–7.

17. Erik Larson, Manfred R. Lehmann, and Lawrence H. Schiffman, "Halakhot," in Joseph Baumgarten et al., *Qumran Cave 4.XXV: Halakhic Texts* (DJD 35; Oxford: Clarendon, 1999), 45–46.

18. *B. Yebam.* 62b; *y. Giṭ.* 83a; *b. Sanh.* 76b; *y. Yebam.* 13:2 (13c). Such a marriage is recorded in Josephus, *Ant.* 12.6.6 (§186).

law complemented each other and together made up the system of Jewish law as understood and practiced by the sect.[19] This system of supplementing the written Torah allowed for derivation of divinely inspired biblical legal interpretations. A few passages in the scrolls indicate that these legal interpretations were considered to be `et va-`et or `et ba-`et, "for each time" (CD 12:21, 1QS 9:13) or *le-fi ha-`ittim,* "for the (specific) times" (1QS 9:13) This indicates a realization that the law develops and changes through this interpretive technique. Apparently, the sectarians were aware that they practiced contemporizing biblical exegesis, even as part of their polemical program against their opponents.

I have tried to illustrate here a number of examples of how the Qumran documents make use of a variety of techniques to effectively update the traditions of the Bible. Techniques of this kind could be illustrated from inner biblical exegesis as well as from later Jewish legal traditions. Exegesis, in every phase of the history of Judaism, was harnessed both to preserve and to develop the heritage of the past. Along with the well-known phenomenon of contemporizing interpretation of the prophets and psalms in Qumran pesher texts, we need to recognize that such exegesis also exists in halakic texts, sometimes even in cases in which the texts claim the opposite. Law, exegesis, and history can never be separated.

---

19. L. H. Schiffman, *The Halakhah at Qumran* (SJLA 16; Leiden: Brill, 1975), 22–32.

# JEREMIAH AND THE "DIASPORA LETTERS" IN ANCIENT JUDAISM: EPISTOLARY COMMUNICATION WITH THE GOLAH AS MEDIUM FOR DEALING WITH THE PRESENT

*Lutz Doering*

Prophets do not normally write letters. When we turn to the Old Testament, there are, however, two exceptions to this rule. One is the prophet Elijah who according to 2 Chr 21:12–15 wrote a letter (21:12: MT מכתב; LXX ἐγγραφή) to King Jehoram of Judah, proclaiming judgment upon the king, his family, and his people. The other, more elaborate and subsequently more important, exception is the prophet Jeremiah.[1] Ever since his alleged letter to the Babylonian exiles in chapter 29 of the Masoretic book of Jeremiah and in chapter 36 of its Septuagint version, Jeremiah and later his companion Baruch have, in Jewish tradition, typically been associated with letter writing. Jeremiah's and Baruch's letters form one part of the correspondence conventionally called "Diaspora letters" in current scholarship.[2] The other part is represented by letters issued by

---

1. It may be argued that the letter of Shemaiah of Nehelam in Jer 29:24–28 (29) was also a prophet's letter; cf. v. 31 נבא *ni*. But the latter seems to be a later Deuteronomistic alignment of the "nonprophetic" Shemaiah with the "false" prophets in the context; cf. Winfried Thiel, *Die deuteronomistische Redaktion von Jeremia 26–45* (WMANT 52; Neukirchen-Vluyn: Neukirchener, 1981), 12–13.

2. Cf. Franz Schnider and Werner Stenger, *Studien zum neutestamentlichen Briefformular* (NTTS 11; Leiden: Brill, 1987), 34–41; Irene Taatz, *Frühjüdische Briefe: Die paulinischen Briefe im Rahmen der offiziellen religiösen Briefe des Frühjudentums* (NTOA 16; Fribourg: Universitätsverlag; Göttingen: Vandenhoeck & Ruprecht, 1991) (preferring paraphrases like "gemeindeleitende [] Briefe ... in die Diaspora" [109]); Manabu Tsuji, *Glaube zwischen Vollkommenheit und Verweltlichung: Eine Untersuchung zur literarischen Gestalt und zur inhaltlichen Kohärenz des Jakobusbriefes* (WUNT 2/93; Tübingen: Mohr Siebeck, 1997), 18–21; Karl-Wilhelm Niebuhr, "Der Jakobusbrief im Licht frühjüdischer Diasporabriefe," *NTS* 44 (1998): 420–43; S. R. Llewelyn, *A Review of the Greek Inscriptions and Papyri Published 1984–85* (vol. 8 of *New Documents Illustrating Early Christianity*; Grand Rapids: Eerdmans, 1997), 127. At a very late stage in the preparation of this article I gained access to Mark F. Whitters's dissertation *The Epistle of Second Baruch: A Study in Form and*

Jewish/Judean³ communities or their authorities, respectively, such as the Passover Papyrus found at Elephantine, the introductory letters to 2 Maccabees, and rabbinic "Diaspora letters."⁴ Among the most important constitutive features for the genre as a whole have been named: attribution to an authoritative addressor; communication with Jews/Judeans in the Diaspora, usually in large areas and broadly addressed; contents dealing with instruction or exhortation; a purpose aiming at strengthening the unity and unique identity of the people of God; and, as has been claimed, the leading role of Jerusalem.⁵

In this paper I will focus on the epistolary communication with the "exiles" fictitiously issued by Jeremiah (and his companion Baruch), thereby providing a comprehensive discussion of all the pertinent evidence available in ancient Judaism.⁶ In each instance I shall highlight questions of form and function. Special

---

*Message* (JSPSup 42; London: Sheffield Academic Press, 2003), which deals with "Diaspora letters" on pp. 86–101. Therefore, I was only able to include brief references to this work in the notes. The use of scare quotes around the term "Diaspora letter(s)" throughout this essay reflects insights regarding description of the genre specified below, section 8.2–3.

3. It seems advisable to speak of "Judeans," not of "Jews," for pre-Maccabean times due to an ethnic-geographic constitution of identity; cf. Shaye J. D. Cohen, *The Beginnings of Jewishness: Boundaries, Varieties, Uncertainties* (Hellenistic Culture and Society 31; Berkeley and Los Angeles: University of California Press, 1999), 69–106.

4. For the *Passover Papyrus:* AP 21, see Bezalel Porten and Ada Yardeni, eds., *Letters* (vol. 1 of *Textbook of Aramaic Documents from Ancient Egypt* (Jerusalem: Hebrew University, 1986), 54–55; for the introductory letters, see 2 Macc 1:1–10a, 1:10b-2:18; for rabbinic "Diaspora letters" see esp. *y. Ḥag.* 2:2 [77d, lines 35–38]; *y. Sanh.* 6:9 [23c, lines 27–30] "From Jerusalem the Great to Alexandria the Little"; cf. S. David Sperling "Fragments of Tannaitic Letters Preserved in Rabbinic Literature," in Dennis Pardee, with the collaboration of J. David Whitehead and Paul E. Dion, *Handbook of Ancient Hebrew Letters: A Study Edition* (SBLSBS 15; Chico, Calif.: Scholars Press, 1982), 183–211, here 204–7; *t. Sanh.* 2:6; *y. Sanh.* 1:2 [18d, lines 13–22]; *y. Ma'aś.Š.* 5:6 [56c, lines 9–18]; *b. Sanh.* 11(a–)b (= letters of Rn. Gamaliel; cf. Sperling, "Fragments of Tannaitic Letters," 189–96]; *MHG* Deut 26:13 [598 Fisch] = *Midr. Tanḥ.* Deut 26:13 [176 Hoffmann] (= letters of Rn. Simeon b. Gamaliel and R. Yohanan b. Zakkai; Sperling, "Fragments of Tannaitic Letters," 184–89).

5. Cf. Schnider and Stenger, *Studien zum neutestamentlichen Briefformular*, 34–35; Taatz, *Frühjüdische Briefe*, 102–10; Whitters, *Epistle of Second Baruch*, 86. Schnider and Stenger include also pseudonymous authorship (38), but even though many of the "Diaspora letters" may be pseudonymous, I do not see why they *necessarily* should be so. Whitters counts Greek language among the genre features (cf. Niebuhr, "Jakobusbrief," 403–31), but he admits that some of the texts show evidence of a Semitic original. The following survey will include texts in languages other than Greek.

6. For the most comprehensive discussion so far see Taatz, *Frühjüdische Briefe*, 46–81. However, two further texts ought to be included now (see below, sections 6 and 7); therefore, at times, Taatz's discussion of Jewish sources is in need of some update and refinement. For a more general study of Jeremiah in early Judaism (and Christianity), see Christian Wolff, *Jeremia im Frühjudentum und Urchristentum* (TU 118; Berlin: Akademie-Verlag, 1976).

attention will be given to the situation of addressors and addressees, if discernible. The assessment of newly available and undervalued evidence will lead us to refine the description of the genre "Diaspora letter." I shall also ask whether there is reason to assume that Judeans or Jews, both in the land and in the Diaspora, perceived themselves as living in an ongoing exile. Thus, I shall clarify how these letters to the "exiles" served as a medium for dealing with the addressees' present. As a starting point I shall briefly discuss the "mother" of all Jeremianic communication with the "exiles," Jeremiah's letter in Jer 29:1–23 (MT) and its version according to the Septuagint.

1. Jeremiah's Letter in Jeremiah 29 (LXX 36):1–23

According to Jer 29:1–3, Jeremiah sent a letter (ספר) "from Jerusalem to the remaining elders among the exiles (אל־יתר זקני הגולה), and to the priests, the prophets, and all the people, whom Nebuchadnezzar had taken into exile from Jerusalem to Babylon" (NRSV), that is, during the deportation of 598/7 B.C.E. The letter is said to be sent "by the hand" (ביד) of El'asah ben Shaphan and Gemariah ben Hilkiah, whom King Zedekiah of Judah had sent to Babylon. It is clearly introduced as divine speech: "Thus says the Lord of hosts, the God of Israel, to all the exiles whom I have sent into exile from Jerusalem to Babylon'" (v. 4; cf. v. 23 נאם־יהוה). The letter then consists of four threads of thought: (1) Verses 5–7 provide encouragement to settle down, build a livelihood, and pray for the welfare of Babylon,[8] since the exile will be more than a short stay abroad. (2) Verses 10–14 contain a promise to the exiles that the deportation will end "when Babylon's seventy years are completed" (thus v. 10), and an exhortation to search for God wholeheartedly. (3) Inserted into that we find in verses 8–9, 15, 21–23 an argument about competing ("false") prophets. (4) In verses 16–19 (20) there is an announcement of disaster for those left in Jerusalem.

Much debated are the questions of whether it is possible to discern a literary kernel around which the other material would have been gathered, and, if so, whether or not such a kernel could be identified as authentically Jeremianic. The absence of verses 16–20 from the text of the Septuagint seems to indicate that they where still missing in the Hebrew *Vorlage* from which LXX Jer was translated (in the middle of the second century B.C.E.?).[9] Further, verses

---

7. The phrase "to Babylon" is lacking in LXX; for a possible corollary see below, n. 42.
8. According to 29:7 MT, the city (העיר); according to 36:7 LXX, the land (τῆς γῆς).
9. This date according to Gilles Dorival, Marguerite Harl, and Olivier Munnich, *La bible grecque des Septante: Du judaïsme hellénistique au christianisme ancien* (Initiations au Christianisme

4–7 in contemporary scholarship are widely thought to go back to Jeremiah,[10] although some authors would not take even this for granted.[11] Several scholars see in verses 10–14 a later addition, mostly because of its longer syntactical units and its Deuteronomistic flavor.[12] Some argue—correctly, to my mind—that the thread concerning "false" prophets in verses 8–9, 15, 21–23 was inserted to link our pericope both with chapters 27–28 and with the context immediately following in 29:24–32.[13] It is likely that in the course of this redaction Shemaiah of Nehelam, whom we see protesting against Jeremiah's letter at verses 24–29, also received the image of a "false prophet" through Jeremiah's claim that he had "prophesied" (v. 31) even though he was not sent by God (see above, n. 1).

For our purpose of tracing the impact of this text on, and its reception within, ancient Judaism, these source-critical theories are only of limited relevance. Interestingly, however, the different strata are virtually identical with the four topical issues distinguished above. In this respect, we must account for the fact that ancient readers of the final form of the text, according to MT and LXX, encountered *both* the encouraging call for adjustment to a long exile (no. 1) *and* the promise of return after seventy years (no. 2). It is this feature of the text, especially, that triggered subsequent reception and rewriting. In its present combination the imperatives in verses 5–7, which may be termed "commands with an implied promise of success,"[14] provide encouragement for a prolonged future in a foreign country, seeking the new beginning within the realm of the family and in the context of the foreign city/land.[15] The announcement of future

---

ancien; Paris: Cerf, 1994 [1st ed., 1988]), 111; Folker Siegert, *Zwischen Hebräischer Bibel und Altem Testament: Eine Einführung in die Septuaginta* (Münsteraner Judaistische Studien 9; Münster: LIT, 2001), 42.

10. Cf. Thiel, *Die deuteronomistische Redaktion*, 11–19; Nelson Kilpp, *Niederreißen und aufbauen: Das Verhältnis von Heilsverheißung und Unheilsverkündigung bei Jeremia und im Jeremiabuch* (Biblisch-Theologische Studien 13; Neukirchen-Vluyn: Neukirchener, 1990), 45, 51. For a more "conservative" position, see Christopher Seitz, *Theology in Conflict: Reactions to the Exile in the Book of Jeremiah* (BZAW 176; Berlin: de Gruyter, 1989), 209–14; and the overview by Pamela Scalise in Gerald L. Keown, Pamela J. Scalise, and Thomas G. Smothers, *Jeremiah 26–52* (WBC 27; Dallas: Word, 1995), 64–65.

11. Cf. Robert P. Carroll, *The Book of Jeremiah: A Commentary* (OTL; London: SCM, 1986), 567, who proposes an "interpretation of the letter(s) of 29 as fabrication(s) within the cycle of 27–29"; Konrad Schmid, *Buchgestalten des Jeremiabuches: Untersuchungen zur Redaktions- und Rezeptionsgeschichte von Jer 30–33 im Kontext des Buches* (WMANT 72; Neukirchen-Vluyn: Neukirchener, 1996), 211 n. 53.

12. Cf. Thiel, *Die deuteronomistische Redaktion*, 14–16; Kilpp, *Niederreißen und aufbauen*, 63–67.

13. Cf. Thiel, *Die deuteronomistische Redaktion*, 13–14; Kilpp, *Niederreißen und aufbauen*, 53–55.

14. Thus Scalise, *Jeremiah 26–52*, 66, referring to GKC §110c.

15. Thus esp. Kilpp, *Niederreißen und aufbauen*, 56–60.

salvation in verses 10–14 corresponds to this promise. It is indeed worthwhile to settle down and to increase in the land of exile, but staying abroad will only be for a limited time. The reference to seventy years, in this respect, forms a link with Jer 25:11–12: "and these nations shall serve the king of Babylon seventy years. Then after seventy years are completed, I will punish the king of Babylon and that nation." Though it has been argued that in 29:10 the seventy years do not refer to the years of the exile but to the Babylonian rule, subsequent references to this number in Bible and Jewish literature, while providing many alterations, show that one cannot distinguish sharply between the two.[16]

Further, we must take into consideration that two versions regarding the issue of "disaster for the Jerusalemites" (no. 4) existed, one of which (represented at least by LXX) lacked this theme. Finally, we note that Jeremiah's letter has a historical aftermath, recorded later in the same chapter: Shemaiah of Nehelam wrote letters (v. 25: ספרים) to Jerusalem, referring to Jeremiah's preceding letter and quoting it in part verbally (v. 28 quotes v. 5). Jeremiah then was ordered by the Lord to "send" (שלח) again to the exiles (v. 31), denouncing Shemaiah as prophesying falsely and announcing his punishment. Thus we see much concern in Jeremiah's correspondence for various features of prophetic activity.

There has been some debate if ספר in Jer 29:1 really means "letter." Thus Pamela Scalise thinks "it is better to characterize the documents in chap. 29" as representing a "'booklet,' which contains a collection of prophecies," similar to chapters 30–31.[17] It is interesting that Jeremiah is associated with writing or dictating in three other pericopae: at 30:2 (ספר) concerning the "book of comfort" (30–31); at 36:2, 4 (מגלת־ספר) concerning the scroll dictated to Baruch; and at 51:60 (ספר) concerning the collection of oracles against Babylon. Only the latter one is sent to Babylon, but it is not directed to the exiles. Thus, we have to distinguish between "books" (ספרים) that were designed for sending and those that were not.[18] What makes an ancient text a "letter" is not the epistolary formulae in the first place—these formulae could have been lost; compare the incorporation of prescript-like formulations into Jer 29:1—it is rather its claim to be a written communication between two locally remote parties.[19]

---

16. Cf. Wolff, *Jeremia*, 100–116. Cf. generally also John Applegate, "Jeremiah and the Seventy Years in the Hebrew Bible: Inner-biblical Reflections on the Prophet and His Prophecy," in *The Book of Jeremiah and Its Reception* (ed. A. H. W. Curtis and T. Römer; BETL 128; Leuven: Leuven University Press/Peeters, 1997), 91–110.

17. Scalise, *Jeremiah 26–52*, 65.

18. For the special case of a "book" (βιβλίον) *secondarily* dispatched, cf. below, section 7 (Baruch LXX).

19. In fact, letters in the Hebrew Bible "are all embedded in narrative passages and lack the clearly formulaic character of the Aramaic letters contained in the book of Ezra" (Pardee,

Several indicators confirm that Jeremiah's writing was perceived as a letter. First, there is the subsequent correspondence in chapter 29, consisting of Shemaiah's reply and Jeremiah's second writing, notably the use of ספר (v. 29) for Shemaiah's letter and of the verb שלח (vv. 25, 28, 31) for the delivery of all three writings. Second, we have the witness of the additional headline in the narrative frame according to LXX 36:1: ἐπιστολὴν εἰς Βαβυλῶνα τῇ ἀποικίᾳ "A letter to Babylon, to the exile." Third, we know that also other texts clearly perceived Jeremiah's writing as a letter. Maybe the prophetic air has made some scholars hesitate in calling the units in chapter 29 "letters," but it is precisely the association of the prophet Jeremiah with letter writing that has affected subsequent texts.

## 2. The Epistle of Jeremiah (Ep Jer LXX)

The oldest one of these texts is the Epistle of Jeremiah (*Epistula Ieremiae*). In the Septuagint this short text of seventy-two verses,[20] dealing mainly with instructions on how to withstand Babylonian idols, comes after Jeremiah, Baruch, and Lamentations (in some manuscripts after Baruch; in the Vulgate it is counted as Bar 6). Dating from the third or second century B.C.E.,[21] it was quite likely originally composed in Hebrew.[22] As Reinhard Kratz has convincingly argued, it was

---

*Handbook*, 169). Cf. the functional definition of letters offered by Dirk Schwiderski, *Handbuch des nordwestsemitischen Briefformulars: Ein Beitrag zur Echtheitsfrage der aramäischen Briefe des Esrabuches* (BZAW 295; Berlin: de Gruyter, 2000), 17: "So soll ... nicht erst dann von einem Brief die Rede sein, wenn ein Mindestmaß an formalen Kriterien erfüllt ist, sondern bereits unter der Voraussetzung, daß der betreffende Text eine bestimmte *Funktion* übernimmt. Diese Funktion besteht darin, *eine aus räumlichen oder sonstigen Gründen verhinderte oder nicht gewollte mündliche Kommunikation zwischen zwei Personen oder Gruppen durch einen schriftlich verfaßten Text zu ersetzen.*" For Greco-Roman letters, cf. Michael Trapp, *Greek and Latin Letters: An Anthology with Translation* (Cambridge Greek and Latin Classics; Cambridge: Cambridge University Press, 2003), 1: "A letter is a written message from one person (or set of people) to another, requiring to be set down in a tangible medium, which itself is to be physically conveyed from sender(s) to recipient(s). Formally, it is a piece of writing that is overtly addressed from sender(s) to recipient(s), by the use of a limited set of conventional formulae of salutation (or some allusive variation on them) which specify both parties to the transaction."

20. I follow the Göttingen Septuagint here: Josef Ziegler, ed., *Jeremias, Baruch, Threni, Epistula Jeremiae* (2nd ed.; Septuaginta: Vetus Testamentum graecum auctoritate Academiae Scientiarum Gottingensis editum 15; Göttingen: Vandenhoeck & Ruprecht, 1976).

21. Cf. Antonius H. J. Gunneweg, "Das Buch Baruch, Der Brief Jeremias," *JSHRZ* 3/2 (1975): 186; George W. E. Nickelsburg, *Jewish Literature between the Bible and the Mishnah* (London: SCM, 1981), 35–42; Reinhard Gregor Kratz, "Der Brief des Jeremia," in Odil Hannes Steck et al., *Das Buch Baruch, Der Brief des Jeremia, Zusätze zu Ester und Daniel* (ATD Apokryphen 5; Göttingen: Vandenhoeck & Ruprecht, 1998), 82.

22. Cf. Gunneweg, "Das Buch Baruch," 185–86; Taatz, *Frühjüdische Briefe*, 57. Kratz is more cautious; he is only convinced by the assumption of two instances of mistranslation from Hebrew at vv. 30 and 71 (Kratz, "Der Brief des Jeremia," 74).

intended as an appendix to the book of Jeremiah, combining the polemics against idols from Jer 10 with a letter by Jeremiah, the model of which is Jer 29:1–23 (MT).[23] Although the Epistle of Jeremiah, except for the use of the second-person plural in addressing the recipients,[24] is virtually devoid of epistolary features, the reference to Jer 29 is evident from the *inscriptio*, as well as from verses 1–2. The *inscriptio* calls the text "a copy of a letter Jeremiah sent to those about to be led captive to Babylon" (ἀντίγραφον[25] ἐπιστολῆς ἧς ἀπέστειλεν Ιερεμίας πρὸς τοὺς ἀχθησομένους αἰχμαλώτους εἰς Βαβυλῶνα). This does not necessarily mean that the letter claims to be identical with the one at Jer 29:1–23;[26] on the contrary, there are indications that it does not.[27] First, there is no definite article with ἐπιστολή; it is a copy of *a* letter, not *the* letter sent by Jeremiah. Second, we know already from Jer 29:30–32 that Jeremiah sent more than one letter to the Golah; thus there is no need to limit the perception of Jeremiah's letter writing to the letter recorded at Jer 29:1–23. Third, the future tense of ἀχθησομένους makes for an important temporal difference. Unlike Jer 29:1–23, sent to the exiles after their deportation to Babylon, the present letter is directed to those for whom the exile is still imminent. When we turn to Ep Jer 2, we can see that the first part of the verse (especially ἔσεσθε ἐκεῖ ἔτη πλείονα καὶ χρόνον μακρόν "you will stay there for many years and long time") takes up the long stay for which Jeremiah provides encouragement at Jer 29:5–7 (thread no. 1 above).[28] The second part of the verse, in turn, refers to the promise of restoration at Jer 29:10–14 (no. 2), although the seventy years have been modified to seven generations. These allusions to, and modifications of, the biblical model betray a keen interest in understanding the present in light of the biblical promise, as we find it later, in a similar but in detail different way, also in Dan 9:2, 24–27. By modifying seven periods of ten years to seven generations—it does not matter for our purpose

---

23. Cf. R. G. Kratz, "Die Rezeption von Jeremia 10 und 29 im pseudepigraphen Brief des Jeremia," *JSJ* 26 (1995): 2–31. That the MT is the model is shown by the headline and v. 1 (mention of Nebuchadnezzar); cf. p. 20.

24. Cf. vv. 1–6; the refrain μὴ (οὖν) φοβηθῆτε / φοβεῖσθε αὐτούς / αὐτά in vv. 14, 22, 28, 64 and 68; and γνώσεσθε in vv. 22 and 71, referring to the situation depicted in vv. 1–6. Cf. Kratz, "Rezeption von Jeremia," 19.

25. For similar use of ἀντίγραφον, cf. 1 Esd 6:7; Philo, *Legat.* 315; Josephus, *Ant.* 12.35, 225; 13.166.

26. Thus Niebuhr, "Jakobusbrief," 425, who then has to cope with the differences between the texts.

27. Cf. Nickelsburg, *Jewish Literature*, 35: "the copy of another letter Jeremiah wrote to the exiles in Babylon."

28. Cf. Shemaiah's interpretation of Jeremiah's words, Jer 29:28 ארכה היא, cf. LXX 36:28 μακράν ἐστιν.

how these were exactly calculated[29]—the author of the Epistle of Jeremiah still places his (implied) addressees[30] within the period of the Babylonian exile.

What is, then, the chronological setting and aim of this letter? Viewed as an appendix to the book of Jeremiah, the Epistle wants to provide those about to be led into exile with useful protection against the idolatry expected in Babylon. It thus claims to be written some time before the letter of Jer 29:1–23. It does not, however, deny or contradict[31] Jeremiah's encouragement to settle down in Babylon, but it does flesh out what a prolonged coexistence with the Babylonians in their land would demand. In literary terms, it goes back and reacts to passages like Jer 16:13, where it states that God will cast the people out to a foreign country where they will serve other gods day and night (ועבדתם־שם את־אלהים אחרים יומם ולילה), or Jer 51 with its variations on the theme "Babylon and her idols." The ingredients for this protective treatment against idolatry are largely being taken from Jer 10:1–16, and secondarily also from other passages.[32] The constant refrain of the Epistle has been gathered from 10:5: "do not be afraid of them, because they are no gods." It is remarkable that in presenting his own paraenesis in the disguise of the exilic prophet, the author takes up several important Jeremianic passages, among them the polemic against idols (without Babylonian reference) at Jer 10, the issue of Babylon and her idols at Jer 51, and the letter at Jer 29; the author then merges them to form a fresh entity matching his needs. Thus we may say that the present is understood, at least in part, through a new synthesis of biblical texts.

---

29. Cf. for the whole issue Kratz, "Rezeption von Jeremia," 23–24 with n. 39 (bibliography).

30. A communication-theoretical model of different levels of "author" and "addressee," which can aptly be applied to the study of pseudepigraphic letters, has been proposed by Hannelore Link. This model distinguishes between (1) the real author(s) and the real addressee(s) on the text-external level; (2) the implied (also known as abstract) author(s) and the implied addressee(s) as encoded in the text; (3) the explicit author(s) and the explicit addressee(s) as named in the text; the fourth aspect concerns the contents. Cf. Hannelore Link, *Rezeptionsforschung: Eine Einführung in Methoden und Probleme* (2nd ed.; Stuttgart: Kohlhammer, 1980), 25–29.

31. Thus, however, Niebuhr, "Jakobusbrief," 425.

32. Cf. Jer 51:15–19; further Isa 40:18–20; 41:6–7; 44:9–20; 45:20; 46:5–7; Pss 115:4–7; 113:15–17; Bel, esp. 4–7. Cf. Kratz, "Rezeption von Jeremia," esp. 7–17. According to Kratz, the Epistle of Jeremiah responds to the doublet of the "idols" issue in Jer 10 (no Babylonian reference) and 51 (Babylon and her idols) in view of the dispersion (cf. 9:15) in order to ward off the threats posed in a passage like 16:13. By warning against the idols the Epistle of Jeremiah fully allows for the (ideally) subsequent letter of Jer 29 with its positive instructions for settling in the country (Kratz, "Brief des Jeremia," 78). This reading is more convincing than the suggestion by Carey A. Moore (following C. C. Torrey) that the Aramaic verse Jer 10:11 "inspired the author of the Epistle to expand upon it": Carey A. Moore, *Daniel, Esther and Jeremiah: The Additions* (AB 44; New York: Doubleday, 1977), 326.

The logic behind fictitiously setting the Epistle shortly before deportation implies, most plausibly, that the letter should be thought of as being taken by the exiles to Babylon and being reread there. Through the extension of the period of exile, the letter can still be of high relevance to its (real) addressees in the third or second century B.C.E. As we know, during that period the Babylonian cults[33] were strengthened by Alexander the Great and subsequently the Seleucids.[34] This suggests that we should look for the addressees precisely in the eastern Diaspora.[35] More specifically, Kratz thinks of the loyal, acculturated Judean population of central Babylonia, and perhaps of the Seleucid settlements in the whole Syrian-Mesopotamian area under Antiochus III. As is well known, while this Seleucid ruler granted special privileges to Jerusalem and its Temple, he also favored the loyal Babylonian Diaspora.[36] According to Kratz, the Epistle polemicizes from the stance of the Judean belief, now authorized by the state, against the Babylonian cults that were themselves promulgated by the state.[37] Both the extension of the period of exile and the Babylonian setting suggest the

---

33. For proof that the Epistle of Jeremiah is directed against Babylonian, not Greek or Egyptian, practice, see Wiegand Naumann, *Untersuchungen über den apokryphen Jeremiasbrief* (BZAW 25; Gießen: Töpelmann, 1913).

34. Cf. Susan Sherwin-White, "Seleucid Babylonia: A Case Study for the Installation and Development of Greek Rule," in *Hellenism in the East: Aspects of the Interaction of Greek and Non-Greek Civilizations from Syria to Central Asia* (ed. A. Kuhrt and S. Sherwin-White; London: Duckworth, 1987), 1–31; Amélie Kuhrt, "Alexander in Babylon," in *The Roots of the European Tradition: Proceedings of the 1987 Groningen Achaemenid History Workshop* (ed. H. Sancisi-Weerdenburg and J. W. Drijvers; Achaemenid History 5; Leiden: Nederlands Instituut voor het Nabije Oosten, 1990), 121–30. Cf. Ps.-Hecataeus *apud* Josephus, *C. Ap.* 1.192–193 for the Jews' opposition to pagan temple restoration and erection under Alexander and the Seleucids. Cf. further the texts for a New Year's ritual (*akitu*) from Babylon and Uruk: *TUAT* 2:212–27, dating from the Seleucid period.

35. It remains debated whether or not we should also look for the author in the eastern Diaspora. Nickelsburg, *Jewish Literature*, 38, views him in the Diaspora; Moore, *Daniel, Esther, and Jeremiah*, 328–29, and Kratz, "Brief des Jeremia," 86, dispute this.

36. For Jerusalem's privileges, see Antiochus's letter to Ptolemy: Josephus, *Ant.* 12.138–144 (Elias Bickerman, "La charte séleucide de Jérusalem," in idem, *Studies in Jewish and Christian History II* [AGJU 9/2; Leiden: Brill, 1980], 44–85), as well as his edict concerning the purity of temple and city in Josephus, *Ant.* 12.145–146 (Elias Bickerman, "Une proclamation séleucide relative au temple de Jérusalem," in idem, *Studies in Jewish and Christian History II*, 86–104); for the loyalty of Babylonian Jews, see his letter to Zeuxis in Josephus, *Ant.*, 12.147–153 (authentic according to Abraham Schalit, "The Letter of Antiochus III to Zeuxis Regarding the Establishment of Jewish Military Colonies in Phrygia and Lydia," *JQR* 50 [1960]: 289–318; but cf. Jörg-Dieter Gauger, *Beiträge zur jüdischen Apologetik: Untersuchungen zur Authentizität von Urkunden bei Flavius Josephus und im I. Makkabäerbuch* [BBB 49; Köln: Hanstein, 1977], 3–151).

37. Cf. Kratz, "Brief des Jeremia," 83–84. Josef Schreiner (in Heinrich Groß, *Klagelieder*; Josef Schreiner, *Baruch* [NEchtB 14; Würzburg: Echter, 1986], 49–50) favors the time of Alexander the Great.

author understood the challenges his addressees faced in terms of the Babylonian exile. Following Kratz, the analogy may have been built on the fact that these inhabitants of the Diaspora were settled roughly as Jer 29:5–7 had advised.[38] Later on, the Epistle of Jeremiah seems to have been received in the Egyptian Diaspora, for which the Greek translation was apparently made.

If these suggestions are correct, then the Epistle of Jeremiah can be grouped with other texts from the Greco-Roman period demonstrating that at least some saw Judeans/Jews in the Diaspora as living in an ongoing state of "exile," despite the restoration in Judea and the rebuilding of the Jerusalem temple under the Persians.[39] Regarding the self-understanding of members of the Diaspora, James M. Scott has recently gathered and discussed some pertinent evidence.[40] He has met, though, the criticism of Erich Gruen, who generally denies an "exilic" self-perception for Diaspora texts and holds that the pertinent lamentations always refer to the Assyrian and Babylonian deportations and never to the present situation, which was often taken with a considerable portion of self-confidence and humor.[41] Gruen may be right for many Diaspora compositions, but some of the evidence quoted by Scott still seems to be relevant; furthermore, unlike Gruen we do not look only at texts *originating* in the Diaspora.[42] Therefore, on

---

38. Cf. Kratz, "Brief des Jeremia," 83.

39. Cf. generally for the notion of a protracted exile (irrespective of the Diaspora) Michael A. Knibb, "The Exile in the Literature of the Intertestamental Period," *HeyJ* 17 (1976): 253–72, discussing *inter alia* Dan 9; *1 En.* 89–90 (Animal Apocalypse); *1 En.* 93:1–10; 91:11–17 (Apocalypse of Weeks); Epistle of Jeremiah (albeit with too-modest conclusions: "an allusion to the fact that many Jews remained in Babylonia after the end of the sixth century" [260]); the *Assumption of Moses; Jub.* 1:9–18; CD; Tob 14:4–7; Baruch; *4 Ezra; 2 Baruch.* Somewhat more reserved is David J. Bryan, "Exile and Return from [*sic*] Jerusalem," in *Apocalyptic in History and Tradition* (ed. C. Rowland and J. Barton; JSPSup 43; London: Sheffield Academic Press, 2002), 60–80, allowing for (at times, subtle) use of the exile theme in *1 En.* 89:72–3, Dan 9, *Assumption of Moses, Psalms of Solomon,* and Philo. He criticizes both N. T. Wright for undue emphasis on the matter (see N. T. Wright, *Jesus and the Victory of God* [London: SPCK, 1996]) and F. Gerald Downing for reserving the notion for the Qumranites only (see G. F. Downing, "Exile in Formative Judaism," in idem, *Making Sense in [and of] the First Christian Century* [JSNTSup 197; Sheffield: Sheffield University Press, 2000], 148–69). For Palestinian Jewry, see also below at nn. 82 and 109.

40. Cf. James M. Scott, "Exile and Self-Understanding of Diaspora Jews in the Greco-Roman Period," in *Exile: Old Testament, Jewish, and Christian Conceptions* (ed. J. M. Scott; JSJSup 56; Leiden: Brill, 1997), 173–218.

41. Cf. Erich S. Gruen, *Diaspora: Jews amidst Greeks and Romans* (Cambridge: Harvard University Press, 2002), esp. 232–52. That Diaspora Jews in the Greco-Roman period had moved from "exile ideology" to a self-understanding in terms of Hellenistic associations has earlier been argued by A. Thomas Kraabel, "Unity and Diversity among Diaspora Synagogues," in *The Synagogue in Late Antiquity* (ed. L. I. Levine; Philadelphia: ASOR, 1987), 49–60.

42. Scott, "Exile and Self-Understanding," points, e.g., at actualization of exilic statements in the Septuagint (see Deut 29:27[28]; 2 Chr 29:9) and the lack of the phrase "to Babylon" in the

the whole the exile motif may be said to be more prominent than the scope of Gruen's study would allow for. In his survey, Scott also criticizes the opposite form, so to speak, of tearing apart "exile" and "Diaspora," as exemplified by Willem C. van Unnik who holds that both terms are incommensurable since Greek διασπορά never translates biblical "exile," but denotes a much more horrible experience.[43] Scott justly cautions that a mainly word-study approach is insufficient for describing the diverse self-understanding of the Jewish Diaspora. The present article, observing a certain transparency of the exile for later generations in part situated in the Diaspora, confirms this criticism and suggests that van Unnik was too quick to dissociate "exile" and "Diaspora."[44]

However, since the Epistle was likely designed and transmitted as an appendix to the (Hebrew) book of Jeremiah, one can also assume early reception in the land of Israel.[45] Here two possible self-perceptions of the readership are in principle conceivable. Potential readers in the land may have shared the notion of a protracted exile, and that Judeans/Jews in Eretz Israel too were part of it; they may have read the Epistle as a warning against idolatry, applicable to any location, for the period of exile. However, another solution seems more appealing here, which may again have been facilitated—whether intended by the author or not—by the future tense of ἀχθησομένους.[46] Since those explicitly addressed by the Epistle's *inscriptio* are still located in the land of Israel, "real" readers of the Epistle in Palestine may, likewise, feel directly addressed. In this perspective the Epistle would provide instructions for dealing with idolatry especially during the infliction of coming hardships. Though such readers would not see themselves directly in exile, they nevertheless would perceive the need to be prepared for the challenge of idolatry.

In sum, both an analysis of the literary techniques and aims of the author and a reflection as to possible early reception of the Epistle show that the present was understood in light of Scripture, especially the role of the exile in the book

---

reference to exile in Jeremiah's letter (LXX 36:4). Cf. also Bryan's article mentioned above and the nuanced discussion of different concepts of "Diaspora" in ancient Judaism by Isaiah M. Gafni, *Land, Center and Diaspora: Jewish Constructs in Late Antiquity* (JSPSup 21; Sheffield: Sheffield Academic Press, 1997).

43. Cf. Willem C. van Unnik, *Das Selbstverständnis der jüdischen Diaspora in der hellenistisch-römischen Zeit* (ed. P. W. van der Horst; AGJU 17; Leiden: Brill, 1993).

44. It may be added with respect to lexical equivalents that, though the translation of "exile" in the LXX is never διασπορά, we do find Aramaic גלותא for "Diaspora" in the third Gamaliel letter, see below, n. 62.

45. Cf. Moore, *Daniel, Esther, and Jeremiah*, 325; Kratz, "Brief des Jeremia," 84–85.

46. For a similar reasoning, see Niebuhr, "Jakobusbrief," 425: "Durch die futurische Formulierung wird den Textrezipienten eine Identifikationsmöglichkeit mit den Briefadressaten angeboten."

of Jeremiah. However, the author's hermeneutic also amounted to a synthesis of Jer 29 with anti-idolatry passages unrelated to Jer 29 within the book itself. A further change is also due to the temporal distance from the days of Jeremiah. To be sure, there are still traces of prophetic authorization in the letter, like the divine instruction in the *inscriptio* (καθότι ἐπετάγη αὐτῷ ὑπὸ τοῦ θεοῦ), or the first-person singular forms in verses 2 (ἐξάξω) and 6 (ὁ γὰρ ἄγγελός μου), referring to God as implied speaker.[47] But there has been a clear shift to paraenetical and argumentative discourse in the Epistle. The prophet still writes, but he only faintly prophesies.

### 3. *Targum Jonathan* on Jeremiah 10:11

Another text clearly relating to Jeremiah's letter in chapter 29 of the biblical book is *Targum Jonathan's* elaboration on Jer 10:11,[48] a verse oddly in Aramaic in the Masoretic Text. Although assigning a date to this text is obviously difficult, there is some reason to assume that it is either prompted by a similar situation as the Epistle of Jeremiah or has, alternatively, some knowledge of this letter (in its Semitic original?).[49] Robert Hayward generally sees the origins of the Targum of Jeremiah "in the land of Israel during, or slightly before, the first century c. e. In fact, *Tg.*'s roots may be even older."[50] However, Codex Reuchlianus, the oldest witness for the Targum to all the Prophets (completed in 1105), quotes the MT and follows it with the targumic letter, which has led Pinkhos Churgin to consider the letter a later addition.[51] But even if Churgin were right,[52] this

---

47. This counterbalances Martin Karrer's statement that the Epistle is "nicht mehr als prophetische Botenrede gekennzeichnet" (Martin Karrer, *Die Johannesoffenbarung als Brief: Studien zu ihrem literarischen, historischen und theologischen Ort* [FRLANT 140; Göttingen: Vandenhoeck & Ruprecht, 1986], 49).

48. For the text, see Alexander Sperber, ed., *The Latter Prophets according to Targum Jonathan* (vol. 3 of *The Bible in Aramaic: Based on Old Manuscripts and Printed Texts;* Leiden: Brill, 1962), 160–61; for an English translation, see Robert Hayward, *The Targum of Jeremiah* (The Aramaic Bible 12; Edinburgh: T&T Clark, 1987), 79.

49. For the latter option, see Kratz, "Rezeption von Jeremia," 8–9 with n. 10, contra Emil Schürer, who denied that the Targum refers to Epistle of Jeremiah; Emil Schürer, *The History of the Jewish People in the Age of Jesus Christ [175 B.C.-A.D. 135]* (rev. and ed. by G. Vermes et al.; Edinburgh: T&T Clark, 1987), 3.2:744.

50. Hayward, *Targum of Jeremiah*, 38.

51. Cf. Pinkhos Churgin, *Targum Jonathan to the Prophets* (New Haven: Yale University Press, 1927), 134–35.

52. He assumes that the letter has "forced out" the MT wording in the text as handed down by all other manuscripts (ibid., 135), but why should not the MT quotation itself, conspicuous for its language, have intruded (as a gloss?) into the text represented by Codex Reuchlianus? The issue needs further study.

would not necessarily point to a late date of the passage, since it could well be an ancient tradition, at first independently transmitted.

At any rate, this letter is even more closely tailored to Jeremiah's letter in Jer 29 than the Epistle of Jeremiah. It claims to be "a copy of the letter that Jeremiah the prophet sent to the remnant of the elders of the exile who were in Babylon." The Aramaic שאר סבי גלותא דבבבל seems to be a rephrasing of the Hebrew יתר זקני הגולה (Jer 29:1). Like Jer 29:1–23 this letter is directed to the exiles after their deportation. Does it thus claim to be the same letter, as some think?[53] Not necessarily, given the inconsequential use of the *status emphaticus* in targumic Aramaic and the observation already noted above that Jeremiah wrote more than one letter to the Golah. Rashi, for one, mentioning the letter in his comments on Jer 10:11, remains quite general in determining its setting. It was, he writes, a letter to Jeconiah and those exiled with him, in order that they may answer in Aramaic when forced to worship the idols. The text of the letter provides a context for the Aramaic verse Jer 10:11. The instruction about what to say to the nations is framed by the case made in the letter: it is thought to be an answer to the request to worship the idols (note the replacement of MT אלהיא "gods" by *Tg.* טעון "idols"). Besides the announcement of their destruction at Jer 10:11, the letter shows that these idols are of no use and have no power; it also draws on the polemics against idols like Epistle of Jeremiah. Again, the merger of Jeremiah's epistolary communication and anti-idol arguments from Jer 10 serves a decidedly pragmatic purpose. The exact nature of this purpose must remain open, however, due to the uncertainties surrounding the history of this passage. Generally it seems to satisfy the need of encouraging the people to stay wholeheartedly with God the creator. The connection with prophetic divine discourse may still be feasible in the larger context of the targumic passage; it is not especially emphasized in the letter itself.

### 4. The Letter of Baruch (*2 Bar.* 78–86)

With the letter of Baruch at the end of the *Syriac Apocalypse of Baruch* (*2 Bar.* 78–86) we encounter an important witness of "Diaspora letters" within the Jeremiah-Baruch circle certainly dating from the period following the destruction of the Jerusalem temple in 70 C.E. According to the prevailing view in contemporary scholarship, the letter forms an integral part of the whole composition.[54] Nevertheless, the situation of textual transmission clearly shows that

---

53. E.g., Hayward, *Targum of Jeremiah*, 79 n. 8.
54. This was argued in detail by Pierre-Maurice Bogaert, *Apocalypse de Baruch: Introduction, traduction du syriaque et commentaire* (2 vols.; SC 144–45; Paris: Cerf, 1969), 1:67–78. Cf. now Whitters, *Epistle of Second Baruch*, 1–23.

chapters 78–86 have early been handed down as an independent letter. Only the manuscript from Milan's *Bibliotheca Ambrosiana* (= c) and an Arabic translation (Mount Sinai Arabic 589) show the complete text of *Syriac Baruch*,[55] while thirty-eight manuscripts contain the letter only. Regarding the date of this writing, most probably of Palestinian origin, opinions range from about 95 to 130 C.E.[56] Often it is assumed that the Greek version from which the Syriac has been translated goes itself back to a Semitic original, but this is far from sure.[57]

The recipients of the letter, which is delivered by an eagle (77:19, 20–26; 87:1 [only c]), are the nine and a half tribes across the River Euphrates, that is, the Assyrian exiles.[58] Since 77:(12), 17–19 and 85:6 mention another letter to the Babylonian exiles, sent by three men, which is, however, not quoted verbally,[59] one can assume that the letter of Baruch is given *pars pro toto* for Baruch's correspondence with the entire Golah. By the time *Syriac Baruch* is written all these areas count among the Jewish "Diaspora," and it is very likely that the letter, through the Golah address, is at least partly directed to inhabitants of the contemporary Diaspora, an issue we will look at more closely toward the end of this section. Contrary to a frequent assumption,[60] there is no reason to think that in the first and second centuries C.E. it was no longer known where the descendants of those deported under the Assyrians lived.[61] Thus, *pars pro toto* should be taken quite strictly as referring to one of two existing parts, given as an example of the whole. What is remarkable in this address, then, is the combination of broadness and differentiation. A comparable feature can also be shown

---

55. For the quality of the text of c, see Bogaert, *Apocalypse de Baruch*, 1:72–73; A. F. J. Klijn, "Die syrische Baruch-Apokalypse," *JSHRZ* 5/2 (1976): 118–19. For the Arabic text, see F. Leemhuis et al., eds. and trans., *The Arabic Text of the Apocalypse of Baruch* (Leiden: Brill, 1986).

56. Early dating (around 95) in Bogaert, *Apocalypse de Baruch*, 1:294–95; late dating (100–130) in Klijn, "Die syrische Baruch-Apokalypse," 114; and cf. the chart in Whitters, *Epistle of Second Baruch*, 155. For location, see Bogaert, *Apocalypse de Baruch*, 1:331–34; Klijn, "Die syrische Baruch-Apokalypse," 114. I remain unconvinced by Rivka Nir's recent attempt to view *2 Baruch* as a Christian text; cf. Rivka Nir, *The Destruction of Jerusalem and the Idea of Redemption in the Syriac Apocalypse of Baruch* (SBLEJL 20; Atlanta: Society of Biblical Literature, 2003).

57. Klijn, "Baruch-Apokalypse," 110–11, favors the assumption of a Hebrew original. Bogaert, *Apocalypse de Baruch*, 1:353–80, remains skeptical: the original may have been in Koine Greek with Hebraisms.

58. For the numbers (against which *2 Bar.* 1:2 divides between ten and two), see Bogaert, *Apocalypse de Baruch*, 1:339–52.

59. Scholars are divided on the reasons for this. See ibid., 1:78–80, for an overview.

60. Cf. Gerhard Delling, *Jüdische Lehre und Frömmigkeit in den Paralipomena Jeremiae* (BZAW 100; Berlin: de Gruyter, 1967), 6–7 n. 12; Taatz, *Frühjüdische Briefe*, 63; cf. also Bogaert, *Apocalypse de Baruch*, 1:339.

61. Cf. esp. Richard Bauckham, "Anna of the Tribe of Asher (Luke 2:36–38)," *RB* 104 (1997): 161–91, esp. 163–78.

in other "Diaspora letters," such as the Gamaliel letters[62] and, as a Christian example, 1 Peter, which is addressed to specific regions of "Diaspora."[63]

The author of the letter is Jeremiah's companion and "scribe" (Jer 36:26, 32) Baruch ben Neriah, writing from Judea (more specifically from an oak tree [*2 Bar.* 77:18]—the same from which he had watched the razing of Jerusalem [6:1]?). Baruch's relation to Jeremiah in *2 Baruch* is a complex issue. In contrast to the portrait in the Hebrew Bible, Baruch is depicted as a prophet himself at the outset (note the *Wortereignisformel* at *2 Bar.* 1:1).[64] However, the remark at 85:3 "and the prophets have lain down (sc. have passed away)" indicates that for the Apocalypse the time of the prophets belongs already to the past. Still, *2 Baruch* does deal with the "prophet" (thus 33:1) Jeremiah. While Jeremiah, to a certain degree, appears to be subordinate to Baruch or, as Bogaert puts it, to play the role of a "silent extra,"[65] we will note that he has quite specific features and functions in *2 Baruch* as soon as we consider also other activities beside direct speech.[66]

From 2:1–2 it emerges that Jeremiah is the most eminent in the group of upright and praying intercessors (including Baruch), commanded to leave the city before its destruction. Further, according to 9:1 it is Jeremiah's heart that "has been found pure from sin." Finally, and most important, Jeremiah is told to "go and support [*dn'zl wnqym*] the captives of the people unto Babylon" (10:2); it is reported that he "went away [*whw dyn 'zl*] with the people" (10:5); and later he is quoted as having "affirmed [*w'tqn*] the rest of our brothers in Babylon" (33:2).

Thus, regarding the roles of Baruch and Jeremiah in *2 Baruch* we should, at least as one factor, account for the tradition of Jeremiah accompanying the exiles

---

62. Cf. t. *Sanh.* 2:6, where the third letter distinguishes between "our brothers belonging to the Babylonian Diaspora (גלותא), and belonging to the Median Diaspora and all the other Israelite Diasporas." For the regions in the first two letters (on the fringes of Eretz Israel), see below, before n. 119. According to Bauckham, the "Median Diaspora" refers to the whereabouts of the northern tribes ("Anna," 166–70, 175–76).

63. Cf. 1 Pet 1:1: "to the elect sojourners of the Diaspora of Pontus, Galatia, Cappadocia, Asia, and Bithynia." For 1 Peter as a Christian "Diaspora letter" see, e.g., Tsuji, *Glaube zwischen Vollkommenheit und Verweltlichung*, 29–32. I am currently working on a monograph on 1 Peter that will deal with this issue more broadly.

64. In part of rabbinic tradition Baruch is considered a prophet (and partly also a priest), cf. *Sipre Num* §78 [74.1–7 Horovitz]; *b. Meg.* 14b–15a; *S. 'Olam Rab.* 20 [331.4 Weinstock]. However, the *Mekilta* disagrees with this view; cf. *Mek.* פסחא בא 1 [5.14–6.10 Horovitz and Rabin]; and cf. Bogaert, *Apocalypse de Baruch*, 1:104–8.

65. Bogaert, *Apocalypse de Baruch*, 1:104 ("comparse muet"). It is Baruch who delivers the word to Jeremiah at *2 Bar.* 2:1; 5:5; 10:2, 4. However, 33:1 speaks of the "orders" Jeremiah imposed on Baruch (*pwqdn' dpqdk*).

66. Cf. Wolff, *Jeremia*, 30–34.

on their way to and (partly, as in *2 Baruch*)⁶⁷ also during their stay in Babylon. This tradition emphasizes the orientating activity of Jeremiah among the exiles,⁶⁸ which is colored in pastoral terms in *2 Baruch* more than in other specimens of the tradition. When we further take into account that in apocalypses the "pseudonymous authors are frequently identified as wise men or scribes,"⁶⁹ Baruch seems to be a first rate choice for authorship of a work placing Jeremiah with the exiles and containing epistolary communication with the Golah from Jerusalem.

The letter has a remarkable prescript and introduction, respectively (78:2): *hkn' 'mr brwk br nry' l'ḥ' d'štbyw rḥm' 'p šlm' nhw' lkwn* "Thus speaks Baruch the son of Neriah to the brothers who were carried away in captivity: 'Mercy and peace be to you!'" The prescript, which plays a significant role in the debate about models for the Pauline epistolary greeting χάρις ὑμῖν καὶ εἰρήνη,⁷⁰ is intimately interwoven with the introduction; it integrates the details regarding the explicit addressor and addressees into a deictic sentence, "Thus speaks." This, however, allows for an important observation. In spite of the archaizing or biblicizing "feel" of the introduction, this letter does not claim to be divine speech. It does not open by "Thus speaks the Lord," but by "Thus speaks Baruch."⁷¹ This evidence is

---

67. *2 Baruch* presupposes indirectly that Jeremiah died in Babylon; see Wolff, *Jeremia*, 92–93.

68. For this tradition, see further below, section 6, and more broadly the article mentioned below in n. 99.

69. John J. Collins, *The Apocalyptic Imagination: An Introduction to Jewish Apocalyptic Literature* (2nd ed.; Grand Rapids: Eerdmans, 1998), 39. Besides Baruch, Collins refers to Enoch, Daniel, and Ezra.

70. Thus the short form 1 Thess 1:1. This is not the place for a detailed discussion of this problem, just a few remarks: (1) I find it more likely that Syriac *rḥm'* translates Greek ἔλεος than Greek χάρις; see Bogaert, *Apocalypse de Baruch*, 1:520; 2:142; Taatz, *Frühjüdische Briefe*, 67; contra Klijn, "Baruch-Apokalypse," 175. Hans-Josef Klauck remains undecided (*Die antike Briefliteratur und das Neue Testament: Ein Lehr- und Arbeitsbuch* [Paderborn: Schöningh, 1998], 212). One indication in favor of Bogaert's view is that the Syriac versions in New Testament epistolary prescripts *constantly* translate χάρις by *ṭybwt'* while reserving *rḥm'* for ἔλεος. (2) This suggests in turn that Paul himself has introduced χάρις into the Jewish greeting formula; see, e.g., Judith M. Lieu, "'Grace to You and Peace': The Apostolic Greeting," *BJRL* 68 (1985–86): 161–78, here 170.

71. Formally this prescript may be a blend of the Greek and the oriental style, depending on the original language assumed. If it were Greek, the prescript would show oriental influence in the peace greeting. If it were in a Semitic language, however, it would be influenced by the position of addressor and addressee in Greek prescripts ("A to B," not originally oriental); cf. Schwiderski, *Handbuch des nordwestsemitischen Briefformulars*, 247–48, 317–18. In either way it is assumed that "Thus speaks" was later prefixed. If, however, the Semitic phrase originally started with "Thus speaks Baruch," one could also assume an inner-oriental variant, similar to the self-introduction of a messenger; cf. Klauck, *Die antike Briefliteratur*, 212; Bogaert, *Apocalypse de Baruch*, 1:70: "typiquement sémitique." Clearly influenced by Hellenistic letter writing are the philophronetic phrases in 86:(1–)3; cf. Karrer, *Johannesoffenbarung als Brief*, 50.

supported by the further observation that there is not even an immediate divine command in 2 Baruch to write the two letters (contrast ἐπετάγη αὐτῷ ὑπὸ τοῦ θεοῦ in Ep Jer *inscriptio!*). On the contrary, the first one is said to be requested by the people (77:12: "Write also to our brothers in Babylon"; cf. v. 17), whereas the second one, to the Assyrian exiles, seems to be Baruch's own completion of this request (77:17: "I shall also write to the nine and a half tribes"). We thus note a significant further move away from the prophetic features of Jer 29. To be sure, there is, as already mentioned, some prophetic coloring of Baruch at the beginning of the Apocalypse[72] (cf. 1:1). Later we find that the (explicit) author of the letter is *generally* authorized as a recipient of revelation (81:4), as being "sent" (84:7), and as charged by God with teaching the people (76:5). As well, the entrance of the eagle symbolizes a special sort of authorization.[73] However, it remains noteworthy that there is no prophetic legitimization in the letter proper; in this respect, the apocalyptic has taken over from the prophet here. Within the scope of his general divine commission Baruch writes on his authority as a divinely inspired teacher located in *Eretz Israel*.

This is also evident from the use of the testamentary genre within the apocalypse. In three instances *2 Baruch* employs the testament form:[74] at chapters 44–46 (an address to Baruch's son, friends, and seven elders); at 77:1–10 (a farewell speech to the people); and in the letter proper (cf. 78:5 "before I die"; 84:1 "as long as I am still alive"). The testamentary genre is excellently suited for preserving exhortation to the law beyond the death of the inspired teacher, especially when it is combined with the epistolary form. These features are still enhanced by the final order directed at the addressees to read the letter in their

---

72. I consider the whole of *2 Baruch* a "historical" apocalypse, with Collins, *Apocalyptic Imagination*, 6–7, 212–25, cf. his view of the apocalyptic genre as *Rahmengattung* (1–42). For the conspicuous combination of various genres within *2 Baruch* (apocalypse, letter, testament), see Whitters, *Epistle of Second Baruch*, 156–59.

73. The eagle as letter carrier recurs in *Paralipomena Jeremiae;* see below, section 5. In Greek literature the eagle is associated with Zeus; see Homer, *Il.* 8.245–252 (with regard to omens); 24.292–298, 310–312 (as messenger [ἄγγελος] and dearest to Zeus among the birds); *Anth. pal.* 9.223 [Bianor] Ἀγγελίην πὰρ Ζηνὸς ἐπεὶ φέρεν ἠεροδίνης αἰετός "As the eagle who circles on high [...] was bearing a message from Zeus"; cf. 9.265 [Apollonides or Philippus] Διὸς ὄρνις "the bird of Zeus" (W. R. Patron, trans., *The Greek Anthology* [LCL; Cambridge: Harvard University Press, 1917], 3:116–17, 140–41). Attitudes of Jews in antiquity to the "king of birds" (Aeschylus, *Ag.* 113; Callimachus, *Hymn.* 1:68; Pindar, *Pyth.* 1:13; *Isthm.* 6:50; Josephus, *War* 3:123; *4 Bar.* 7:9; *b. Ḥag.* 13b [נשׁר]) were ambiguous: once knocked off the Herodian temple (Josephus, *War* 1:648–655; *Ant.* 17:149–167) and experienced as the sign of the victorious Romans (*War* 3:123; 5:48; 6:316), representations of eagles were later adopted on synagogue lintels and furnishings (see the illustration in *EJ* 6:337–38 [Gush Halav, Sardis]).

74. Cf. Bogaert, *Apocalypse de Baruch*, 1:120–26, and now Whitters, *Epistle of Second Baruch*, 44–46, 156–68.

assemblies and to contemplate it especially during their fast-days (86:1–3; cf. also 84:7, the letter as "testimony," and 84:9, the order to pass the letter and the law on to the children). Further, this later sample of a "Diaspora letter" within the Jeremiah-Baruch circle is already cross-influenced by features of the "community type" letters to the Diaspora mentioned at the outset of this article. The most conspicuous feature in this respect is the designation of the addressees as "brothers" (*2 Bar.* 78:2, 3, [5]; 79:1; 80:1 etc.).[75] This underscores the emphasis on the cohesion and integrity of the people resident both in the land of Israel and in the Diaspora. The contents of the letter of Baruch match such a paraenetical function. Summarized in 78:5, they can be described as an account of the disaster (chs. 79–80), comfort in the current situation (chs. 81–83), and the acknowledgement of divine judgment (chs. 84–85). From a more pragmatic perspective, the letter can be characterized as a blend of Torah paraenesis, consolation, and revelation.[76]

How is the present being read in light of Scripture in this text? Karl-Wilhelm Niebuhr has pointed out that the letter with its *pars pro toto* Diaspora address, its direction toward the future destiny of the people, and its being issued by a recipient of revelation made it suited to "function" as an authoritative "Diaspora letter" issued from Eretz Israel. "Die Identifikation der Textrezipienten mit den Briefempfängern ist hier besonders naheliegend."[77] The letter, as well as the apocalypse as a whole, betrays the keen interest in the "exilic" characters of Jeremiah and Baruch after the destruction of the temple in 70 C.E. that has been emphasized by Christian Wolff in his classic monograph.[78] As in *4 Ezra* (cf. 3:1–2, 28–31; 10:20–24, 44–49), a text closely related to *2 Baruch*, 70 C.E. "was being read" in terms of 587 B.C.E.[79] Similar to the earlier event, "70" was

---

75. See n. 4 above for these texts. Cf. for the "brothers" address AP 21:1, 10; 2 Macc 1:1; the Gamaliel and Simeon ben Gamaliel-Yohanan letters; further Acts 15:23–29 (v. 23b), a Christian "Diaspora letter." I remain unconvinced, though, by Whitters's recent proposal (*Epistle of Second Baruch*, 81–85) to classify *2 Bar.* 78–87 proper also as a *festal* letter (see below, n. 120). Passages such as 84:7–9 and 86:1–3 do not seem to promulgate any one specific Jewish feast or fast but rather to make provisions for reception of the letter and its exhortation, as argued above.

76. Cf. Bogaert, *Apocalypse de Baruch*, 1:126. For Torah paraenesis in *2 Baruch*, see Wolfgang Harnisch, *Verhängnis und Verheißung der Geschichte: Untersuchungen zum Zeit- und Geschichtsverständnis im 4. Buch Esra und in der syr. Baruchapokalypse* (FRLANT 97; Göttingen: Vandenhoeck & Ruprecht, 1969), 208–22.

77. Niebuhr, "Jakobusbrief," 429; cf. the preceding context on pp. 428–29.

78. Cf. Wolff, *Jeremia*, e.g., 95–98, 188, 189–92.

79. Cf. ibid., 34; Bogaert, *Apocalypse de Baruch*, 1:102–3; Knibb, "Exile," 269–71 (who points also at the differences between the two texts). The parallelism of the two temple destructions is also evident in the dating of both on the same day of the year; see Jer 52:12 (10th Ab) (but cf. 2 Kings 25:8–9: 7th Ab) with Josephus, *War* 6:249–250 (250: ἡ εἱμαρμένη χρόνων περιόδοις ἡμέρα "the fated day in the revolution of the years," i.e., 10th Loos, equivalent to Ab; he further reports that

perceived as a catastrophe imposed by a foreign power, leading to a situation for which guidance was necessary, and epistolary communication modeled on Jeremiah's letter was an efficient means for this. However, the details in form and contents have changed from prophetic to paraenetical, consolatory, and revelatory discourse.

Further, it is intriguing to observe the interplay of tenses and temporal markers throughout the letter. While the references to Moses (84:2–5) and the prophets (85:1–3) are dominated by the perfect tense (in Syriac), we find, especially in chapter 85, statements concerning the future in the imperfect tense (e.g., 83:2–3; 85:4–5, 7, 12), paraenetically supplemented by the cohortative (83:4–5; 85:9) and the imperative (83:8; 85:11). In the middle between these tenses, so to speak, we find a conspicuous reiteration of the temporal marker "now" (*[d]hš*; cf. 82:3; 83:5, 10–15, 17–20, 22; 84:5; 85:3). It is obvious that this "now" invites the addressees to read it as immediately referring to their own present, thus suggesting again transparency of the "exile" for later generations. More specifically, by this application the addressees become indeed integrated into the "present" of the "exilic" letter. This process can be best described as a mutual penetration or "melting" of temporal horizons. Thus, we find elements of the addressees' contemporary outlook incorporated into the text, such as the notion, mentioned above, that the prophets have passed away and that the people have nothing except God and his law (85:3).[80] Again we observe that the letter, with its testamentary elements, being received, (re-)read, and passed on by the addressees, is a very efficient medium for such a hermeneutic process. All this would work best with addressees actually located in the Diaspora.[81] However, we should note that 2 *Baruch* views *all* tribes of Israel in exile (cf. esp. 78:4; 85:3, with Baruch writing, "*We* have left our land"). If this were also to be

---

on 8th Loos [70 C.E.] the temple was already set on fire: 220–35); *t. Ta'an.* 4 [3]:9; *b. Ta'an.* 29a; *b. 'Arak.* 11b (the rabbinic texts harmonize the biblical data [and those as reported by Josephus?—thus Bogaert, *Apocalypse de Baruch*, 1:173] and, as is well known, reckon the 9th Ab as the date of both destructions). Bogaert has argued that over against this 2 *Baruch* takes the end of the siege on 8th Elul as starting point for its internal calculations; see Bogaert, *Apocalypse de Baruch*, 1:163–76.

80. See already Harnisch, *Verhängnis und Verheißung*, 214–15. This seems to be a better explanation of this statement than Wolff's suggestion (*Jeremia*, 33) that 85:1–5 belong to an older text unit. Regarding the notion of time in the Gospel of John, Jörg Frey (*Das johanneische Zeitverständnis* [vol. 2 of *Die johanneische Eschatologie*; WUNT 110; Tübingen: Mohr Siebeck, 1998], 247–68, 287, 290–91, 296) has noted a similar *Horizontverschmelzung*: retrospective verbal forms are anachronistically integrated in Jesus' farewell speech (and other passages), imputing the Johannine perspective to Jesus.

81. For this, see the considerations in Bogaert, *Apocalypse de Baruch*, 1:335–52.

understood as a qualification of Israel in the author of *2 Baruch*'s own time, the assumption of a comparable reception in Palestine would make no less sense.[82]

### 5. Baruch to Jeremiah and Jeremiah to Baruch according to *Paralipomena Jeremiae* (*P. J.* [*4 Bar.*] 6:17–23; 7:23–29)

Next, mention should be made of the two letters in *Paralipomena Jeremiae*, a work probably of Palestinian origin, dating from the first third of the second century C.E. and closely related to *2 Baruch*.[83] The two letters on first sight seem to be merely a private correspondence: in chapter 6 from Baruch to Jeremiah and in chapter 7 from Jeremiah to Baruch.[84] However, both letters, which were specifically designed for their literary context, have broader implications. While in *Paralipomena Jeremiae* Jeremiah stays with the exiles in Babylon, the Ethiopian Abimelech falls asleep for sixty-six years. When he awakes, the figs he has been ordered to carry are ripe—though it is out of season—and they are still fresh (3:9–10, 15–16; 5:1–6:10). Abimelech finds Baruch at a tomb close to Jerusalem (4:11; 6:1; 7:1), and the latter wishes to report the sign of the figs to Jeremiah in Babylon. An angel appears to Baruch and commands him to write a letter to Jeremiah (6:11–13). The angel even outlines the contents of this letter: Jeremiah shall speak to the children of Israel that everyone who has become "a foreigner" (ξένος [6:13])[85] must separate himself for fifteen days. Thereafter, God will lead the people back to Jerusalem; those not separating themselves from Babylon will neither come into Jerusalem nor be received back by the Babylonians (6:13–14). The following letter of Baruch

---

82. See Whitters, *Epistle of Second Baruch*, 52: *2 Baruch* views Palestinian Jews as "living in a spiritual and moral exile"; and Bogaert, *Apocalypse de Baruch*, 1:334: "L'exil de l'auteur … est donc sprituel et moral."

83. For the date and location, see Berndt Schaller, "Paralipomena Jeremiou," *JSHRZ* 1/8 (1998): 678–81. I consider *Paralipomena Jeremiae* (a title I prefer over *4 Baruch*) essentially a Jewish work, except for the Christian closing in ch. 9; see Schaller, "Paralipomena Jeremiou," 665–66, 677–78; Jens Herzer, *Die Paralipomena Jeremiae: Studien zu Tradition und Redaktion einer Haggada des frühen Judentums* (TSAJ 43; Tübingen: Mohr Siebeck, 1994), 159–76.

84. Text and numeration according to J. Rendel Harris, *The Rest of the Words of Baruch: A Christian Apocalypse of the Year 136 A.D.: The Text Revised with an Introduction* (London: Clay, 1889). In Codex Barberini (= a) and in the Slavonic version Sla the letters are not reproduced verbally; see Schaller, "Paralipomena Jeremiou," 734 (n. d on 6:16). For Jeremiah's letter, A B C ArmC SlB have a shorter text (Schaller, "Paralipomena Jeremiou," 741 [n. a on 7:23]); the longer variant (C I Aeth) is to be preferred (689 n. 180). Sigla according to Schaller, "Paralipomena Jeremiou," 689–92.

85. The meaning seems to be "become an apostate"; thus, e.g., Schaller, "Paralipomena Jeremiou," 733.

(6:17–23), however, differs to no small degree from this sketch and must rather be called complementary.[86] It mentions God's mercy and covenantal faithfulness, the people's sturdiness, and a conditional promise of return that Jeremiah is to deliver to the people and that differs in detail from the angel's outline. As in *2 Baruch*, Baruch sends the letter, together with fifteen figs from Abimelech's basket, through an eagle.

The prescript of the letter is somewhat odd: Βαροὺχ ὁ δοῦλος τοῦ Θεοῦ γράφει τῷ Ἰερεμίᾳ· Ὁ ἐν τῇ αἰχμαλωσίᾳ τῆς Βαβυλῶνος, χαῖρε καὶ ἀγαλλιῶ "Baruch, the servant of God, writes to Jeremiah: While your are in the captivity of Babylon, be glad and rejoice" (6:17). To begin, χαῖρε should not be considered a variant of the greeting formula χαίρειν,[87] since in the few examples of formulaic χαῖρε it always comes at the beginning and is followed with a vocative.[88] The occurrence of γράφει is also peculiar; it is not normally found in Greek prescripts.[89] This has been explained as the relic of a messenger formula.[90] But, it is significant that a verb indicating speech has been replaced by one denoting written communication. This emphasis is further advanced by the report-like way this letter refers to divine speech: "For he [sc. God] has sent me his angel and told me (καὶ εἶπέ μοι) these words, which I am *sending* (ἀπέστειλα)[91] you " (6:19). Likewise, at 6:20 Baruch merely *reports* "the words the Lord, the God of Israel, *has* said (εἶπε Κύριος [aorist!])," i.e., through the angel (even if this is at variance with the angelic speech at 6:13–14, see above). The one single occurrence of λέγει Κύριος in Baruch's letter (6:22) therefore most probably belongs to the angelic speech (thus also 6:13, 14). However, alongside this emphasis on mediation of divine speech we nevertheless gather Baruch's divine authorization to write the letter

---

86. Thus Klauck, *Die antike Briefliteratur*, 218, who points out that both letters aim at further supplementation at 8:2–3, which is one of the main indications for their purely "literary" existence in *Paralipomena Jeremiae;* see Herzer, *Paralipomena Jeremiae*, 118.

87. Pace Taatz, *Frühjüdische Briefe*, 79.

88. See Francis X. J. Exler, *The Form of the Ancient Greek Letter: A Study in Greek Epistolography* (Washington, D.C.: Catholic University of America, 1923), 35–36; Heikki Koskenniemi, *Studien zu Idee und Phraseologie des griechischen Briefes bis 400 n. Chr.* (AASF Ser. B 102.2; Helsinki: Suomalainen Tiedeakatemia, 1956), 164–67. Further, the nominative ὁ suggests that χαῖρε should not be joined with the dative τῷ Ἰερεμίᾳ but rather with καὶ ἀγαλλιῶ. It thus belongs to a part of the letter equivalent to a "prooemium"; see Klauck, *Die antike Briefliteratur*, 218. For links with the context, esp. with 6:3, see Herzer, *Paralipomena Jeremiae*, 117.

89. The one example noted by Schaller is late and in Coptic: Schaller, "Paralipomena Jeremiou," 734 (n. b on 6:17), referring to Adolf Deissmann, *Licht vom Osten* (4th ed.; Tübingen: Mohr Siebeck, 1923), 188–89.

90. Thus Taatz, *Frühjüdische Briefe*, 79.

91. An epistolary aorist; see BDR §334.

from his self-designation as "servant of God"[92] and, again, the delivery of the letter by an eagle.[93]

While all letters discussed so far have allegedly been sent from Jerusalem or its vicinity, Jeremiah's response (*P.J.* 7:23–29) is sent from Babylon to Jerusalem. Though formulated in a more personal tone and virtually devoid of normal epistolary features (starting with υἱέ μου ἀγαπητέ "my beloved son" [7:23]), it is not a private letter.[94] It recalls both the suffering of the people in Babylon and the threat of apostasy, inviting those in Judea to pray for the return of the exiles, especially that they may hear the words of Jeremiah which—according to Baruch's preceding letter (6:22)—is the prerequisite of restoration. This letter also emphasizes the unity and mutual responsibility of the people. In line with the evidence so far, it does so without any employment of prophetic speech.[95] At the same time, this reply from Babylon to Jerusalem is a first indication that "Diaspora letters" do not function only from Judea to the Diaspora, but may follow also others paths of communication.

Both letters with their context allude to the biblical model of Jeremiah's letter, but they are also shaped by variations on other Jeremianic materials (e.g., Abimelech [Ebed-melech in Jer 38:7, etc.]), by independent elaboration (e.g., the fig miracle, mutual prayer, and the probe with Jordan water [6:23]), as well as by features deriving either from *2 Baruch* (thus Jens Herzer)[96] or from a source common to *2 Baruch* and *Paralipomena Jeremiae* (thus Berndt Schaller).[97] Most notable among these latter features are Baruch's role as one of the letter writers and the eagle as the letter carrier. On the other hand, in *Paralipomena Jeremiae* we again see Jeremiah as (the other) letter writer. This composition may further be viewed as developing and modifying thread number 2 (see §1 above) of Jeremiah's letter in Jer 29, dealing with restoration from exile. The figure of sixty-six years too may be related to the seventy years of exile according to Jer 29:10, although the issue remains debated.[98] It is clear, however, that the temporal situation of both letters differs from that of Jer 29 (and of *2 Bar.* 78–86), since these

---

92. Cf. New Testament epistolary prescripts: Rom 1:1; Titus 1:1; Jas 1:1; 2 Pet 1:1.

93. Karrer, *Johannesoffenbarung als Brief*, 52, points out that Baruch's letter is in need of special authorization: the eagle both introduces the letter at its delivery (7:15) and certifies it by reviving a dead man (7:17), and its contents are repeated in direct divine discourse at 8:2–3. It is, nevertheless, not useful to call this letter "ein eher privates Schreiben."

94. Contra Taatz, *Frühjüdische Briefe*, 81: "persönliches Klageschreiben."

95. See also Karrer, *Johannesoffenbarung als Brief*, 52: "Verzicht auf jede spezifisch prophetische Redeform."

96. Cf. Herzer, *Paralipomena Jeremiae*, 33–77; cf. also Bogaert, *Apocalypse de Baruch*, 1:186–221.

97. Cf. Schaller, "Paralipomena Jeremiou," 672–75.

98. Cf. the opinions recorded in Schaller, "Paralipomena Jeremiou," 724 (n. d on 5:1).

letters claim to be issued close to the end of the exile. As in *2 Baruch*, the events of 70 C.E. and of 587 B.C.E. are equated, although *Paralipomena Jeremiae* seems more removed from the catastrophe. In sum, though the Jeremianic account still provides some light, the present is also read in light of further developments within the Jeremiah-Baruch tradition. Jeremiah's reply invites us to look for other examples of "Diaspora communication" also not issued from Jerusalem. The following two texts bring us back to the second century B.C.E.

### 6. Jeremiah Writes (?) from Egypt to the Babylonian Exiles (4QApocryphon of Jeremiah C$^d$ [4Q389] 1)

This piece of evidence has only recently come to our knowledge, and is only beginning to be included into the discussion of "Diaspora writings."[99] It is a text from Qumran, published by Devorah Dimant in 2001, termed 4QApocryphon of Jeremiah C.[100] Limited space does not permit us to discuss the complex relationship of this text with other fragments, mainly dealing with the prophet Ezekiel. It will suffice to note here that for the time being I assume that Dimant is right in separating this text from the fragments dealing with Ezekiel.[101]

This text represents the tradition of Jeremiah accompanying the exiles on their way to Babylon ("until ]the river" [4QApocrJer C$^a$ (4Q385a) 18 i:7]) and subsequently staying in Egypt (4Q385a 18 ii), where he exhorted the captives to remember the covenant, abide by the law, and abhor the idols.[102] Another fragment, 4QApocrJer C$^d$ (4Q389) 1, which according to Dimant has to be located at the beginning of the composition,[103] recounts how Jeremiah does something "from the land of Egypt" (line 5: מארץ מצר[ים). The text then continues (lines 5–7): "[And it was] / [in the thi]rty-sixth year of the exile of Israel, they read [these] things (or: words) [ before] / a[ll the Children of I]srael upon the

---

99. See Lutz Doering. "Jeremia in Babylonien und Ägypten: Mündliche und schriftliche Toraparänese für Exil und Diaspora nach *4QApocryphon of Jeremiah C*," in *Frühjudentum und Neues Testament im Horizont Biblischer Theologie: Mit einem Anhang zum Corpus Judaeo-Hellenisticum Novi Testamenti* (ed. W. Kraus and K.-W. Niebuhr; WUNT 162; Tübingen: Mohr Siebeck, 2003), 50–79.

100. Devorah Dimant, *Qumran Cave 4.XXI: Parabiblical Texts, Part 4: Pseudo-Prophetic Texts* (partially based on earlier transcriptions by J. Strugnell; DJD 30; Oxford: Oxford University Press, 2001).

101. The arguments of Dimant and her critics are assessed at greater length in Doering, "Jeremia in Babylonien und Ägypten," 51–54.

102. See for these passages Dimant, DJD 30, 159–66; Doering, "Jeremia in Babylonien und Ägypten," 56–65.

103. Dimant, DJD 30, 220–23.

river Sur in the presence (or: while standing) [...]."¹⁰⁴ The crucial word here is קראו "they read." This word has not been read properly before, therefore the text has been misunderstood. In her edition Dimant rightly justifies this reading with reference to one of the better photographs (PAM 42.509). The original of the fragment in Jerusalem has become very dark, but a recent infrared photograph prepared by Israel Antiquities Authority shows that the reading is correct.¹⁰⁵

What is the impact of this reading? The exiles have assembled at the shore of the river Sur; someone is reading aloud "these things (or: words)" before them, probably "in the presence (or: while standing)." Which things (or: words)? It seems most appropriate to assume a connection with Jeremiah's action from Egypt, mentioned immediately before. Since other options, as

The crucial word is in the second line from the bottom, the second word from the left.

for example his coming from Egypt, are virtually excluded by the sequence of Jeremiah's whereabouts according to 4Q385a 18, the most probable solution is that Jeremiah *wrote* to the exiles from Egypt. However, except for the reference to "reading," we do not know anything specific about this hypothetical document. Judging from 4Q385a 18 (see above), we may speculate that this piece of writing would also deal with exhortation and Torah paraenesis. At any rate, this text shows, together with other evidence from Qumran,¹⁰⁶ that Jeremiah did not

---

104. [ויהי] / [בשל]שים ושש שנה לגלות ישראל קראו הדברים] האלה לפני] / כ]ל בני י[שראל על נהר סור במעמד ד]. I deviate from Dimant in that I reconstruct the beginning of the passage as a temporal sentence. See Doering, "Jeremia in Babylonien und Ägypten," 65–67 (where the erroneous ויהי should be corrected to יהי). For another possible deviation, see. n. 105.

105. The inserted picture is a detail of the crucial passage in the photograph of Mus. Inv. 349 (Jerusalem, 1 July 2003; courtesy Israel Antiquities Authority). We may consider that in place of the hole to the right of the letters, visible on the photograph, there was once a *waw* (ויקראו), which would yield a slightly better syntax.

106. Assembled in Doering, "Jeremia in Babylonien und Ägypten," 75–76.

only become an important figure after 70 C.E., as has been claimed by Christian Wolff and others, but that he already played an orientating role in the crises of the second century B.C.E. The circles responsible for 4QApocrJer C, identified by Dimant with some forerunners of the *yaḥad*,[107] saw their own present still within a ten-Jubilee period (i.e., of 490 years) of iniquity (cf. 4QApocrJer C[b] [4Q387] 2 ii:2–4) that started around the beginning of the Babylonian exile and may have been related, as is the case in Dan 9:2, 24, to the seventy years of Jer 25:11–12; 29:10.[108] This suggests a notion of ongoing exile that is also evinced by the terminology of sojourning and exile in other texts from Qumran.[109] Jeremianic letter writing, combined with further paraenetical development of the Jeremiah tradition, seems to have been regarded as especially apt for dealing with such a present. However, it must be admitted that it is not clear whether the hypothesized piece of writing exists only on the fictional level of the text, whether it was embedded in the Apocryphon, or whether it should be identified with the Apocryphon itself, similar to the book of Baruch.[110] We shall now briefly turn to this text, which is the last specimen of "Diaspora communication" to be discussed here.

### 7. The Book of Baruch (LXX)

Recent scholarship on the book of Baruch, preserved in Greek in the Septuagint, is divided on the issue of its literary unity. Some conceive that the book is a unitary composition, in which the (prosaic) prayer of repentance (1:15aβ–3:8), the (poetic) exhortation to turn back to the divine law (3:9–4:4), and the (equally poetic) promise of return of all exiles (4:5–5:9) form a coherent unfolding

---

107. Paleographically, the MSS date from ca. 50–20 B.C.E., whereas the composition comes from the second century B.C.E., as is suggested by close ties with pre-*yaḥad* texts such as *Jubilees*, the Enochic Animal Apocalypse (*1 En.* 84–90), or the Apocalypse of Weeks (*1 En.* 93:1–10; 91:11–17). See Dimant, DJD 30, 107–16.

108. Cf. ibid., 179–85, referring also to *1 En.* 89:59–90:13.

109. See the overview by Martin G. Abegg Jr., "Exile and the Dead Sea Scrolls," in Scott, *Exile*, 111–25. It is, however, debated if the *yaḥad* still considers itself in exile (thus Abegg) or if, e.g., the author of CD "considered the exile to have ceased … with the foundation of his own community" (thus Jonathan G. Campbell, "Essene-Qumran Origins in the Exile: A Scriptural Basis," *JJS* 46 [1995]: 143–56, here 148).

110. These uncertainties should urge some caution vis-à-vis the recent proposal to reckon fragments containing first person account by Jeremiah, classified by Dimant as 4QApocrJer A (4Q383), as part of this "letter"; thus Armin Lange with Ulrike Mittmann-Richert, "Annotated List of the Texts of the Judaean Desert Classified by Content and Genre," in *The Texts from the Judaean Desert: Indices and an Introduction to the* Discoveries in the Judaean Desert *Series* (ed. E. Tov; DJD 39; Oxford: Clarendon, 2002), 115–64, here 127 n. 12.

of the (prosaic) programmatic introduction (1:1–15aα).[111] Others claim that the different parts were later combined and prefaced by an introduction,[112] which according to some also shows certain literary tensions.[113] For our purpose these problems are of rather minor importance, given the fact that both the advocates of Baruch's unity and recent supporters of the thesis of literary growth tend to concur in placing the composition as a whole in the Maccabean period.[114] Such a date is now supported by the close traditio-historical ties between the introduction and 4QApocrJer C$^d$ (4Q389).

According to its introduction (1:1–15aα), Baruch is a piece of writing that Baruch allegedly composed (ἔγραψεν [1:1]) in Babylon and read (ἀνέγνω [1:3]) in front of Jeconiah and the people at the river Sur, a locality now also known from 4Q389. The Greek text, a translation from the Hebrew—most scholars agree on this at least for the prosaic part 1:1–3:8[115]—has the misspelling Σουδ (1:4), which can be corrected from the Syriac version (*swr*) and 4Q389. Subsequently the book is sent, apparently by the people (cf. ἀπέστειλαν [1:7], ἀπεστείλαμεν [1:14]), together with the temple vessels and money for offerings, from Babylon to Jerusalem. It is thus unclear if the book should be imagined as designed for dispatch from the outset. The switch from "Baruch" to "they" and "we," respectively, speaks against this view. On the other hand, the opening of the book recalls, in part literally, the beginning of the biblical letter of Jeremiah (cf. Bar 1:1 καὶ οὗτοι οἱ λόγοι τοῦ βιβλίου οὓς ἔγραψεν Βαρουχ with Jer 29:1 MT [36:1 LXX]). It is thus likely that Baruch, even if not strictly a letter or at least *not only* a letter, wants itself to be seen as based on the model of Jeremianic communication between Jerusalem and Babylon. Odil Hannes Steck has suggested that also the tripartite corpus of the book refers to Jeremiah's letter. According to

---

111. Thus Jonathan A. Goldstein, "The Apocryphal Book of I Baruch," *PAAJR* 46/47 (1979/80): 179–99; Odil Hannes Steck, *Das apokryphe Baruchbuch: Studien zur Rezeption und Konzentration "kanonischer" Überlieferung* (FRLANT 160; Göttingen: Vandenhoeck & Ruprecht, 1993), esp. 253–65.

112. Thus the majority of scholars: e.g., Gunneweg, "Buch Baruch," 168–69; Moore, *Daniel, Esther, and Jeremiah*, 258–61; Schreiner, *Baruch*, 45; Otto Kaiser, *Die alttestamentlichen Apokryphen: Eine Einleitung in Grundzügen* (Gütersloh: Kaiser Gütersloher Verlagshaus, 2000), 54–56.

113. Overview and critique in Steck, *Das apokryphe Baruchbuch*, 7.

114. Steck, *Das apokryphe Baruchbuch*, 290–303, and Goldstein, "I Baruch" opt for 164–62 B.C.E. Kaiser, *Die alttestamentlichen Apokryphen*, 56–57 favors more broadly 168–39 b.c.e. Cf. further David G. Burke, *The Poetry of Baruch: A Reconstruction and Analysis of the Original Hebrew Text of Baruch 3:9–5:9* (SBLSCS 11; Chico, Calif.: Scholars Press, 1982), 27–32. A Pompeian date has recently been proposed by Schreiner, *Baruch*, 46–47.

115. For 1:1–3:8, see, e.g., Emanuel Tov, *The Septuagint Translation of Jeremiah and Baruch: A Discussion of an Early Revision of the LXX of Jeremiah 29–52 and Baruch 1:1–3:8* (HSM 8; Missoula, Mont.: Scholars Press, 1976), 111–33. For the whole book, see Burke, *Poetry of Baruch*, passim; Steck, *Das apokryphe Baruchbuch*, 249–53.

Steck, the prayer of repentance (1:15aβ–3:8) corresponds with Jer 29:5–7 (thread no. 1 above) in that it concerns the whole period of exile until restoration, the exhortation (3:9–4:4) corresponds with Jer 29:8–9 (no. 3, warning against "false" prophets), and finally the promise of return (4:5–5:9) corresponds with the promise at Jer 29:10–14 (no. 2).[116] Admittedly, this proposal is more convincing for the last issue than for the first two. But even in a more limited form it would underscore the references of (the final form of) Baruch to Jeremiah's letter.

It seems that the notable differences vis-à-vis Jer 29 (Baruch as author; first recited by Baruch and only later sent by the people; direction from Babylon to Jerusalem) demonstrate that Baruch wants to be read both in the Diaspora (cf. 1:3–6) and in Jerusalem (1:7, in the temple: 1:14). In this way it provides orientation in a situation perceived as a protracted exile, both in the Diaspora and at home, an implication of the book's Deuteronomistic outlook on history.[117] Again we witness the correspondence between the book's own present and the exile, this time irrespective of distinctions between land and Diaspora, which is aptly elaborated upon by a piece of writing in the Jeremianic tradition.

We must further note that Baruch is neither authorized as prophet nor scribe, but is simply referred to by his name and a genealogy based on five further names. This aims at rooting Baruch firmly in the people of God,[118] which matches nicely with the book's emphasis on the cohesion and integrity of the people at both locations.

## 8. Summary

8.1.

There is a well-established tradition of written communication with the Golah fictitiously issued under the authority of Jeremiah and Baruch. Most of these letters are embedded in larger compositions (§§3, 4 [except for the MSS offering the letter only], 5; maybe also the Epistle of Jeremiah [§2], provided it was indeed intended as an appendix to Jeremiah). The book of Baruch (§7) is a special case since it presents itself as a book written and recited in exile and later on sent to Jerusalem; the nature of the piece of writing in 4QApocrJer C (§6) remains obscure. While we cannot discern a distinct letter form for these

---

116. Cf. Steck, *Das apokryphe Baruchbuch*, 10.
117. Cf. ibid., 21: "Die nach wie vor andauernde Epochensituation der Zerstreuung Israels und deren Überwindung ist das dominierende Thema von Bar, zu dem Israel allerorten in der Diaspora (Babylonien) und zuhause (Jerusalem) folglich durch ein versendbares Buch orientiert werden soll." Cf. ibid., 10–11 with n. 31, 263–64; also Knibb, "Exile," 268, 271.
118. Cf. Steck, *Das apokryphe Baruchbuch*, 17.

texts, we have seen that all of them refer, implicitly or by allusions, in part even literally, to Jeremiah's letter in Jer 29 MT (36 LXX). With respect to the main characteristics of "Diaspora letters" in general, it emerges that all the texts reviewed here clearly feature an attribution to an authoritative addressor, communication involving Judeans/Jews outside the land of Israel (in various settings, see below), letter contents dealing with instruction or exhortation, and an emphasis on the unity of the people of God.

8.2.

While classification as "Diaspora letters" may thus be justified, we should, however, be aware that these texts recall the setting of the Babylonian (and, in §4, the ongoing Assyrian) exile. In some of the texts, "exile" is transparent for the situation of the real addressees located in what was considered "Diaspora" at the time (§2, maybe §§3, 4; in part also §7). In others, however, the exilic setting serves to deal with the present situation of readers who must be located also (thus §7; maybe §§2, 4) or mainly in the land of Israel (§5; probably also §6), as suggested by general reflections on the compositions in which the texts are embedded. The Jeremiah-Baruch type of literary communication with the Golah thus employs the exilic setting on two levels: in a more "local" sense referring to Judeans/Jews living in the Greco-Roman Diaspora, and in a rather "qualitative" sense referring to Judeans/Jews seeing themselves in a situation of ongoing exile. It seems that where the "local" sense is present we always find the second level employed, too. While some of the texts allow no more than to state that the present was understood "in terms of the exile," there are indications, especially in *2 Bar.* 78–86 (§4), of a "melting" of temporal horizons, that is, the integration of the readers' present into the "present" of the "exilic" letter.

8.3.

Further, letters or pieces of writing of this type could have been sent also from places other than Jerusalem. We have both a letter (*P.J.* 7:23–29 [§5]) and a book (Baruch [§7]) issued from Babylon to Jerusalem (we may speak of "inverse Diaspora communication"), and we have apparently a piece of writing sent from Egypt to Babylon (§6). At least for the Jeremiah-Baruch type of the "Diaspora letters," this casts doubts about the established assumption that the emphasis is on the leading role of Jerusalem. In describing the genre, emphasis should be shifted from the centrality of Jerusalem to the key issue of the unity and coherence of the people.

At this point, it may be worthwhile to consider another shift in the description of the genre, even though this has not been the focus of the present paper. This shift concerns the "Diaspora letters" dealing with administrative, calendar, and legal issues. Not all of them are directed to the Diaspora in the strict sense. Good examples are the Gamaliel letters of rabbinic literature. Of the three letters only one is addressed to the Diaspora proper, while the destinations of the two others are areas on the fringes of Eretz Israel (Upper and Lower Galilee, Upper and Lower South). This is even more obvious in the two letters of Rn. Simeon ben Gamaliel and R. Yohanan ben Zakkai. Both letters are directed to remote areas in Palestine.[119] The emphasis is again more on the unity of a people scattered over various areas than on clear distinction between these areas.[120]

8.4.

A gradual replacement of divine discourse by paraenetical speech can be observed throughout the sources. While at the outset we still find traces of divine instruction and direct divine discourse (§2), prophetic forms of speech become virtually absent from later letters. Sometimes divine speech is merely reported by the letter writer (see §5, where it has been revealed to the writer by an angel). Though the writers remain either generally charged by God (§4) or at times legitimized as "prophet" (§3) or "servant of God" (§5), there is a shift away from specifically prophetic activity to the role of an authoritative letter writer providing exhortation, comfort, and Torah paraenesis. Since we could discern interference with the second type of "Diaspora letters" issued by leaders of Jerusalem or Judean Jewry (see above, §4), it may be considered that this shift too was influenced by this type of letters.

8.5.

The texts discussed here work on the presumption that Jeremiah and/or Baruch can provide orientation for a present that may be perceived, in some way or another, as analogous to, or protracting, the exile. While the situation after 70 C.E. seems especially apt for such a reading (§§4 and 5), it has become clearer by new evidence and by reevaluation of somewhat neglected texts that in addition the Babylonian Diaspora of the third to second century B.C.E. (§2) and especially the critical situation of both the Diaspora and the land of Israel in mid-second century B.C.E. (§§6, 7) could be addressed, too.[121] The prominence

---

119. For these texts, see the sources specified in n. 4 above.
120. Some of these second type "Diaspora letters" are also "festal letters" (AP 21; 2 Macc 1:1–2:18; see n. 4). In light of the foregoing discussion it may be asked if "festal letters" issued *in* the Diaspora, like Esth 9:20–28 and (though different in LXX and absent from the L-text) 9:29–32, should not be considered as closely related.
121. Differences between the two modes of "analogous situation" and "protraction of the exile" cannot be further addressed in this article. The discussion above suggests that the texts after

of Jeremiah and Baruch as letter writers is thus earlier and more widespread than has been normally thought before, and the fixation with the post-70 situation, still prevailing in contemporary scholarly judgment, should be given up.

---

70 C.E. emphasize analogy, although one wonders whether all of them would have shared the view that restoration after the Babylonian exile had indeed been successfully completed.

# Justifying Deviance: The Place of Scripture in Converting to a Qumran Self-Understanding

*George J. Brooke*

## 1. Introduction

Few nowadays would deny that the members of the Qumran community, and also probably those in the wider movement of which Qumran was a part, were a minority in late Second Temple Judaism, even among the educated elites in Palestine. A case can be made that the Essenes were a well-recognized and widespread part of Judean society,[1] but they should not be seen as the main Jewish party of the time.[2] In short, the minority status of the Qumran group suggests that those who became members could well be considered by others, or have considered themselves, as deviating from normative Jewish behavior in certain ways. In part, I attempt in this essay to discover how those joining the Qumran group, or the Essene movement from which it had emerged, justified their behavior to themselves and to others.[3]

In addition to this concern with how new members justified their deviation from normative Jewish behavior, I present an additional thesis: that it is appropriate to describe the move made by those joining the Qumran community, or Essenism in general, as one of conversion. This can be demonstrated from the

---

1. See esp. the writings of Brian J. Capper, "The Palestinian Cultural Context of the Earliest Christian Community of Goods," in *The Book of Acts in Its Palestinian Setting* (ed. R. Bauckham; The Book of Acts in Its First Century Setting 4; Grand Rapids: Eerdmans, 1995), 323–56.

2. Hartmut Stegemann, "The Qumran Essenes—Local Members of the Main Jewish Union in Late Second Temple Times," in *The Madrid Qumran Congress: Proceedings of the International Congress on the Dead Sea Scrolls, Madrid 18–21 March, 1991* (ed. J. Trebolle Barrera and L. Vegas Montaner; STDJ 11; Leiden: Brill, 1992), 83–166. His view depends on some considerable amount of special pleading and the identification of the "scribes" of the New Testament as Essenes.

3. Of course, people in any age seldom describe themselves as deviant; as has been pointed out, for example, by Erich Goode, deviance neutralization by the deviant involves "the reflexivity of the self, the integrity of identity, and the need for a positive self-image": Erich Goode, *Deviant Behavior: An Interactionist Approach* (Englewood Cliffs, N.J.: Prentice-Hall, 1978), 71.

fact that in the movement's own terms the root שוב plays a significant technical role: "The Priests are the converts of Israel who departed from the land of Judah, and (the Levites are) those who joined them" (CD 4:2–3).[4] The term also occurs in a less technical usage: "And this is the Rule for the men of the Community who have freely pledged themselves to be converted (לשוב) from all evil and to cling to all His commandments according to His will" (1QS 5:1).[5] And each member who approaches the Council of the Community is described as entering "the Covenant of God in the presence of all who have freely pledged themselves. He shall undertake by a binding oath to return (לשוב) with all his heart and soul to every commandment of the Law of Moses in accordance with all that has been revealed of it to the sons of Zadok" (1QS 5:8–9).[6]

The dominant motif of turning, of conversion, in those sectarian compositions which speak of new members, and even of the ongoing practices of existing members, can be taken as a signal that modern discussions of conversion may be applied to those joining the Qumran community in ways which might illuminate the processes of becoming a member. In particular, the general understanding of conversion put forward by Lewis Rambo in his landmark empathetic study, *Understanding Religious Conversion*,[7] is relevant:

> Through conversion an individual may gain some sense of ultimate worth, and may participate in a community of faith that connects him or her to both a rich past and an ordered and exciting present which generates a vision of the future that mobilizes energy and inspires confidence. Affiliating with a group and subscribing to a philosophy may offer nurture, guidance, a focus for loyalty, and a framework for action. Involvement in mythic, ritual, and symbolic systems gives life order and meaning. Sharing those systems with like-minded people makes it possible to connect with other human beings on deeper intellectual and emotional levels.[8]

In his overarching description of the processes of conversion Rambo acknowledges the insights of other analysts, notably John Lofland and Rodney Stark.[9] Lofland and Stark's work is based on the analysis of some of those who

---

4. Geza Vermes, trans., *The Complete Dead Sea Scrolls in English* (London: Penguin, 1998), 130; interpreting Ezek 44:15.
5. Ibid., 103.
6. Ibid., 104.
7. Lewis R. Rambo, *Understanding Religious Conversion* (New Haven: Yale University Press, 1993).
8. Ibid., 2.
9. Especially John Lofland and Rodney Stark, "Becoming a World-Saver: A Theory of Conversion to a Deviant Perspective," *American Sociological Review* 30 (1965): 862–75; I am grateful

converted to a small millenarian religious cult. This makes their insights all the more pertinent to some of the features of the sectarian compositions found at Qumran which housed what some observers might well describe as a small millenarian religious cult. I shall use some aspects of the seven-stage framework of conversion proposed by Lofland and Stark to suggest that conversion theory may help us better understand how the Qumran community, and especially its new members, read the present. At several points Lofland and Stark's insights will, however, be modified by reference to Rambo's more nuanced and open-ended descriptions. In fact, Rambo's empathetic stance may be especially suited to the description of things concerning Qumran because he engages with his topic on the basis of his own personal experience in the Church of Christ, which he readily labels as a religious sect. "I found," he states, "that the Church of Christ stressed knowledge of the Bible and obedience to God's will: 'correct' knowledge and 'right' behavior were essential."[10] He goes on to observe that emotional issues were regarded as secondary or irrelevant alongside knowledge and action for all that he subsequently came to recognize that such knowledge and action are motivated by fear, self-loathing, and insecurity, emotional issues if ever there were any.

However, the straightforward application of theories of conversion are not the concern of this collection of essays. Rather, it is my task, in using such modern theories, to ask questions about the place of scripture at each stage in the conversion process. I will look at how at each stage in that process the converts may have justified their behavior or had it justified for them through appeal to scripture. In what follows I suggest that various features of the use of the Jewish scriptures in the sectarian compositions found at Qumran are illuminated when juxtaposed with some aspects of modern theories constructed for the better understanding of conversion, not least as those theories are suggestive of the move that is being made from the more normative to the less normative or deviant form of behavior.[11]

---

to my colleague F. Gerald Downing, Honorary Research Fellow in the Centre for Biblical Studies at the University of Manchester, for indicating the value of Lofland and Stark's work and making other valuable bibliographical suggestions.

10. Rambo, *Understanding Religious Conversion*, xiii.

11. Sociological theories concerning deviance itself are not as helpful as conversion theory, largely because most deviance theory has been concerned with the causal explanation of crime, delinquency, and mental illness and with discovering means for correcting deviant behavior; see the theoretical discussion of this by David Matza, *Becoming Deviant* (Englewood Cliffs, N.J.: Prentice-Hall, 1969). Though attempting to describe the opponents of the author of the Pastoral Epistles, rather than the processes of conversion to a deviant form of religious behavior, Lloyd Keith Pietersen has suitably catalogued the various theoretical perspectives in the sociology of deviance and

## 2. The Seven Stages of Conversion

Lofland and Stark outline what they describe as seven necessary and sufficient factors for conversion. Converts must (1) experience enduring, acutely felt tensions (2) within a religious problem-solving perspective (3) that leads them to define themselves as religious seekers, (4) encountering the new group at a turning point in their lives, (5) wherein an affective bond is formed with one or more converts (6) where extracult attachments are absent or neutralized (7) and where, if they are to become deployable agents, they are exposed to intensive interaction. Let us consider each of these in turn.

### 2.1. Tension

At the outset Lofland and Stark observed that a potential convert must experience enduring, acutely felt tensions.[12] It is impossible to gauge what might best describe the tensions that could have characterized the circumstances of the average convert to Essenism or its Qumran form. Nevertheless we can assume that there was a felt discrepancy between some imaginary, ideal state of affairs and the circumstances in which potential community members saw themselves as caught up. At least for some converts, as Lofland and Stark observed for the converts to the cult at the center of their investigation, there might be "a frustrated desire for a significant, even heroic, religious status, to 'know the word of God intimately,' and to be a famous agent for his divine purposes."[13] Lofland and Stark describe several kinds of preconversion tension experiences: nota-

---

attempted to apply them to the reading of ancient texts: see Lloyd Keith Pietersen, "Teaching, Tradition and Thaumaturgy: A Sociological Examination of the Polemic of the Pastorals" (Ph.D. diss., University of Sheffield, 2000), 52–63.

12. "Just as tension can have myriad consequences, its sources can also be exceedingly disparate. Some concrete varieties we discovered were: longing for unrealized wealth, fame, and prestige; hallucinatory activity for which the person lacked any successful definition; frustrated sexual and marital relations; homosexual guilt; acute fear of face-to-face interaction; disabling and disfiguring physical conditions; and—perhaps of a slightly different order—a frustrated desire for a significant, even heroic, religious status, to 'know the mind of God intimately,' and to be a famous agent for his divine purposes" (Lofland and Stark, "Becoming a World-Saver," 864–65). To what extent any of these bases of tension may have lain behind the motivation for individuals to begin their conversion process to the Qumran community will remain a secret, though presumably anyone with any kind of acute physical disfigurement would not have been able to proceed very far before finding themselves unwelcome. It is intriguing to note that two of the three nets of Belial described in CD cover wealth and sexual matters, items that feature significantly in Lofland and Stark's list here and that may have required explicit comment by the community's authorities not least because of the motivating experiences of new converts.

13. Ibid., 864–65.

ble among them were hallucinations of various kinds or speaking in tongues, trances, and so on—all factors that reinforced the experience of frustrated aspiration somewhat acutely and over long periods of time.

Rambo is concerned to suggest that the context for the kinds of tension or crisis that Lofland and Stark describe as at the outset of the processes of conversion is extremely diverse and dynamic.[14] It seems to me that three features relating to the place of scripture resonate with this stage of conversion. To begin with, it is commonly suggested that those likely to engage in the journey to conversion will be experiencing some form of alienation and confusion. Such forms of tension are more readily experienced in settings characterized by pluralism of any sort. Perhaps the kinds of pluralism represented by the fragmentation of Judean society after the Maccabean revolt facilitated the moves to conversion that were needed to have new members sign up to a movement such as the one at Qumran. Intriguingly, the pluralism of the age is also visible in the variety of scriptural text-types attested at Qumran. Such variety is not the result of sectarian readings of the tradition,[15] like that found among Samaritan Jews, but is a reflection of what is available to elites more broadly.

But, second, while such pluralism in scriptural text-types might be a contributing factor to the kinds of pluralist experience that create confusion and alienation and promote conversion to deviant groups, it is also the case that we know of such textual pluralism from within the movement to which converts were moving. Rambo observes that congruence is an important determinant of whether conversion will occur. In other words, it is possible to have one's cake and eat it in this instance, because the same textual pluralism that is a feature of the confusion that motivates converts can also be found within the movement in a reassuring way. Rambo defines such congruence grandly: "elements of a new religion mesh with existing macro- and microcontextual factors."[16] This is not to insist that the Qumran community deliberately preserved diversity of text-types to encourage or facilitate the conversion process of new members, but it does not seem to have engaged in very careful restrictive practices.

A third feature of this initial stage of conversion to a deviant perspective becomes apparent through Peter Berger's analysis of the contemporary religious

---

14. Rambo, *Understanding Religious Conversion*, 44–55.

15. See George J. Brooke, "*E pluribus unum*: Textual Variety and Definitive Interpretation in the Qumran Scrolls," in *The Dead Sea Scrolls in Their Historical Context* (ed. T. H. Lim et al.; Edinburgh: T&T Clark, 2000), 107–19, esp. 116–17; Eugene Ulrich, "The Absence of 'Sectarian Variants' in the Jewish Scriptural Scrolls Found at Qumran," in *The Bible as Book: The Hebrew Bible and the Judaean Desert Discoveries* (ed. E. D. Herbert and E. Tov; London: British Library, 2002), 179–95.

16. Rambo, *Understanding Religious Conversion*, 37.

scene in *The Heretical Imperative*.[17] Berger asserts that three religious options are available: deductive, reductive and inductive:

> Deductive religiosity is based on some authority, such as the Bible or a religious leader, that provides "legitimate" interpretation of life and God. Followers acknowledge the revelation derived from these authorities and follow their dictates explicitly. In the deductive orientation, conversion is regulated by norms that delineate specific requirements for change in belief, behavior, and feeling.[18]

Though an analysis of the modern situation, Berger's viewpoint suggests that those most likely to start on the conversion process to the Qumran community or its parent group would already be inclined towards respect for authority of some sort, and among such authorities sacred text can claim pride of place. More can be said about this in relation to other stages of the conversion process, but this perception endorses the view that the lack of political or religious institutional power in Essenism generally was more than compensated for by the more highly developed place given to the authority of the scriptures compared to other forms of contemporary Judaism. It was, therefore, not the case that scripture just happened to play a significant role in the life of the Qumran community; rather, it played a necessary role as conveyer of authority, especially once the founding figure was no longer available.

2.2. Type of Problem-Solving Perspective

Converts to deviant religious groups also need to perceive that the perspective within which they can best make sense of the tensions in their lives are neither psychiatric, nor political or sociopolitical, but rather religious. In understanding conversion in late antiquity it is not sensible to distinguish in an over-sophisticated way between these perspectives, since it is far from certain whether Jews of late Second Temple times would categorize their worldview as concerning religious and nonreligious matters. However, the important matter for our present purposes is to realize that converts do not seem to desire to manipulate the self or reorganize their immediate social surroundings. According to Lofland and Stark, they want to see "both sources and solutions as emanating from an unseen and, in principle, unseeable realm";[19] there is a "general propensity to impose religious meaning on events."[20]

---

17. Peter L. Berger, *The Heretical Imperative* (Garden City, N.Y.: Doubleday, 1979).
18. Rambo, *Understanding Religious Conversion*, 29–30. Here he summarizes and applies Berger's insight that the most important aspect of modern Western secularization is pluralism.
19. Lofland and Stark, "Becoming a World-Saver," 867.
20. Ibid., 868.

Rambo proposes that although it is not uncommon for converts to be largely passive in the face of missionary zeal, in many instances converts are active agents at the stage of crisis in their conversion process. It is, of course, impossible to interview new converts to the Qumran community or to read the transcripts of such interviews. Rambo's experience, however, which is endorsed by other analysts, is that many conversions are based on the kind of extraordinary experience that might be called mystical.[21] As some justification for his own conclusions he appeals to the Acts of the Apostles and the case of Saul of Tarsus. But other kinds of experience can also be equally significant—such as recovery from an illness—which may be relevant in considering conversion to a group apparently interested in healing. However, we cannot know precisely what kinds of experiences a convert to the Qumran movement might have had. All that we can stress at this stage is that at the base of the experiences of the modern converts examined is the way in which the experiences are interpreted as providing a religious perspective on life. They provide a basis for meaning in the transcendent.

What emerges as striking out of the sectarian documents found at Qumran is that the sense of identity within the group seems to be very largely derived from particular readings of scripture. The community has no clearly identifiable founding moment which is celebrated in some way, and the founding figure remains hidden behind an epithet. In other words the religious perspective provided for the prospective convert is based on interpretations of scripture, rather than on political events, historical moments, or founding figures. So, for example, the exhortations at the opening of the *Damascus Document* are epitomes of scriptural narratives interpreted so as to provide the hearer or reader with negative and positive examples from the past. The opening lines of the *Rule of the Community* in its Cave 1 form recall the summary instruction of Deut 6:4–5. The scriptures and their suitable interpretation take pride of place in the construction and reconstruction of the world. This provides the authoritative religious perspective that enables the convert to move from crisis to quest. The convert can transition from the experience of tension toward creative and active agency in the move from one situation or group to another.

---

21. It could be that the quasi-mystical description of some worship at Qumran, which might be implied through what is summarized in the *Songs of the Sabbath Sacrifice*, is indicative of the kinds of experience a member of the community might have continued to have which would have been very largely congruent with his preconversion experiences.

## 2.3. Seekership

The preconverts whom Lofland and Stark investigated all found conventional religious institutions inadequate as a source of solutions. Each became a seeker, a person searching for some satisfactory system of religious meaning to interpret and resolve his or her discontent. Among the converts investigated there was a persistent refusal to accept dogma, but an equally persistent search for the truth in personal experience, even in the mystical or occult realms. Intriguingly, Lofland and Stark even record an interview with one pair of preconverts who described their interest in the Dead Sea Scrolls as part of their own search for meaning.[22]

All preconverts believed that spirits of some variety came from an active supernatural realm to intervene in the material world. The supernatural realm might be experienced in the weather, in political affairs and national disasters, or in individual lives.[23] Such spirit entities could, sometimes at least, break through from the beyond and impart information, cause experiences, or take a hand in the course of events.[24] Furthermore, there is a persistent teleology among preconverts, an understanding that each person has a purpose within the overall purposes for which everything was created.

Rambo has underlined the importance of the quest: it is an ongoing process, but one that will greatly intensify during times of crisis. Rambo assumes that converts are commonly active agents in their own conversion. What might lead one to conclude that converts to the Qumran community were actively engaged in their own quests for meaning? One possible clue rests in the fact that, whereas most of the manuscripts containing sectarian compositions are penned in an orthography that has become identified as belonging to the Qumran scribal school, most of the manuscripts that contain copies of scriptural books are not penned in that way. This suggests that such manuscripts were brought to Qumran from elsewhere. Some of these copies of the scriptures may have been brought by those joining the community. If that was the case, then it seems that at least some of those joining were already predisposed to constructing their outlook on the world on the basis of scripture. That this may have been quan-

---

22. Part of the interview runs: "My wife and I became interested in the revelation of Edgar Cayce and the idea of reincarnation which seemed to answer so much, we read searchingly about the Dead Sea Scrolls, we decided to pursue Rosicrucianism, we read books on the secret disclosures to be gained from Yogi-type meditation" (Lofland and Stark, "Becoming a World-Saver," 868).

23. The presence at Qumran of compositions like 4QZodiology and Brontology ar (4Q318) may suggest that the outlook of some or many at Qumran was consonant with such a perspective that might have lain behind their conversion.

24. Lofland and Stark, "Becoming a World-Saver," 869.

titatively and qualitatively different from many other Jews may be indicated by comparing Qumran ideology and use of scripture with that of the Wisdom of Ben Sira. Ben Sira makes little explicit use of scripture in his extensive writing and even comes to rely on non-Jewish sources for some of his instruction. Such is not the case at Qumran.

Three other matters involving scripture may well be important at this stage in the move to deviancy through joining Essenism more generally, or the Qumran group in particular. Each of these matters might also have had a role at other stages, but from a different perspective. In the first place, it is noteworthy that it is only scripture as interpreted that offers a suitable religious construction of the world. The real significance in this matter is that the interpretation is not plain to everyone, but divinely inspired. The skilled interpreter has to reveal the significance of the law. Some matters are indeed available to all, inasmuch as the text of the law is revealed (נגלה), but the interpretation exegetically discloses what is hidden (נסתר). In relation to both the *Damascus Document* (CD 3:12–16) and the *Rule of the Community* (1QS 5:7–12; 8:15–16; 9:13–14, 18–20) the comments of Lawrence H. Schiffman are worth repeating in this context:

> The *nigleh*, then, is nothing more than Scripture, while the *nistar* is sectarian interpretation of it.... *nistar* is derived only through divinely inspired biblical exegesis. It would appear that, like the Sadducees and the later Karaites, the Qumran sect relied exclusively on interpretation of the Bible for the derivation of its *halakhah*.[25]

The same case can be made with regard to the interpretation of the prophets. According to the Habakkuk Commentary, the Teacher of Righteousness was the one "to whom God made known all the mysteries of the words of His servants the Prophets."[26]

Second, the tendency toward a predestinarian outlook in the preconvert as observed by Lofland and Stark corresponds with some features of the sectarian compositions at Qumran. The notions of election and predestined membership of the covenant people resonate with scriptural allusions (1QS 9:14; 1QpHab 5:4; 1QHª 15:13–19). Converts actively engaged in their own quests, and who were eventually admitted to the community, would have understood themselves as divinely preselected. Nevertheless, daily life within the new group would,

---

25. Lawrence H. Schiffman, *The Halakhah at Qumran* (SJLA 16; Leiden: Brill, 1975), 32; the point remains valid, even if some of the terminology used to express the matter might now be different.

26. Vermes, *Complete Dead Sea Scrolls in English*, 481.

no doubt, have been marked by all kinds of regular decision-making processes which might indicate that God's hand did not control every action.[27]

Third, the standard ingredient in the convert's quest of recognizing that conventional religious institutions are inadequate as a source of solutions suggests that alternative sources of authority are common to the convert's outlook. Together with sensing the divine origin of the interpretations and perceiving themselves predestined in some way for their new lives, converts could well have acknowledged implicitly or explicitly that the texts of scripture themselves were an increasingly significant authoritative institution. This authority could replace the temple or other political structures and the allegiances such institutions required. It is perhaps, then, no accident that the moves towards the institutionalization of scripture are now best attested in this sectarian movement.

2.4. The Turning Point

The encounter with the new group occurs at what Lofland and Stark identify as a turning point for people, especially young adults. Old obligations and lines of action have diminished for various reasons and new lines of involvement have become desirable and possible. It is impossible to say much about the moment of encounter, but it is clear from Rambo's nuancing of Lofland and Stark's work that the ways in which the advocate[28] of a particular group and the potential convert reciprocally meet each other's needs is an area that requires careful exploration. I have already suggested that in relation to the Qumran community and those who might be interested in joining, part of this reciprocity rests in a common interest in the scriptures as a source of identity and of hope. The scriptures are the agreed upon basis on which a perspective on the world can be suitably constructed. In the turning point many other factors also need to be taken into account, such as commonalities in ethnicity, class, social background, economic status, lifestyle, and the like, as well as the way in which the community member might be able to offer inducements of various kinds to encourage the wavering convert.

It is not possible to outline in any significant way what part scripture might have played at the turning point, but a few suggestions can indicate the sort of role the scriptures could have occupied. It is clear that scripture could have been a significant part of the missionary strategy of the advocate. Some particu-

---

27. See the realistic assessment of this by E. P. Sanders, "The Dead Sea Sect and Other Jews: Commonalities, Overlaps and Differences," in *The Dead Sea Scrolls in their Historical Context* (ed. T. H. Lim *et al.* Edinburgh: T&T Clark, 2000), 7–43, esp. 29–30.

28. Rambo, *Understanding Religions Conversion*, 66–86, devotes two chapters to outlining the role of advocates and their strategies.

lar piece of interpretation might have been found especially attractive by the prospective convert and been a major contributory factor at the turning point. Scripture could also have been part of the inducement to join. Perhaps rumors of long periods of extensive study of and deliberation about scripture were seen as attractive. Maybe the prospect of possible involvement in the production of manuscripts of scripture was also appealing.[29]

2.5. CULT AFFECTIVE BONDS

The circumstances surrounding the fifth stage in the conversion process are particularly significant for its outcome. The important factor at this stage is the satisfaction derived from some form of personal encounter or connection with a member of the community or sect. Many converts reported intellectual reservations about the group but nevertheless developed strong personal bonds with members of the group.

Again, it is impossible to gauge quite how a convert to the Qumran community might have developed strong personal bonds with members of the group. It may be that in relation to Qumran it is incorrect to separate this stage from the following stage inasmuch as it seems that the most obvious way in which personal bonds were established between long-standing members and new converts was through various forms of communal living, even if such living was often structured very hierarchically. Rambo provides a fuller understanding of this stage by describing what Arthur Griel and David Rudy have labeled the encapsulation processes.[30] These processes involve four components (relationships, rituals, rhetoric, and roles), but, all four of these matters can also be readily identified as playing a significant part also in the sixth stage.[31] The pesharim and other commentary sections could have been used to encourage

---

29. Which is the well-known understanding of the principal function of the Qumran settlement according to Hartmut Stegemann, *The Library of Qumran: On the Essenes, Qumran, John the Baptist, and Jesus* (Grand Rapids: Eerdmans, 1998), 51–55, esp. 52: "This construction plan reflects a clear center of interest: the *production of scrolls*, together with all preliminary stages of obtaining and working the leather from which the scrolls were made."

30. Arthur Griel and David Rudy, "Social Cocoons: Encapsulation and Identity Transformation Organizations," *Sociological Inquiry* 54 (1984): 260–78; as adapted by Rambo, *Understanding Religious Conversion*, 103–8.

31. To what extent the findings of Chana Ullman, "Cognitive and Emotional Antecedents of Religious Conversion," *Journal of Personality and Social Psychology* 43 (1982): 183–92, that converts commonly had relational and emotional problems in childhood, adolescence and immediately prior to their conversion, especially that they had absent, weak, or abusive fathers, can be translated to the circumstances of late antiquity is difficult to know. See the discussion in Rambo, *Understanding Religious Conversion*, 111.

identification with the community and its supposed scripturally ordained history and circumstances in this stage or in either of the subsequent ones, just as their divinely inspired exegesis might have played a role in convincing the potential convert of the heavenly origin of the religious view of the world which they constructed.

2.6. EXTRACULT AFFECTIVE BONDS

At a sixth stage extracult bonds are negated or neutralized and significant commitment is apparent. In Qumran it is not surprising that there was a fictive kinship element[32] and a widespread disparagement of the temple cult as practiced by others. Within a newly constituted Israel at the foot of Sinai, the convert joins the community[33] and becomes variously part of both sanctuary and priesthood as divinely intended. Although these scripturally based identity markers may have been variously used during the history of the movement, the possibilities in such phrases as "sanctuary of men/Adam" (מקדש אדם)[34] and "sons of Zadok" are manifold. In addition as part of the use of such identity markers there is a very strong rehearsal of purity regulations and a separatist ideology, endorsed not least by various statements from or the general ethos of Genesis, Deuteronomy, and Isaiah. It is this scripturally justified separation that apparently results in Jewish nonmembers of the community being labeled in ways similar to non-Israelites in scripture. Thus in the ceremony of admission, people are divided into those who are among the blessed and those who are cursed (1QS 1:21–2:18). The language pattern of the blessings and curses of Deuteronomy demarcate who is an insider and who is an outsider. Once on the inside and adequately cleansed, the convert then can receive instruction that will enable a more profound understanding of the precepts of God. The separation from the habitation of the unjust is given a scriptural motivation; such separation is to enable the preparation of the way of the Lord in the wilderness. This is a way which is itself "the study of the Law which He [God] commanded by the hand of Moses, that they may do according to all that has been revealed

---

32. This is most obvious in the use of "fathers" and "mothers" in 4Q270 (4QD$^e$) 7 i 13–14.

33. As James VanderKam has recently suggested, even the language of the self-designation of the community as יחד is derived as a neologism from scripture: see James VanderKam, "Sinai Revisited," in *Biblical Interpretation at Qumran* (ed. M. Henze; Studies in the Dead Sea Scrolls and Related Literature; Grand Rapids: Eerdmans, 2005), 44–60.

34. See, e.g., George J. Brooke, "Miqdash Adam, Eden and the Qumran Community," in *Gemeinde ohne Tempel—Community without Temple: Zur Substituierung und Transformation des Jerusalemer Tempels und seines Kultes im Alten Testament, antiken Judentum und frühen Christentum* (ed. B. Ego et al.; WUNT 118; Tübingen: Mohr Siebeck, 1999), 285–301.

from age to age, and as the Prophets have revealed by His Holy Spirit" (1QS 8:15–16).[35]

The rejection of others has its counterpart in a sense of rejection by others that can be confirmed in a number of ways. The ongoing use of the Hodayot within the community probably encouraged members to identify repeatedly with the persecution and rejection experienced by the author, who was readily recognized as a founding figure within the movement with an ongoing significance. In such a way new converts and even long-standing members are equipped with and internalize a rhetoric that justifies their deviance. The hymnody that encapsulates such a sense of rejection is replete with scriptural allusion. Most obviously in 1QH[a] 12:7–9 we hear echoes of the servant song of Isaiah and the suffering motifs of the psalms of lament when we read:

> Teachers of lies [have smoothed] Thy people [with words], and [false prophets] have led them astray; they perish without understanding for their works are in folly. For I am despised by them and they have no esteem for me that Thou mayest manifest Thy might through me. They have banished me from my land like a bird from its nest; all my friends and brethren are driven far from me and hold me for a broken vessel.[36]

2.7. INTENSIVE INTERACTION

Total conversion, according to Lofland and Stark, only comes about after intensive interaction with full members. Such interaction, requiring physical proximity, has to be concrete and may involve the daily or even hourly accessibility of full members. Such intensive interaction can take several forms. It can be based on continuous reminders and discussion about the need to make other converts. But this does not seem to have been the case at Qumran.

At Qumran total conversion is endorsed positively and negatively. On the positive side a year or two of probation passes in which the kind of association needed for total conversion is made entirely possible. Scripture plays its part: "and the Many shall be on watch together for a third of each night of the year in order to read the book, explain the regulation, and bless together" (1QS 6:7–8).[37] The study of scripture and its correct interpretation do not seem to have been undertaken solely for academic edification, but so that those of lesser rank

---

35. Vermes, *Complete Dead Sea Scrolls in English*, 109.
36. Ibid., 263.
37. Florentino García Martínez, trans., *The Dead Sea Scrolls Translated: The Qumran Texts in English* (Leiden: Brill, 1996), 9.

or newer membership may have their allegiance constructed through scripture. It is enough to regulate that it happens; the specific content does not need further definition.

On the negative side, this total conversion is endorsed through the careful repetition of the delimitation of the group, and particularly of those who can be full participants. Those who are excluded and those included are based upon the repetition of scriptural models, interwoven in complex patterns.[38] As in Deut 23:2–4, so in 4QMMT restrictions are applied to the Ammonite, the Moabite, the bastard, and the man whose testicles have been crushed or whose penis has been cut off. In 1QS$^a$ 2:4–9 restrictions based on Lev 5:3; 7:21; Deut 23:11–12; Exod 19:10–15; and Lev 21:16–24 are applied to any man smitten with any human uncleanness, any man smitten in his flesh, or paralyzed in his hands or feet, or lame, or blind, or deaf or dumb; the old and tottery are also carefully restricted. In 1QM 7 similar restrictions are applied to the community in its cosmic struggle. No man who is lame or blind or crippled or afflicted with a lasting bodily blemish or smitten with bodily impurity shall march out to war with them. In 4Q174, again following Deut 23:2–4, it is the unclean, the uncircumcised, the Ammonite, the Moabite, the half-breed, the foreigner, and the stranger who are refused access to the community because of the presence in it of holy ones (angels).

Initial tentative assent becomes a language device for interpreting everyday events in the convert's life. The convert is placed at the center of the battle between good and evil spirits. Lofland and Stark observe that the sect which the convert is joining "has a variety of resources for explicating everyday events in terms of a cosmic battle between good and evil spirits."[39] Since all the cult's "interpretations pointed to the imminence of the end, to participate in these explications of daily life was to come more and more to see the necessity of one's personal participation as a totally committed agent in this cosmic struggle."[40]

A physical relocation, such as a move into communal buildings, often accompanies and endorses this move toward total conversion. On the basis of conversion theory it is likely that a very suitable understanding of the primary purpose of the Qumran buildings themselves is that they functioned as the place where new converts were made into total converts. Furthermore, it is perhaps no accident that in the form of the *Rule of the Community* found in the exemplar from Cave 1 (1QS), the ritual of admission is followed in columns 3 and 4 by the so-called treatise on the two spirits. In light of theories of conversion, it

---

38. As with all the lists of texts in this essay, it is unlikely that all were used at the same time; nevertheless, certain motifs are constantly repeated in various compositions and in various guises.
39. Lofland and Stark, "Becoming a World-Saver," 873.
40. Ibid.

seems as if the editors of 1QS recognized that new members would need thorough cultural transformation within the cosmic dualism of the spiritual outlook of the community.

3. Conclusion

In this short study I have suggested that consideration of the processes of conversion as analyzed by recent theorists can help describe how a Jew might become a member of the Qumran community or the wider movement of which it was a part. Many factors would have been involved as a Jew moved from one form of Judaism to that found in the shifting sands of the sectarian writings of the Qumran community. Not all the factors involved would have been based in scripture or justified scripturally. However, attention to these conversion processes enables modern readers of the sectarian compositions found in the Qumran caves to recognize that several features of the variety of ways in which scripture was used in the Qumran community and the wider movement of which it was a part were perhaps in the form that they were, or functioned as they did, because they underlined the move from the moment of crisis or tension to the total conversion of the new member. Conversion theory contributes toward explaining in some cases why scripture was used in the way that it was. Converts whose very conversion was a move toward deviancy found their move strategically supported by the ways in which they were encouraged to read the present through their use of scripture. In many respects, for the convert to, and for the continuing member of, the Qumran community scripture justified deviance and endorsed a particular reading of present experience.

# PART 2:
## ANCIENT JUDAISM

# "READING THE PRESENT" IN THE ANIMAL APOCALYPSE (*1 ENOCH* 85–90)

*L. T. Stuckenbruck*

## 1. INTRODUCTION

The question addressed here shall ultimately be: How has the present shaped the way the document, here the Animal Apocalypse in *1 En.* 85–90, has presented the past (salvation history) and the future (eschatology)? However, to refer at all to "the present" in the Animal Apocalypse is not a straightforward matter; it brings to mind a number of issues that arise when considering any "historical apocalypse" ascribed to a remote idealized figure of the past.

The Animal Apocalypse and several portions of Daniel (chs. 7–12) provide us with some of the earliest Jewish accounts, composed during the mid-160s B.C.E., which we may designate pseudepigraphal prophecies *ex eventu*.[1] The stories variously relayed in these writings[2] consist of a selective retelling of past and future events. Such stories are told from two simultaneously different vantage points, both of which surface in the narrative: (1) the perspective of the purported author (which reflects the literary or "fictive" present) and (2) the perspective of the composition's real author (which corresponds to the "real" present). Although these discernible "presents" are chronologically remote from one another—in the Animal Apocalypse, they are as remote as the time between

---

1. In addition to these works, we may also include other roughly contemporary compositions, however of less certain date: Apocalypse of Weeks (*1 En.* 93:1–10; 91:11–17); *Jubilees* (esp. 23:8–32; cf. 32:21 and 36:1–11); and the fragmentary "pseudo-Jubilees" (esp. cf. frag. 2) and "pseudo-Danielic" materials from Qumran Cave 4 (4Q243; 4Q244–245).

2. In the Animal Apocalypse such "prophecy" is presented one unbroken and detailed account, while in Daniel it occurs several times in much shorter segments (7:1–28; 8:1–27; 9:1–27; and 10:1–12:4). The main material difference between the Enochic Animal Apocalypse, on the one hand, and those in Daniel, on the other, is that the former selects events from the fictive past of the purported author (Enoch), whereas in Daniel none of the visions focus are concerned with events prior to the time of the "Daniel" in the sixth century.

the antediluvian Enoch and the years of the Maccabean revolt—authors of such works did not, of course, choose their temporal frameworks arbitrarily. In the case of the *1 Enoch* documents, the authors found in the crisis-laden time of the antediluvian patriarch an analogy that, at least for them and those sympathetic to their ideas, helped them interpret contemporary circumstances.

With respect to the Animal Apocalypse, the author(s) found in "Enoch" a way to coordinate the inner frames of *Urzeit* and *Endzeit:* during a remote era of increasing destruction and evil, Enoch is made to recount visions that anticipate a decisive divine intervention in the Great Deluge. By analogy, a real writer, as "Enoch," was interpreting contemporary events to support his conviction that a final eradication of evil powers and the reestablishment of a new world order were imminent.

However, in the Animal Apocalypse this analogy between the fictive and actual contemporary horizons inevitably and eventually breaks down in the narrative. What the real author(s) envisioned of the eschatological future, of course, bears a finality that the first major intervention by God through the flood did not produce. After the deluge, the new establishment described within the story of Israel is neither cosmological nor universal in scope; it is, rather, an account about how God's revealed purposes for God's people are carried forward on the shoulders of specially designated figures and groups who are given prominence in the story. Moreover, the punishment of antediluvian evil, for all its decisiveness, remains incomplete, whereas the author expected eschatological judgment to eradicate injustice altogether. Finally, in the Animal Apocalypse the time of the real author(s) is interpreted as an era during which divine intervention is already being manifested. This is especially true if allusions to the contemporary activities of Judas Maccabeus in *1 En.* 90:12, 13–14 are taken into account. By contrast, the antediluvian period, except for the "human" Noah and his sons who survive the deluge on the boat (89:1), is more lacking in such signs of hope.

These discontinuities aside, correspondences between fictive and real time in the Animal Apocalypse raise the question of precisely which "present" should be taken as a point of departure for our study. To do this, we need to consider each in turn more closely. First, there is the literary present purported in the document. This in itself is complicated because of the frame of the vision (85:1–3a; 90:39–42). The vision is framed within a setting in the life of the young, as yet unmarried, Enoch who in this phase of his life recounts what he sees (85:3; cf. 83:2). It is this young Enoch who sees a vision on his bed (85:3) and who, after the same vision, wakes up praising God and weeping as a result of its content (90:40–42). However, in the document it is not simply the young Enoch who recounts his vision. The broader narrative framework for his account consists of a conversation between the much older Enoch and his son Methuselah. This is clear from 85:1–2, according to which Enoch asks Methuselah to pay attention to the dream vision he is about to recount, while in 90:42, after the vision, the same setting is implied as Enoch explains how "on that night" he remembered what he had seen in the first dream as well (cf. chs. 83–84). Thus we have to do with a narrative in which two voices converge: one of the older Enoch and that of the younger one. Since in the larger literary context of *1 Enoch* we may identify attempts by some compilers of the tradition to place several of the visions into a "testamentary" setting in which the departing patriarch is made to communicate last words of instruction to his progeny, the fictive present of the Animal Apocalypse is itself best located in the young Enoch's life.[3] From this vantage point, the fictive "past" consists of all those events that have occurred between the time of Adam's appearance as a "white bull" (85:3: *wakona zeku lahm sa'ada*) and the time that three "humanlike figures" from heaven, with four others accompanying them, remove the young Enoch from the earth to a "high place" (*makan nawax*). This literary present for young Enoch occurs before the flood and comes after the tumult brought on by violence committed on the earth by the gargantuan offspring of the watchers against human beings (86:1–6). From his lofty position, the young Enoch is allowed to view what is to happen in "the future" (87:5), which includes events both immediate (the flood and its aftermath) and remote (extending into the ideal future). The text thus assumes that once the vision is finished, Enoch will "return" to his real-life setting. Enoch's premarital status may be significant. Did the real author of the Animal Apocalypse wish to suggest that Enoch's status, for the sake of having the vision, connotes a purity superior to that of one who is married? This is a possible inference, though what this means in relation to any view that would have regarded celibacy as an ideal state is hard to infer. Enoch is, after all, not so much depicted

---

3. Cf. esp. *1 En.* 82:1–2 (at the conclusion of the Astronomical Book); 91:1–3 (as an introduction to the Apocalypse of Weeks and Epistle of Enoch); 83:1–2 and 85:1–2 (to the first vision and Animal Apocalypse in the Book of Dreams); and, more vaguely, 1:2 (at the beginning of the Book of Watchers). George W. E. Nickelsburg (*1 Enoch 1* [Hermeneia; Minneapolis: Fortress, 2001], 25–26) argues that the formation of the early Enochic corpus of writings was shaped along the lines of a testament before it was expanded (175–150 B.C.E.) to include the Book of Dreams (esp. chs. 85–90), the whole of chs. 92–105 (which was written with the testamentary form in mind), and the Birth of Noah tradition (chs. 106–107). The collection finally took the form of *1 Enoch*, with additions over time of the Astronomical Book (inserted before the a testamentary scene in 81:5–82:3), the Similitudes (chs. 37–71), and another work by Enoch for Methuselah preserved only through the Ethiopic tradition (ch. 108). Since the testamentary form only opens, and does not conclude, the Animal Apocalypse, we take the more immediate frame of visions given to the young Enoch as our point of departure here.

as a representative for implied readers as he is *singled out* as one to whom the vision is granted.[4]

Second, there is the "real" present of the author or authors who composed and redacted the document. The key passage is, of course, 90:6–19, which in its present form[5] depicts the transition from identifiable historical events from the time of the writer—these relate to the advent of Seleucid rule and successes of the Maccabean revolt—through to the scenario of eschatological judgment. The introduction of a "sheep" whose activity is accompanied by a the opening of the eyes of other sheep (v. 9) being persecuted by "ravens" (vv. 8,11) and who enjoys some military success against the ravens (vv. 12, 14) places the account squarely within the time frame of Onias III's career and that of Judas Maccabeus.[6] Beyond this, precision is difficult to come by because of the likelihood that the Animal Apocalypse was edited soon after it was originally composed. If, for example, the content of 90:12 is taken as a point of departure, then the unsuccessful attempts of the gathered ravens to remove the horn of the ram may well be taken to refer to Judas Maccabeus's early victories against Apollonius and Seron in 166 B.C.E. (1 Macc 3:10–12, 13–26; 2 Macc 5:24–27). Given these as the last discernible events within the "original" work, then the Animal Apocalypse may be thought to have been composed soon thereafter, perhaps 165 B.C.E. If, however, the point of departure for dating is to be found in 90:13–14, then the time of composition may be placed slightly later. The mention in 90:14 of requested assistance given to the "ram" by the angelic "man"[7] (who elsewhere in the document acts as a scribe who records transgressions of God's commands)

---

4. Not clear is whether Enoch's being unmarried serves to underscore the "purity" of his visions in chs. 83–84 and 85–90. While J. T. Milik has argued that this is indeed the case (*The Books of Enoch: Aramaic Fragments from Qumrân Cave 4* [Oxford: Clarendon, 1976], 42), Patrick A. Tiller (*A Commentary on the Animal Apocalypse of 1 Enoch* [SBLEJL 4; Atlanta: Scholars Press, 1993], 231) and Nickelsburg (*1 Enoch 1*, 370) caution that this detail may be little more than "a chronological indicator." In any case, one is not to infer that the real author was himself an advocate of celibacy.

5. Inconsistencies in the narrative have led Nickelsburg (*1 Enoch 1*, 396–98) to argue that this passage represents the welding of two layers of tradition, one composed either at the end of the third century B.C.E. or just after the death of Onias III (169 B.C.E., if 90:8 alludes to this death) and a later one that alludes to the successes of Judas Maccabeus before his death in 160 b.c.e. (90:11, 13–15); contra Tiller, *Commentary on the Animal Apocalypse*, 67–79, who considers the latter to have been composed as part of the original vision. If Nickelsburg's view is correct, then the interpolator attempted to locate his community socially within the tumult and ambiguities surrounding more contemporary events. Though the author welcomes the successful activities of Judas Maccabeus, this does not mean unconditional support. See further below.

6. See the previous note.

7. Those referred to as "man" or "men" in the Animal Apocalypse are angels, while the human or demonic figures are represented as animals.

may be reminiscent of Judas Maccabeus's defeat of Lysias at the battle of Beth-zur recorded in 2 Macc 11:6–12, a battle that is inspired by the appearance of a "horseman" in answer to prayers that God "send a good angel to save Israel" (2 Macc 11:6; cf. 1 Macc 4:26–35). As nothing is said about Judas's death in 160 B.C.E., one may—especially given the hope associated with events of which he is a part—assign the *terminus ad quem* of both the composition and redaction of the Animal Apocalypse to that year.

Whatever one makes of these allusions to contemporary events, it is clear that author(s) regarded the Maccabean revolt, indeed the career of Judas Maccabeus himself, as one endowed with divine activity. In Judas, the writer believed, God's purpose unfolds not only for the people of God, but also for the world at large. Judas participates in one of the stock themes of the Animal Apocalypse when his ascendancy to leadership as "one great horn" over the sheep (Israel) is synchronized with a time when "their [i.e., the sheep's] eyes were opened" (*1 En.* 90:9: *wa-takašta 'a'yentihomu*), a point that is repeated twice in the passive in quick succession.[8] The passive is in itself important: the author did not attribute to Judas Maccabeus himself the opening of the sheep's eyes but simply notes the contemporaneity between the advent of his leadership and divine revelation to (some of) the sheep. In other words, despite Judas's military following from other sheep and rams (v. 10), the author's support of Judas Maccabeus is by no means unconditional. In this connection, it may be interesting if we observe that nothing during the Judas's career is said about the temple. Neither the temple's desecration nor its cleansing and rededication are mentioned, momentous events indelibly stamped on the memory of Jews and recorded in other literature.[9] It could be argued, however, that not too much should be made of the lack of mention of the purification of the temple; assuming that the angelic assistance mentioned in 90:13–14 refers to what happened at Beth-zur, only in 2 Maccabees does the restoration of the temple cult (2 Macc 10:1–9) occur *before* the angelic intervention (see 2 Macc 11:1–12 [esp. vv. 6, 8]) and could, therefore, be regarded as a deliberate omission in the Animal Apocalypse. The sequence in 1 Maccabees, however, has the purification (1 Macc 4:36–61) follow immediately after the battle (4:26–35). More significant, in any case, would be the text's neglect to mention or even allude to the violation of the temple

---

8. The alternatives of an active "he opened their eyes" or passive "their eyes were opened" relate to whether or not the final vowel of the verb is long; the manuscript evidence diverges. Given that the Gt form for the verb more likely reflects a passive rather than active meaning, the translation in the passive is to be preferred (with Tiller, *Commentary on the Animal Apocalypse*, 349; contra Isaac's main translation in OTP 1:70).

9. See, respectively, 1 Macc 1:41–64; 4:36–61; and 2 Macc 6:1–6; 10:1–8.

cult. While temple ideology is by no means absent in the Animal Apocalypse (cf., e.g., 90:50–51, 54 concerning the "house" during the time of Solomon), nothing suggests that the author(s) had special affinity to the Second, present Temple, even during the time God was seen to be acting on behalf of Judas and those fighting with him. The author(s) and early redactor(s) of the document thus belonged to a group of Jews whose piety does not seem to have disallowed military engagement allied to Judas, but who nonetheless subscribed to a different expression of religious ideology, especially as regards the present temple.

## 2. The Animal Apocalypse as Shaped by the Present

These observations of *1 En.* 90:6–19 allow us to characterize the "real present" for the author(s) of the Animal Apocalypse in several, somewhat overlapping, ways. First, the present is a time when, once more in the story, *divine revelation has been disclosed to a certain group* distinguishable from those immediately associated with Judas. We do not go far wrong to suppose that the author(s) identified with such a group, a community that traced its identity to a recent disclosure of divine guidance and/or revelation. Second, *in terms of Judas and the cult of the Second Temple, the author(s) gave principled, and perhaps even practical and military, support* without entirely locating therein their present pragmatic aims. Support for the cult and Maccabean military activity is not unqualified. Third, the present is a time when *the lines between the forces of evil, on the one hand, and those acting as human and divine agents on behalf of God, on the other hand, are clearly drawn*. This clear-cut distinction holds despite the possible misgivings of the community behind the Animal Apocalypse over against Judas and the temple. These three features that characterize the present for the author(s) do not simply emerge "out of the blue" in *1 En.* 90:6–19; what we may infer from the vision about perception of contemporary circumstances and events may help us understand why the visionary account of salvation history and eschatological future has been given its particular shape. In what follows, I briefly elaborate how each of the emphases observed in 90:6–19 feature in the document as a whole.

First, in the Animal Apocalypse we encounter the notion of the present as a time of *divine disclosure that has constituted a community with which the author(s) identified*. As mentioned already, this revelation occurs in tandem with the advent of the Judas Maccabeus as leader of the resistance against the Seleucids ("ravens"). It is described as "the opening of the eyes" (90:9), that is, as an event in which something was "seen" that had not previously been perceived. The revelation, however, may go back further, that is, to a time when such revelation to "small lambs" is said to have been ignored by sheep to whom they cried out, presumably for help (90:6).

This community-defining event is not an isolated occurrence within the narrative; it comes as the culmination of a series of similar disclosures made in the past to favored groups of people and individuals in the narrative (cf. 89:28, 40, 41, 43; 90:6). We review these instances here, noting also the image with which it is contrasted: blindness and going astray. In the period following the great deluge, the first group to be given revelation are the "sheep" (Israelites) who were rescued from the "hyenas" (Egyptians) at the waters of the Red Sea. According to the text, which is partly extant in the Aramaic text of 4Q206 frag. 5 col. iii, "their eyes [were] opened and they began to see" while being without water or "grass" (i.e., food) in the desert (89:28a). As a result, the Lord of the sheep provides them with sustenance (89:28b), and they become able to see the Lord's "mighty and great and fe[arful] appearance" (89:30). Ironically, however, this vision of God concludes with the statement that "they began to be blinded and to go astray" (89:32) after they declare to their leader [Moses] their inability to look at the Lord (89:31). The condition of blindness, which ironically mirrors the state attributed to the Egyptians in 89:21, is mentioned again when Moses returns from the rock's summit; this state is ascribed to a majority who face (or at least observe) a decisive form of divine punishment (89:35). The second mention of eyes being opened again occurs in combination with "blinding." Following Knibb's translation of *1 En.* 89:41, we read a general summary that characterizes the existence of the sheep who had come to "a pleasant and glorious land" (Canaan) as follows: "sometimes their eyes were opened, and sometimes blinded, until another sheep rose up and led them, and brought them all back, and their eyes were opened."

Here the allusion is to the ups and downs associated with the time of the judges. The "ups" occur when Israel worships God, and the "downs" correspond to times when Israel's faith is characterized by idolatry. Thus, as with the Israelites in the wilderness, the people to whom divine disclosure has been granted do not remain irreversibly in such a state. Implied is the strong sense of accountability that accompanies the reception of revelation from God. The third passage differs from the others in that the eyes opened are those of an individual. In this case, the reference is to the prophet Samuel who is enabled to see that Saul has renounced the path or glory given to him by God (89:44). Between the time of Samuel and the beginning of the period leading up to the Maccabean crisis, none of the textual witnesses makes any further mention of eyes being opened. Instead, in two instances, both relating to the temple cult, people are said to be blinded. In 89:54 a state of blindness, initially introduced in the Animal Apocalypse to characterize the Egyptians (89:21[10]), is here associated

---

10. In 89:25 there is a further reference to the Egyptians (designated "hyenas," possibly "bears" in the Aramaic: 4QEnoch[e] = 4Q206 4 iii 15 to 89:27) who did not see the Israelites at the Red Sea

with the complete abandonment of "the house of the Lord of the sheep and his tower" toward the end of the divided monarchy. This behavior is punished with a slaughter that may allude to the fall of the northern kingdom (89:55) and, ultimately, if this refers at all to the cultic aberrations of Manasseh, with the destruction of the temple itself (89:56, 66–67). The other instance of blindness occurs after the Second Temple was built after the exile (89:73). The account is careful to note that the table before this rebuilt "tower" was impure, a state that then characterizes the condition of the returnees whose eyes are blind, as well as the condition of those "shepherd" figures who are given oversight over their punishment (so 89:74; more below). Again, the result of blindness, which manifests itself through the improper observance of the cult, is "destruction," that is, oppression and violence suffered at the hands of the Hellenistic rulers in the wake of Alexander the Great. For this post-exilic community there is no divine intervention.

Finally, at the beginning of the passage that introduces the Maccabean revolt, the text refers to "small lambs" who "began to open their eyes, and to see, and to cry to the sheep" (90:6). The revelation given to this group falls on the deaf ears of sheep who, like their post-exilic predecessors, are much blinded (90:7). In the narrative, this conflict marks the emergence of the real author's recently formed community, who came to distinguish themselves over against other Jews who refused to heed their message (90:8).

In the eschatological future, the restoration of Israel to the "new house, larger and higher than that first one" (90:29) culminates in the statement about the sheep within the house: "And the eyes of all of them were opened, and they saw well, and there was not one among them that did not see" (90:35). The temple cult is now expected to be properly observed,[11] and Jerusalem will be restored to its rightful glory (so that 90:29 contrasts with the state described in 89:73). The author anticipates that this restoration will, in turn, result in a widening participation of God's plan: the various species of animals who are now subordinated to the victorious white bull (cf. 90:37) will themselves all be transformed into "white bulls" (90:38).

---

(cf. *Ps.-Philo* 10:6). This is not, however, linked in the text to the more profound "darkening" of the eyes in v. 21 that leads the Egyptians to pursue the Israelites; see Tiller, *Commentary on the Animal Apocalypse*, 284–86.

11. Of course, the reference in text to an "old house" (with pillars, beams, ornaments) in 90:28 may also more broadly include the replacement of the old with a new Jerusalem, called a "new house, larger and higher than the first one" (with new pillars and ornaments) in 90:29 (compare with 89:50 and especially 89:72–73). It is best not to interpret the imagery and vocabulary too precisely, that is, as applying either to a "new city" or to a "new temple" (contra Tiller, *Commentary on the Animal Apocalypse*, 376, who overstates the distinction), as the reference to Jerusalem does not exclude that here the temple or, more specifically, the cult is in view.

The author has read the enlightened status of his community both backwards and forwards into the narrative. Both the past and future stories are made contemporary through language that reflects the present righteous community's understanding of itself. Having eyes opened is expressed in the story through the proper use of divinely ordained responsibility. However, such privileged status implies a warning of forfeiture. When this is squandered through the abuse of privilege, punishment follows. In particular, the metaphor, the opposite of which is "blindness" and the related image of wandering astray denote discernment. In the case of Saul, this means recognition of the abuse of kingship by Saul (89:44). On the flipside, blindness is the condition that leads to a neglect of the temple cult as God has set it up to be (89:54), and it is blindness that leads to the misguided belief that Second Temple bears God's unequivocal stamp of approval (89:73). The association of a complete, divine disclosure to the restored Israel in a new Jerusalem and temple in the ideal future age suggests that the community behind the Animal Apocalypse harbored a temple ideology that they believed neither be adequately addressed nor catered to during the career of Judas Maccabeus. For the time being, the community had to find ways of expressing piety apart from immediate participation in the temple cult. This suspicion would have been confirmed if indeed, as recorded in 2 Maccabees, it was through letters from Antiochus V to Lysias and to the Jewish "senate" and "other Jews" that the temple and ancestral customs were restored to the Jews (2 Macc 11:22–33).

The second feature we have identified regarding the "present" behind the Animal Apocalypse *is the notion of support for what is divinely appointed, though not without qualification.* Specifically, I have already referred to the Second Temple and to the leadership of Judas Maccabeus. However, the question arises: How does this principle manifest itself elsewhere in the narrative? Here it is appropriate to refer to the "seventy shepherds" introduced into the narrative, partly stitched together from images known through Ezek 34 and Zech 11.[12] These shepherds are first referred to in a legitimate capacity: In the wake of Israel's preexilic abandonment of the temple and their ensuing punishment, these shepherds are summoned to take over the responsibility of destroying some of the sheep in accordance with the Lord's command (89:60–61). The shepherds, however, overstep the bounds prescribed for their activities and, contrary to God's intention, end up meting out punishment in excessive amounts. Significantly, they (and not God) are ultimately held responsible for the destruction of the First Temple (89:66–67). In the narrative, special care is taken to describe how each of these shepherds, assigned with responsibility for a fixed

---

12. On this see Nickelsburg, *1 Enoch 1*, 391.

number of sheep, destroy in excess of their limit (89:68-69).[13] Despite the lack of avowed support in the Animal Apocalypse for the Second Temple, the destruction brought by the shepherds against those who undertook the project of re-establishing a defiled version of the cult is regarded as excessive (89:74). These shepherds, assigned to respective periods, continue to function in such a manner until the time of the Maccabean revolt (90:1-5). In the narrative, they function as heirs to the "stars" (that is, the angels) which fell before the time of the flood (86:1-3). The author did not attempt to speculate about the prehistory of the stars, and so the narrative says nothing specifically about whether or not they were originally "good." Important here, however, is that the shepherds who were initially assigned legitimate areas of responsibility for the discipline of God's people, are to suffer no less a punishment than the demonic stars before them: they too are to be thrown into the abyss of fire (90:24-25). The author expects that this kind of eschatological punishment is even reserved for the blinded sheep (90:26-27) referred to earlier in the story.

The third characteristic of the real "present" for us to note is *the clear-cut lines drawn between forces of evil, on the one hand, and the Lord and those acting as the Lord's responsible agents, on the other.* Because the present it seen as a time of major military conflict between the Jewish sheep and the Seleucid ravens, the entire salvation history that precedes, especially from the flood onward, stresses the division through religio-political conflict. Unlike the Book of Watchers in *1 En.* 1-36 (cf. esp. 15:1-16:4), in the Animal Apocalypse there is little reflection on or interest in anthropological dimensions to the problem of evil. Indeed, whereas in the Book of Watchers, the offspring sired by the rebellious angels, the giants, are allowed to go on existing in the form of spirits that afflict human beings after the time of the flood (*1 En.* 15:8-11; cf. also *Jub.* 10), in the Animal Apocalypse these giants—called "elephants, camels, and donkeys"—are completely annihilated by the deluge (89:6). The absence of reflection on interiorized struggles that could be faced by the Lord's people means that any group or individual is represented as either wholly compliant or wholly noncompliant to the purposes of God at any given time. Significantly, it is the *unfolding of time*, within God's design for the world, that determines whether or not faithfulness is going to last. Faithfulness calls for nothing more than more of the same.

This "simplification" of cosmic evil over against the earlier Enochic tradition may come as a surprise, given the ambivalence we may attribute to the document's attitude towards Judas Maccabeus. How does the removal of ambiguities in the face of evil fit with the ambiguous relationship implied between

---

13. In the "shepherds" we have a personification of limited time periods, perhaps of seven years' duration each; regarding such periods, see the "seventy weeks" of years in Dan 9:24.

the community behind the Animal Apocalypse and Judas and those allied to his cause? The response to this question could be that, for the community, the jury on what Judas would ultimately become was still out. The author of the document interpreted the time of his community as one of hope, hope that the contemporary events would somehow usher in a judgment through which those figures who either embodied evil or had been disobedient to the Lord would be held accountable (90:17,20–27) and through which military vengeance against political oppressors in the story would be given to the sheep (90:18–19). Despite this hope, Judas is given no role whatsoever in ushering in the eschaton.

## 3. Conclusion

The writer(s) of the Animal Apocalypse regarded their "present" as one characterized by violence and oppression worse that at any time since the flood (90:17; the last twelve shepherds had caused greater destruction than even their predecessors). The dimensions of antediluvian evil show themselves once again, though with a different face. On this point the fictive and "real" horizons of the present converge.

The present is, however, also conceived as a time of unprecedented hope, stirred by (1) the identity of the document's community as a renewed locus in which the ultimate divine purpose and plan for God's people has been disclosed and by (2) the military successes of Judas Maccabeus. Both these reasons for optimism are interpreted as manifestations of divine intervention. In the case of Judas, help in the struggle against the Seleucids came through the angelic scribe who until now in the narrative had been able to do no more than simply record the excessive abuse of responsibility by the shepherds.

The question remains: What did these acts of God in recent history give the author(s) reason to anticipate? In the Animal Apocalypse these divine disclosures have brought about an irretrievable momentum toward resolution: the contemporary oppressive forces against God's people, which have been read into and out of the past as resulting from the shepherds' disobedience, will be dealt the ultimate blow of destruction, alongside demonic fallen stars bound up in the abyss since the deluge. In this way, the nature of the stars functions at once to demonize fomenters of the current religio-political crisis and to assure that their annihilation is a foregone conclusion.

Although the community of the author(s) was critical of the Second Temple (to such a degree that their participation in the polluted cult would have been out of the question), it cannot be described as having been "sectarian." In a strict sense, the "sheep" are and remain a group larger than those whose eyes have been opened (as in the account of salvation history). These are, in the first instance, the elect people of God. Furthermore, the designation of God as "Lord of the sheep" has this larger community of God's covenant people in view; it is *among them* that God's ultimate plan is being worked out. This is a plan that in the past and eschatological future is portrayed in terms shaped by the narrower concerns of the enlightened community behind the document.

# WHY HAS DANIEL'S PROPHECY NOT BEEN FULFILLED? THE QUESTION OF POLITICAL PEACE AND INDEPENDENCE IN THE ADDITIONS TO DANIEL

Ulrike Mittmann-Richert

## 1. The Hermeneutical Problem

"Reading the Present"—this rather unusual combination of terms is meant to disclose a hermeneutical process in which the human conception of life in its actual historical environment is shaped by an ongoing scriptural interpretation. What might be called the need for an exegetical contextualization of history, however, is not as easy to define as it may seem from the outside, since Scripture—as the hermeneutical key to history—is always in need of being interpreted itself. As to the question, therefore, of how "the present" was transformed into literature in ancient Judaism, the modern-day reader of ancient texts finds himself hermeneutically navigating through a world in which the borders move, as our changing understanding of history redraws the hermeneutical map to Scripture. The interpretation of this map is quite different, however, as the belief in God as the lord of history and the transcendent source of scriptural revelation reveals an emotional topography in personal faith and understanding.

How, then, does one come to a meeting point between faith and history? One has to bear these aforementioned hermeneutical reflections in mind when turning to the Additions to Daniel, because these Additions constitute a very special hermeneutical problem, as, at first glance, they don't at all seem to be answerable with the question just stated. This problem emerges from a radical opposition of scriptural and historical facts: what is to be done, when there is seemingly no way to hermeneutically bridge the gap between Scripture and the actual historical situation?

This question of a crucial incompatibility of history and Scripture immediately leads to yet another question which has to be answered before one can even try to understand the problems with which the author or the authors of the

Additions to Daniel are coping or even struggling.[1] It is the question of the historical situation itself: What kind of situation in early Jewish history could have caused such hermeneutical problems that the scriptural witness was in danger of losing its credibility and reliability? The answer might be a surprise, because it was not a time of grief and suppression that led to this intellectual struggle, but a time of freedom and new political independence for the Jewish people, as will be explained later, the most peaceful period of the Hasmonean era, very probably the time of Simon (142–135/4 B.C.E.).

That freedom and peace could cause a serious theological problem is even more surprising when one takes into account that for the Jewish people the first half of the second century B.C.E. had been a time of tremendous suffering. It reached its peak when, in the religious crisis under Antiochus IV, Jerusalem was transformed into a Greek *polis* by force, the Jewish temple on Mount Zion was dedicated to Zeus Olympios or Baʿal-šamem and Jewish worship was abolished; Judaism itself was on the edge of being extinguished.[2] One would assume, therefore, that following the Maccabean war and the rededication of the temple, the period of political peace and independence under Hasmonean rule would be celebrated as the fulfillment of eschatological expectations. Yet it was not. Because the overwhelming and hitherto unknown danger that the Jewish people had to face by almost losing their religious identity had forced eschatological expectations to such tense apocalyptic heights, whatever followed this period of deadly suppression and persecution was certain not to fit the picture. Hasmonean rule, although it guaranteed political and religious freedom in that period, was far from what Daniel had foretold, namely, God's everlasting victory over the nations and the establishment of his kingdom on Mount Zion.

It was not, of course, the first time in Jewish history that Israel was confronted with seemingly unfulfilled eschatological expectations. The Babylonian captivity had once yielded expectations of a second exodus leading to God's final and everlasting enthronement on Mount Zion (e.g., Isa 52:11–12; 55:12–

---

1. It should be noted at this point that this essay, which deals with a *hermeneutical* problem, does not start with a survey of the textual evidence (as one would expect), but rather with an argumentation that is based on a foregoing analysis of the text. The historical picture that is now being outlined should not be understood as the premise used to conduct the textual analysis but rather as the result of such an analysis, which now has to be confirmed through a second look at the text. For the exegetical analysis underlying the argumentation, see Ulrike Mittmann-Richert, "Einführung zu den historischen und legendarischen Erzählungen," *JSHRZ* 6/1 (2000): 114–38.

2. For the historical situation, see Emil Schürer, *The History of the Jewish People in the Age of Jesus Christ*, 175 B.C.–A.D. 135 (rev. and ed. G. Vermes et al.; 3 vols.; Edinburgh: T&T Clark, 1973), 1:137–63. Cf. Mittmann-Richert, "Einführung," 24–31, 34–35, 37–38, 49–55.

13; 60:1–22; Jer 51:45), expectations that were deeply disappointed because of the political problems with which those who returned to the Holy Land had to cope. But whatever suffering and despair Israel had undergone as an exiled nation in Babylonian times, it was exceeded by the catastrophe brought upon the Jewish people under Seleucid rule. Not only were the outward political conditions of Jewish life, which were preserved in a heathen surrounding, destroyed, but the inner foundations of Jewish religion were also toppled. That which no one had ever thought possible had occurred: God himself, the God of Israel, had been overthrown, and his holy temple had been taken over by a heathen God from Babylon, whom the book of Daniel, taking up his Semitic name Ba'al-šamem, calls *šiqqûz mešômem* (wing of abominations, Dan 8:13; 9:27; 11:31; 12:11). Jerusalem had become Babylon. In earlier times the Babylonian siege and tearing down of the temple could be (and by the prophets actually was) interpreted as *God's own* forsaking of the temple and willing departure from Mount Zion because Israel had forsaken him. The installation of the Greek cult of Zeus Olympios in Jerusalem under the ruler of "Babylon," Antiochus IV, and the destruction of Jewish religion as such could not, however, be rationalized by means of such conceptions of judgment alone. In Daniel's words, Antiochus IV had reached for the stars of heaven and succeeded in throwing them down to earth (Dan 8:9–12; 7:21, 25). Desperation and skepticism were gaining ground and forced religious yearning to a point where, in the eyes of true believers, nothing short of God's own transcendent intervention on earth would suffice to prove God's might and power over the nations. National and individual hopelessness was only overcome by the hope expressed in the book of Daniel that the religious oppression under the rule of Antiochus IV was part of the eschatological drama resulting in God's mighty and unexpected overthrow of the evil on earth. God would not earn his victory over the heathen forces, so it was believed, by politically strengthening his people Israel, but by universally shattering the image of human power from his transcendent realm. In Dan 11:40–45, the eschatological picture evolves. The end of the demonic reign of Antiochus IV is foretold in a vision of God's triumphant victory over the unified powers of Egypt and Babel. Both of them were archetypes of the power of evil in whose realm Israel once had to dwell as an exiled nation and which, in trying to overcome even God himself, suffers its eschatological defeat.[3] Yet the reality was quite different. Judas Maccabeus had

---

3. In this account of the eschatological victory over the powers of evil, the book of Daniel combines the age-old Egyptian threat with the memory of the disastrous defeat at the hands of the Babylonians in order to emphasize the destructive might of the heathen powers in the most dramatic way. There could be nothing worse for the author than the eschatological reunion of

certainly succeeded in recapturing Jerusalem and restoring the temple and the temple cult. But whatever followed, even the constitution of an independent Jewish state, was the result of a political maneuvering and of taking advantage of changing alliances; it was not the result of God's triumphant and forceful victory over his enemies.

It is essential to realize the urgency and the seriousness of the religious problem implied in these historical developments in order to reach a thorough comprehension of the Additions to Daniel. It is possible, however, to understand the religious problem as a scriptural one: Why have Daniel's prophecies not been fulfilled? Why have they not been fulfilled exactly as it was revealed to the prophet?[4]

The designation of Daniel as a prophet implies that the book of Daniel has a scriptural status which needs further consideration. Since, however, the hermeneutical process underlying the growth of the Daniel tradition cannot be verified other than through exegetical results,[5] the question of the prophetic

---

those powers which in the course of history had almost succeeded in extinguishing the people of Israel. The combination of the Egypt typology and the Babylon typology is anticipated in Dan 3, where the furnace, as a symbol of the Egyptian menace, is located in Babylon. The insertion of poetic texts into this chapter is, therefore, highly significant. However, it should be noted that in most modern interpretations of the book the allusions to Egypt and to Israel's original experience of global oppression are mostly ignored or quickly passed over. For a thorough investigation and typological interpretation of the allusions to Egypt and Babylon in the book of Daniel, see Hartmut Gese, "Das Geschichtsbild des Danielbuches und Ägypten," in idem, *Alttestamentliche Studien* (Tübingen: Mohr Siebeck, 1991), 189–201, whose insights are applied to the interpretation given in this study. Cf. Hartmut Gese, "Die Bedeutung der Krise unter Antiochus IV. Epiphanes für die Apokalyptik des Danielbuches," in idem, *Alttestamentliche Studien*, 202–17.

4. The necessity to deal with disappointed eschatological expectations is so urgent that, seen from a modern scholarly point of view, it is most astonishing that, with respect to Daniel, the question of unfulfilled prophecy has never been answered by integrating exactly those texts into the picture that reframe the book of Daniel in later tradition. They do not get any consideration, although scholarship is quite aware of the textual hints to other prophetic books. The reason for this neglect of influential traditions is to be found in a one-sided methodology in applying redaction criticism. It can generally be observed that wherever redaction critical standards are applied, the interpretation of the Additions is guided by the conviction that all textual elements seemingly contradicting the flow of thought of the stories and revealing an implicit meaning are to be judged as secondary additions to the original text. The focus of redaction critical work is the LXX version, as it contains most of those elements and hints to other prophetic traditions that make the stories difficult to understand. So it is generally concluded that, if the theological superstructure is torn down, one comes to the very foundations of the Daniel tradition which are supposed to be even older than those pieces of text of the book of Daniel that are identified—methodologically in exactly the same way—as "old material." The anachronism of this application of fixed standards, however, has not been a topic of scholarly discussion yet.

5. See n. 1.

rank of the book of Daniel must be left open and answered in the light of the interpretation of the person and universal role of Daniel expressed by the Additions to the book. But whatever the exact classification of Daniel's words may be, the question as stated above remains: Why have Daniel's words and visions not come true? Or have they, despite the fact that instead of God being the only king and ruler on earth the Hasmoneans have established themselves as rulers of the Jewish people, and this in the midst of heathen powers that continue to exert their might on earth?

In approaching the question of unfulfilled prophecy, the modern exegete, in taking a seat among the exegetes of old, becomes part of a fascinating discussion. Its starting point, however, is *not* the question as it has just been stated in order to disclose the hermeneutical problem as such; its starting point is a hermeneutical credo: Scripture cannot be false. God's revelation to his prophets has to be trusted, however things may appear. So what is to be done to bridge the gap between Daniel's words and present history? Scripture needs to be studied more deeply. Indeed, the hermeneutical process that underlies the Additions to Daniel may be seen as a movement from Scripture to history and back to Scripture again. In coping with the actual historical situation, the author or the authors of the Additions to Daniel tried to read Scripture in the light of Scripture, which means they reread the book of Daniel in the light of the prophetic traditions that form the background of Daniel's prophecy, the most important being the prophecies of Jeremiah, Habakkuk, and Hosea. From these earlier prophets, a new understanding of the book of Daniel was gained, an understanding that helped to preserve and even strengthen the authority of Daniel and finally established the rank of the book of Daniel as a prophetical. At the same time it manifested the conviction that God had proven to be the true ruler of history in everything that had occurred since Antiochus IV had tried to gain power over the world and its God.

The following analysis of the Additions to Daniel is an attempt to present a new look at these texts that are mostly regarded as simple tales without theological depth and quality or, in the case of the hymns, as pieces of literature that originally did not belong to the Daniel tradition. It will also show that all of the Additions, as reflections of the time that has just been recalled, belong together thematically and do not contain old material.[6] They are not texts that had, as

---

6. The fact that the Additions thematically belong together has not been recognized so far because scholarship has confined the categorization of the prose texts to only two possibilities: since they are fictional in character, but at the same time contain scriptural allusions, they are either classified as legendary tales or as midrashim to certain prophetic texts. A third possibility of classification does not even get considered: the possibility that the texts in question are witnesses of a scriptural discussion led on the basis of a whole *complex* of traditions. As will be shown in this investigation,

scholars suppose, led a life of their own before they were collected and attached to the book of Daniel,[7] but grew out of the transformation of the Daniel tradition.

Closely tied to the question of textual transmission is the question of manuscript transmission, which, because of its complexity, cannot be discussed in this essay. Here it must suffice to state the author's conviction that, although among the existing versions the so-called Theodotion (θ) version had gained canonical status in the early church,[8] the text transmitted by the

---

the Additions are the result of a transformation of certain traditions, which was necessitated by the historical developments in Hasmonean times. This formation of traditions corresponds to the Old Testament process of transforming and reshaping traditions, even if the lines that separate the biblical texts from legendary material are at some points transgressed. An exception among recent studies of the Additions is that of Marti J. Steussy, *Gardens in Babylon: Narrative and Faith in the Greek Legends of Daniel* (SBLDS 141; Atlanta: Scholars Press, 1993), which also tries to integrate the complete picture of biblical references into her exegesis of the texts. Her failure in coming up with a historical-theological synthesis is due to her neglect of the poetic pieces that are pivotal for the understanding of the whole picture.

7. See especially Ingo Kottsieper, *Zusätze zu Daniel*, in O. H. Steck et al., *Das Buch Baruch, der Brief des Jeremia, Zusätze zu Ester und Daniel* (ATD, Apokryphen 5; Göttingen: Vandenhoeck & Ruprecht, 1998), 211–19, who not only applies a most complicated model of the genesis of the texts to the interpretation of the Additions but also supplies the reader with a highly developed reconstruction of various stages of the formation of the texts, which, in the case of Bel and the Dragon, reaches back to the fifth century B.C.E. In fact, Kottsieper is sure that, by starting with θ at the end of the chain of textual transmission, which the author recognizes as a Sadducean redaction of the first century C.E., he can trace back the way of every single narrative element of the stories over a period of five hundred years up to their Babylonian and Persian beginnings (248–56). See also Andreas Wysny, *Die Erzählungen von Bel und dem Drachen: Untersuchungen zu Dan 14* (SBB 33; Stuttgart: Katholisches Bibelwerk, 1996), 172–81, who applies a similar model of textual genesis. The story of Susanna is dated in Persian times by Carey A. Moore, *Daniel, Esther and Jeremiah: The Additions. A New Translation with Introduction and Commentary* (AB 44; Garden City, N.Y.: Doubleday, 1977), 91–92. This hypothesis is in contrast with the opinion that the story of Susanna is of younger origin and mirrors the conflict between Pharisees and Sadducees under Alexander Jannaeus (103–76 B.C.E.). Compare D. M. Kay, "Susanna," *APOT* 1:643–44, who summarizes the discussion of his time. This overview may suffice to show that in recent studies of the Additions the discussion about the genesis of the texts has become increasingly hypothetical in character. Therefore, scholarship is far from any consensus in terms of date and origin of the Additions. The same is true for the question of provenance, concerning which the spectrum of answers ranges from the Babylonian diaspora over Palestine to Egypt. Cf. Mittmann-Richert, "Einführung," 117–18. Only the prayer of Azariah seems easy to date and localize, as it contains concrete hints to an evil king oppressing the Jews (Dan 3:32–33 LXX) and to the cessation of the temple cult (Dan 3:38 LXX), which both point to the crisis under Antiochus IV and to Palestine as the place of origin. Cf. Hans-Peter Rüger, "Apokryphen I," *TRE* 3:298–316; and K. Koch, *Deuterokanonische Zusätze zum Danielbuch: Entstehung und Textgeschichte* (2 vols.; AOAT 38; Kevelaer: Butzon & Becker; Neukirchen-Vluyn: Neukirchener, 1987), 2:80.

8. Cf. Hieronymus, *Praefatio in Danielem Prophetam* (PG 28:1357–60).

LXX[9] has to be taken as the older and more original one.[10] Nevertheless, with respect to the hermeneutical problem the *content* of the Additions is the primary interest.[11]

---

9. Only two Greek manuscripts have been preserved: Pap. 967 (cf. Winfried Hamm, *Der Septuaginta-Text des Buches Daniel [3–4] nach dem Koelner Teil des Papyrus 967* [Papyrologische Texte und Abhandlungen 21; Bonn: Habelt, 1977]), and *Codex Chisianus* (88). Among the translations, only the *Syrohexapla* contains the text of the LXX version.

10. Helmut Engel, *Die Susanna-Erzählung: Einleitung und Kommentar zum Septuaginta-Text und zur Theodotion-Bearbeitung* (OBO 61; Fribourg: Universitätsverlag; Göttingen: Vandenhoeck & Ruprecht, 1985), and Wysny, *Erzählungen*, 33–141, also follow the assumption that the LXX version represents an older stage of text transmission than the Theodotion version; against Jürgen Lebram, "Daniel/Danielbuch und Zusätze," *TRE* 8:342, who is convinced that the LXX version is a paraphrase of the text transmitted by θ. See also Otto Plöger, "Zusätze zu Daniel," *JSHRZ* 1/1 (1973): 65–69; Moore, *Daniel, Esther and Jeremiah*, 30–34; Koch, *Deuterokanonische Zusätze zum Danielbuch*, 1:13–14; Dominik Helbling, "Transzendierung der Geschichte: Dan 3,57–90 LXX als hymnische Exegese," *BN* 14 (2002): 7–10; and Mittmann-Richert, "Einführung," 116–17. The problem of text transmission is further complicated by the fact that there is no consensus on the question of the original language of the texts. Despite the lack of manuscript evidence, a Semitic origin of the Additions is held probable by many exegetes. Cf. Moore, *Daniel, Esther and Jeremiah*, 25–26. The discussion about the original language of the Additions, however, is not just a modern one, but has its roots in the early church. Cf. the correspondence between Julius Africanus and Origen (*Epistola Africani ad Origenem de historia Susannae; Epistola Origenis ad Africanum de Susannae historia* [PL 11:41–86]), in which arguments are exchanged as to whether or not the pun in Sus 54 und 58 is a significant clue to the original language of the story. See Engel, *Susanna-Erzählung*, 17–24 (with bibliography). The theory that 4QDanSuz? ar (4Q551) is an Aramaic fragment of the story of Susanna is held by Jósef-Tadeusz Milik, "Daniel et Susanne à Qumrân?" in *De la Tôrah au Messie: Études d'exégèse et d'herméneutique biblique offertes à Henri Cazelles pour ses 25 années d'enseignement à l'Institut Catholique de Paris (Octobre 1979)* (ed. M. Carrez et al.; Paris: Desclée, 1981), 337–59. This hypothesis, however, has not met with much approval. An Aramaic text of the Additions to Dan 3 is also found in the medieval chronicle of Jerahmeel, which at the end of the nineteenth century was held to be the original text by Moses Gaster, "The Unknown Aramaic Original of Theodotion's Additions to the Book of Daniel," *Proceedings of the Society of Biblical Archaeology* 16 (1894): 280–90, 312–17; 17 (1895): 75–94; by the same author: *The Chronicles of Jerahmeel* (London: Royal Asiatic Society, 1899), 1–9. Gaster's hypothesis has long been refuted, since the Aramaic text proved to be a retranslation of the Theodotion version. In more recent times, only Koch, *Deuterokanonische Zusätze zum Danielbuch*, 1:19–39, has tried to invigorate Gaster's thesis of an Aramaic original by objecting that, in earlier studies, the textual details had not found due attention. For a general overview, see David A. deSilva, *Introducing the Apocrypha: Message, Context, and Significance* (Grand Rapids: Baker, 2002), 222–25.

11. The novelty in the methodological approach followed in this study, whose results were already presented in the introductory hermeneutical discussion, lies in the fact that the historical picture presented in the Additions is not drawn from historical allusions in the texts, which tend to be symbolic in character and ambiguous because of the typological literary methods employed. The historical picture is drawn, rather, from the *theological* focus of the Additions, which, despite their differences in form and content, ties them all together. This goes against the general

## 2. The Additions as Witnesses of a Scriptural Rereading of the Book of Daniel

A first glance at the Additions to Daniel shows that the major obstacle for a coherent interpretation of the texts is their formal variety. The stories of Susanna and of Bel and the Dragon are prose narratives, very similar to those in Dan 1–6, but there are also two pieces of poetry inserted into chapter 3 of the book of Daniel. These are two psalms, each of a different genre: the prayer of Azariah (Dan 3:26–45 LXX), which is a psalm of lamentation;[12] and a hymn of creation, which is known to modern readers as the Song of the Three Young Men (Dan 3:52–90 LXX). The title of the poem recalls the story in Dan 3, which tells about the rescue of three young Jewish men who refuse to worship the idol erected by Nebuchadnezzar and, when cast into the furnace, the symbol for Egypt (Deut 4:20; 1 Kgs 8:51; Jer 11:4),[13] are saved from the flames by the angel of God. In this context, the inserted psalms not only highlight the change of situation from deadly peril to miraculous deliverance, but also serve to point out the fact that what happens in the story relates to all of Israel (Dan 3:28–41, 83–87 LXX). They reflect the historical situation of the nation as a whole: a people rescued from the abyss of death, a people rescued from the Seleucid furnace.

In contrast to these psalms whose literary function is to deepen and theologically accentuate an existing tale, the stories of Susanna and of Bel and the Dragon contain new narrative material,[14] material very different from that found in the book of Daniel.[15] In each of these stories Daniel appears in a new role. In the story of Susanna Daniel is presented as the judge of his people who frees his nation from the abuse of power exerted by Israel's authorities. By skillfully inves-

---

assumption that the Additions to Daniel owe their existence to a certain extent to chance; cf., e.g., Moore, *Daniel, Esther and Jeremiah*, 12.

12. Only in θ is Azariah portrayed as an individual. In the LXX, the psalm is a common prayer of the three young men with Azariah as their leader.

13. Cf. Mittmann-Richert, "Einführung," 121.

14. In the LXX, both stories are placed after Dan 1–12, while in θ the story of Susanna becomes the introduction to the book of Daniel as a whole. This is probably done because in Sus 45 Daniel is called a juvenile, which suggests that his rescuing Susanna was the beginning of his public career.

15. The growth and multiplicity of the Daniel tradition is also documented by the extant material from Qumran: 4Q243–246 (George Brooke et al., *Qumran Cave 4.XVII: Parabiblical Texts, Part 3* [DJD 22; Oxford: Clarendon, 1996], 95–184). As far as content and genre are concerned, however, this material has nothing in common with the Additions transmitted in Greek. For the classification of 4QFour Kingdoms[a-b] ar (4Q 552–553) as a further Daniel Apocalypse, see Armin Lange with Ulrike Mittmann-Richert, "Annotated List of the Texts from the Judaean Desert Classified by Content and Genre," in *The Texts from the Judaean Desert: Indices and an Introduction to the* Discoveries in the Judaean Desert *Series* (ed. E. Tov; DJD 39; Oxford: Clarendon, 2002), 126–27 with n. 11.

tigating the case of Susanna, who was accused on the false testimony of two of Israel's elders of having committed adultery, he saves her from being sentenced to death and thus establishes justice in Israel. In the double story of Bel and the Dragon, the image of Daniel is changed again. Now he appears as a priest (Bel 2 LXX) who, in serving the true and only God, brings to light the powerlessness and worthlessness of the heathen Gods.[16] The irony in these tales—at some points even heightened to ridiculousness—cannot be missed: the fact that Bel's existence is purely a material one and the statue itself no more than a handcrafted idol is criminologically proven by the footprints of the heathen priests who secretly take away the food prepared for the god. Likewise, the animal nature of the dragon is brought to light by a simple trick. The dragon, who consumes the food that Daniel has prepared for him from pitch, fat, and hair, bursts asunder. Instead of worshiping the God of Israel, however, the king throws Daniel into the lion's den where he is miraculously fed by the prophet Habakkuk, and from which he is released after seven days, unhurt by the beasts.

Simple tales, yet the simplicity of the composition should not deceive the exegete into neglecting the theological depth of the narratives and their fervor, both of which arise from an ongoing process of scriptural reflection. Thus, by taking another, deeper look at the story of Bel and the Dragon, one finds striking parallels to Jer 50 and 51, the great announcement of the downfall and destruction of Babylon.[17] There is hardly any motif in this Daniel story that is not part of Jeremiah's prophecy, the most prominent being the extermination of the Babylonian idols, above all of Bel (Jer 50:2; 51:17, 44, 47, 52). In Jeremiah it is stated again and again that the idols have neither life nor breath, a statement which, in the story of Bel and the Dragon, serves as the hidden starting point for everything that happens (Bel 5–7, 24–25, 27). Likewise, in Jeremiah the reader meets the dragon as a symbol of the devouring Babylonian power. Here too, it is foretold that the dragon will be destroyed because of his own voracity (Jer 51:34–35). Finally, lions appear as symbols of the Babylonians' violent lust for power and universal might (Jer 51:38–39). Not only do the theological leitmotifs in the story of Bel and the Dragon correspond exactly to those in the Jeremiah passage, but the narrative even follows Jeremiah in taking over the idea that the idols are mocked and ridiculed and finally trapped by God himself (Bel

---

16. Like the stories in Dan 1–6, the story of Bel and the Dragon belongs to the set of confrontation stories in which Daniel proves the powerlessness and ineffectiveness of the heathen gods. The difference, however, lies in the fact the demise of idol worshiping in the Additions is not caused by the hubris of the heathen king but by Daniel himself.

17. Moore, *Daniel, Esther and Jeremiah*, 122–23, who only considers Jer 51:34 as a reference text for Bel and the Dragon, ignores the general importance of Jer 50 and 51 for the formation of the Additions.

7, 19, 27). In Jer 51:17–18 it is written: "Every goldsmith is put to shame by his idols, for his images are false, and there is no breath in them. They are worthless, mere mockeries. They will perish at the time of their punishment."[18] Then, appropriating the concept from Jer 50:24, the author of the Daniel story portrays Daniel as cunningly trapping the dragon and the priests of Bel (Bel 13–22, 25, 27): "I set a trap for you and you were taken, O Babylon!"

What does it mean when, in the story of Bel and the Dragon, the overthrow of the Babylonian idols, which Jeremiah *foretells*, is not only paralleled but described as a *past event*? It means that Jeremiah's eschatological vision has become truth. Jeremiah's prophecy is fulfilled, and Daniel, who like Jeremiah had awaited the downfall of the Babylonian god Bel (or Baʿal-šamem), has become God's instrument of salvation.

Here one gets a first glimpse of the rationale underlying the Additions to Daniel, the unity of which is also revealed by their close connection to Jer 50 and 51. There is yet another striking parallel to be named: in Jer 51:15–16 the mockery of the heathen idols, their lifelessness, worthlessness, and ineffectiveness, is tied to the praise of the Creator, the only one among the gods having life and exerting power over the elements of nature (rain and wind, thunder and lightning, Jer 51:15–16; cf. Dan 3:64–65, 73 LXX). If Jer 51:48 is also taken into consideration, which foretells creation's universal praise and joy at the time of Babylon's destruction, then it becomes clear why the Additions contain a hymn of creation. In the Song of the Three Young Men (Dan 3:52–90 LXX), wind and rain, storm and thunder, and the other elements of nature, with all creatures of the earth, are called to join Israel's praise to God. The Song of the Three Young Men is meant to be the hymn of praise of a people that has experienced God's help while in danger of being burned by the flames of the furnace; it is meant to be the joyful song of the people having overcome the Seleucid oppression.[19]

---

18. Cf. Jer 10:14 and 10:11.

19. The reason it is generally held impossible that the psalms in Dan 3 LXX were composed in the process of a scriptural transformation of the Daniel tradition is because the composition of liturgical texts is not considered to be an exegetical scribal undertaking. It is rather assumed that the psalms originated from a "no man's land" called "temple tradition," in which the only literary work done with biblical traditions consisted in the adaptation of older liturgical pieces. It is therefore important to gain a new historical understanding of the urgent need for scriptural reflection and theological discussion in Hasmonean times and the impact it had on the formation of religious texts, especially in the area of liturgy. The detailed study of Helbling, "Transzendierung der Geschichte" (see n. 10), in which the author analyzes the Song of the Three Young Men according to Pap. 976 on the basis of the biblical traditions alluded to in the psalm, is a good first step. Helbling also dissociates himself from the assumption that the psalm in question is just an adaptation of unknown earlier traditions and instead states that the poem is the product of a thorough exegesis of certain Old Testament materials, especially the Daniel tradition, for which there was a

In the end, Babylon itself is consumed by the flames (Jer 51:58; Dan 3:47–48 LXX).[20] Again, the fact that the hymn of praise that Jeremiah had announced as resounding from the mouth of creation at the time of God's victory over the power of Babylon is now actually addressed to God by his people and the whole of creation signifies not only a historical change but also a change of mind. Israel in Hasmonean times acknowledges the fulfillment of everything Jeremiah—and with him Daniel—had foretold and, along with the whole of creation, gratefully praises God for helping the nation overcome the religious crisis.

The connection between the hymn inserted into Dan 3 and the story of Bel and the Dragon is also evident in the theological message of these texts. They both express the conviction that creation is not to be worshiped itself, as is done by the adherents of the dragon, but points to him who alone is to be adored: the God of Israel, the Creator of the universe. As they stand together, these texts prove to be witnesses of an ongoing historical-theological reflection, whose scriptural foundations are the prophecies against Babylon, *including*, by encompassing it, Daniel's prophecy. By taking both the announcements of Jeremiah and the words of Daniel as predictions of the same event, the downfall of Babylon in Seleucid times, a hermeneutical key was found to open the door for a new understanding of the book of Daniel.

However, only part of the prophetic picture has been disclosed so far. The appearance of yet another prophet in the story of Bel and the Dragon shows that there is more to be found. Habakkuk appears at the end: flying, carried by an angel to Babylon, where he feeds Daniel with bread and wine. Like Jeremiah, Habakkuk belongs to those prophets who warned Israel of its imminent overthrow by Babylonian forces, cruelly punishing the people for having left their God. The LXX contains a further allusion to Habakkuk: in its opening words, the tale as a whole is identified as a piece of prophecy from Habakkuk. Both references to Habakkuk have caused interpreters a lot of trouble, and to date the question of Habakkuk's role in the story has, by and large, confounded any explanation. An explanation can be found, however, if the hermeneutical key that was used by analyzing the references to Jeremiah in the Additions to Daniel is applied to the book of Habakkuk.

In chapter 3, this rather short prophetic work ends abruptly with a personal statement: in the midst of grief and sorrow caused by the Babylonian oppression, the prophet expresses his firm conviction that God will grant him salvation

---

historical need. See esp. Helbling, "Transzendierung der Geschichte," 57–58, in which the author calls this process of transformation of traditions "hymnische Exegese [hymnic exegesis]."

20. See also Mal 3:19–21, where the rescue from the furnace goes along with the extermination of the godless.

and strengthen him, raise him up and lead him over the heights of the earth. This is truly an open end.[21] In a time when the reversal of history for which Habakkuk had waited and for which he had pleaded had come, this ending must have forced narrators to develop it further.[22] The Habakkuk scene in the story of Bel and the Dragon certainly is such an extension of the book and denotes the fulfillment of the Habakkuk prophecy. This is true not only because the words themselves are taken up and Habakkuk is pictured on his mission to Daniel as being carried over lofty heights[23] but also because the violent picture of the fruit of the fields being destroyed, which is also part of Hab 3, is taken up and reversed: in Bel and the Dragon, the fields are ripe to be reaped and the harvest is brought in (Bel 33–39). Since the earth bears fruit again, Habakkuk, who had desperately mourned over Israel's fields and vineyards lying waste, is now able to provide Daniel with bread and wine.[24] Again, the point cannot be missed: the bringing of bread and wine signifies, against the historical backdrop of the book of Daniel, a situation totally changed. It is the sign of the reversal of history and denotes the end of the Babylonian peril, which of course means the end of the persecution and religious oppression under Seleucid rule.

It is evident how the author or authors of the Additions transformed Daniel's prophecy by personally integrating him into the picture of the earlier prophecies about Babylon, while at the same time adapting them to the present time. Daniel's apocalyptic announcements were reviewed with the help of well-known eschatological categories, and Daniel arises to serve as the mediary of God's everlasting will as laid down in Scripture. Since Daniel, according to the book of Daniel (Dan 1:1; 2:1; etc.), is supposed to have lived at the time of the Babylonian king Nebuchadnezzar, and therefore to have been a contemporary of Jeremiah and Habakkuk, the theological concept of the Additions to Daniel is quite in line with Scripture itself.

However, the transformation of the visionary elements in the book of Daniel does not mean that they lose their eschatological character. This becomes quite clear when one considers the feeding motif in the story of Bel and the Dragon, which recurs three times: Bel is fed, the dragon is fed, and

---

21. The LXX translation of the verses in question clearly shows that the tenses in the Hebrew text were understood to be in the future and to imply that God will guide Habakkuk to a better end.

22. Similarly Steussy, *Gardens in Babylon*, 159.

23. Here the combination of prophetic traditions also includes Ezekiel's experience of being lifted up by God's spirit and carried to Jerusalem (Ezek 8:3).

24. The mention of the wine is not a secondary addition to the text, as is generally assumed (cf., e.g., Wysny, *Erzählungen*, 122), but is an original and essential part of the scene. The bringing of bread and wine to Daniel, which presupposes that the vine did bear fruit, is meant to be the positive counterpart to Hab 3:17, where the fruitlessness of the vine is the sign of the time of judgment.

finally Daniel is fed by God himself. Although this triple feeding has rarely caught the attention of interpreters, it is most important to note the difference in thought underlying the feeding scenes. While the heathen gods *need* to be fed *by their adherents* (who think that the gods' consumption of food proves that they are living, Bel 6, 24 LXX), the God of Israel does not need to be fed but is, rather, the one who provides his people with everything they need to live. The story would lose its point, if, as most scholars suggest, the Habakkuk episode were detached from the other pieces of the tale as a secondary element of unknown origin. That Israel's God is the living and only God is *not* proven by the fact that the priests of Bel are shown to be deceitful, and it is *not* proven by the dragon's bursting asunder; it is only shown by God's might to give and sustain life as he does when he supplies Daniel with the food he needs.[25] In granting Daniel life, God reveals himself as the Creator.

The eschatological picture, however, evolves from the *combination* of creation motifs. It is certainly not by chance that Daniel has to dwell in the lions' den for seven days and is fed exactly on the sixth day, which, in the creation story, is the day on which man was created (Bel 32; cf. Gen 1:26–31). But the prophet is not only kept alive and thus saved by his Creator, he is also granted the everlasting peace of creation, which is represented by his dwelling with the lions without being hurt.[26] This is clearly an eschatological image establishing Israel's eschatological hopes. Israel, in the figure of Daniel, having been saved from the mouth of the Babylonian lion Antiochus IV, is granted everlasting sustenance by the Creator himself, which, in the period of peace following the Maccabean war, must have appeared to be a precious gift. Since the concept of Israel and creation dwelling in peace is also found in 1 Maccabees (1 Macc 14:4–15), where it is enlarged by messianic images and historically connected to the time of Simon, one must search for the origin of the Additions to Daniel in the time of this Hasmonean ruler. The time of Simon was a time of rest

---

25. In the Old Testament prophetic tradition, the reference to the nonexistence and inefficacy of the idols is always combined with the praise of God's might to give and sustain life and the power he exerts as the Lord of history. See Jer 51:15–19; Pss 98:5; 115:3–7; 135:6–7, 15–17; Isa 41:19–20, 29; 44:6–20; Hos 8:4–5, 14. This makes it even more impossible to think of the distinct episodes in Bel and the Dragon as originally independent tales; against Wysny, *Erzählungen*, 121–22, 172–80, and Kottsieper, *Zusätze zu Daniel*, 248–49, who, in another context, also points out that satirically unmasking the idols alone does not provide the basis for the belief in the one and only living God (op. cit., 269). The literary unity of the story is held by John J. Collins, *Daniel: A Commentary on the Book of Daniel* (Hermeneia; Minneapolis: Fortress, 1993), 409. Collins, however, regards the attribution to Habakkuk in the heading of the text as secondary. He is also convinced that the story originated independently from Dan 6.

26. Cf. also Isa 58:13–14, where the promise is given to those who sanctify the seventh day that they will ride upon the heights of the earth and will be fed by God.

and new prosperity and was, therefore, an appropriate time to be highlighted theologically.[27] In the story of Bel and the Dragon, this was done by a scriptural integration of Daniel's eschatological visions into the actual experience of political freedom regained and peace firmly established. But it can also be stated the other way around. The author of the story of Bel and the Dragon is eager to confirm that Israel's peace is established by the fulfillment of everything Daniel and Habakkuk, as they are seen together, had foretold.[28] In Hab 3 the final judgment is described as a consuming fire which will lead to the destruction not only of Israel but also of the elements of creation (Hab 3:6, 8–11). This establishes the coherence of the story of Bel and the Dragon and the poetic Additions to Dan 3 by confirming that the eschatological image of creation's peace is in fact a historical picture,[29] not one appropriated from unknown sources.

Yet the picture is not complete, and there are still some aspects left to be dealt with if a full comprehension of the hermeneutical process underlying the Additions to Daniel is to be reached. The transformation of apocalyptic hopes was certainly not accomplished only by an intellectual endeavor, which is the major impetus behind a scriptural revaluation of history, but also by an emotional reestablishment of the relationship between the Jewish people and their God, which is accomplished in the cult. The integrity of the cult was a sign of the integrity of the nation as a whole and its dwelling safely in the promised land under the protection of God. So the transformation of Daniel's expectation of God's kingdom on earth could only be accomplished by spiritualizing the concept of the kingdom itself and by celebrating God's presence on earth as a cultic truth. But again, this transformation was not carried out without Scripture as a guide.

The key for a new understanding of the events following the downfall of the heathens is found yet again in the book of Habakkuk. His prophecy about Babylon reaches its theological climax in a passage directed against the heathen idols (Hab 2:18–19). Their having neither life nor might is not contrasted, as

---

27. See Schürer, *History of the Jewish People*, 1:189–99; cf. Mittmann-Richert, "Einführung," 35–36.

28. The integration of Daniel into the growing Habakkuk tradition was probably influenced by Hab 2:2–3, where Habakkuk is commanded by God to write down what is shown to him until the time of fulfillment. In this passage Habakkuk gets commissioned and authorized by God in a similar way to Daniel.

29. The fact that Dan 3 and the story of Daniel in the lions' den (Dan 6 resp. Bel 31–42) theologically belong together is also confirmed by 1 Macc 2:59, where the three friends are called by their Hebrew names, just as in the Additions. The parallels in 1 Macc 2:61 and Dan 3:40 LXX should also be noted. It seems as if the author of 1 Maccabees had drawn on a version of the Daniel tradition in which the text of Dan 1–12 had been enlarged by the Additions to Dan 3 and perhaps even by Bel and the Dragon.

in Daniel, with the power of the living God but rather with God's presence in his holy temple. The message, as it was heard in post-Seleucid times, is clear: the overthrow of Babylon is only accomplished when God comes to dwell in his temple anew. So the words of Habakkuk help to form an understanding of the rededication of the temple by Judas Maccabeus as an eschatological event. It was obviously the event of which Habakkuk spoke. Now it becomes clear why Daniel is presented as the priest of his people in the story of Bel and the Dragon. Only as a priest could he preserve Israel's cult from being destroyed by heathen influence, and only as a priest was he able to secure the permanence of Jewish worship on Mount Zion. As a priest, Daniel himself confirms the truth of what was revealed to him in the visions laid down in the book of Daniel![30]

It becomes evident once more, then, why liturgical pieces were added to the Daniel tradition. Since God grants his presence only to those turning to him and taking part in his worship, the integrity of the Jewish community is only established by Israel's worship of God, in which the young men in Dan 3 take part as representatives of their people.[31] With these psalms, inserted into Dan 3 and put on the lips of faithful Jews, the cultic meeting of God and his people is portrayed.[32]

But the question of the cult—newly established after a period of desuetude—is also dwelled on in these texts themselves, especially in the Prayer of Azariah. This psalm is woven from allusions to the prayer of Solomon on the occasion of the dedication of the First Temple (1 Kgs 8:14–53).[33] In this prayer, God is asked to forgive his people if, should they ever fall into sin and aberra-

---

30. Interestingly enough, in Bel 1 LXX, the prophet Habakkuk is also described as being of priestly descent. The fact that Habakkuk is called a Levite may be explained by Hab 3, where the prophet appears as a psalmist. Since the recitation of psalms in the temple was carried out by the Levites, according to the books of Chronicles (cf., e.g., 1 Chr 16:4; 2 Chr 5:11; 7:6), Habakkuk's recitation of a psalm could be understood as an allusion to his priestly office.

31. In the Song of the Three Young Men, Israel is not just represented by its priests and God's servants (Dan 3:85 LXX) but also comes together with all of creation to worship God sitting on his throne. This corresponds to the view of the temple as the place where the faithful cross the boundaries of transcendence and where the all-encompassing power of God as Creator of heaven and earth becomes manifest. The much-debated question whether Dan 3 refers to the earthly or to the celestial temple is therefore beside the point. For the integration of the poetic texts into the prose text of Dan 3 in the LXX and in θ, cf. Mittmann-Richert, "Einführung," 133–34.

32. Presumably the book of Habakkuk has also influenced the formation of the psalms in Dan 3, as it is one of the peculiarities of the book of Habakkuk that it ends with a psalm of lamentation (Hab 3), in which Habakkuk presents himself as one who prays for God's mercy in times of judgment. Cf. also the end of the book in the LXX (Hab 3:19 LXX), where Habakkuk is foretelling God's victory (τοῦ νικῆσαι) ἐν τῇ ᾠδῇ αὐτοῦ.

33. This text also served as the model for the prayer of repentance in Dan 9. Cf. esp. Dan 9:5 with 1 Kgs 8:47.

tion and be led into exile and captivity (1 Kgs 8:46; Dan 3:29 LXX), they turn back to their God in prayer and repentance (1 Kgs 8:47–48; Dan 3:41–43; cf. 1 Kgs 8:60 and Dan 3:45 LXX). And just as they are in the Daniel tradition, these images themselves are woven together, and the experience of deliverance from exile and destruction is compared to the exodus and the rescue from the flames of the Egyptian furnace (1 Kgs 8:51). Because of this parallelism, the prayer of Azariah cannot be considered a traditional prayer. The function of the prayer becomes clear if one realizes that its reader takes part in a double movement of thought. Azariah refers to Solomon's prayer and thereby to the dedication of the temple, while at the same time he mourns over the past defilement of God's temple caused by Israel's sin. In so doing, he fulfils what Solomon had once made a condition for the restitution of the cult: turning back to God in an attitude of repentance. In the context of the Daniel tradition as a whole, Azariah's prayer of repentance denotes Israel's turning back to God[34] and thereby points to the fact that the temple had actually been rededicated again. Temple worship itself, however, appears newly established in the young men's hymnic adoration, which they, as representatives of all of Israel, address to God in the presence of his angel (cf. Dan 3:53–55, 83–87 LXX).[35]

With the liturgical adoration of God, performed by faithful Israel from the midst of the furnace, the cycle of motifs connecting the Additions to one another is finished. The rededication of the temple confirms Israel's vic-

---

34. The fact that the prayer is made on behalf of all of Israel is only clear in the LXX version, where the prayer gets spoken by the three friends together. Since, however, in the context of Dan 3 the three young men are the only people who remain true to God in such a time of peril, most interpreters of the text state that it is inappropriate for them to confess their sins and that the psalm must have therefore originated in another context. As it has been shown above, this interpretation ignores the Old Testament references in the psalm. For in Solomon's prayer on the occasion of the dedication of the First Temple, it is stressed explicitly that "there is no man who does not sin" (1 Kgs 8:46.) The acknowledgement of this fact by Israel, as represented by Azariah and his friends, and the subsequent confession of their sins are the preconditions for God's universal reversal of history as it is manifest in the rededication of the Second Temple. Against Koch, *Deuterokanonische Zusätze zum Danielbuch*, 2:35; Moore, *Daniel, Esther and Jeremiah*, 40–41; and Kottsieper, *Zusätze zu Daniel*, 231. For further details on the Song of the Three Young Men, see also Mittmann-Richert, "Einführung," 131–33. For the theology of the Prayer of Azariah and the Old Testament references in the Theodotion version, see M. Gilbert, "La prière d'Azarias (Dn 3,26–45 Théodotion)," *NRTh* 96 (1974): 561–82.

35. The restitution of the cult is also alluded to in Ps 103, which has been integrated into the Song of the Three Young Men (cf. Dan 3:54, 57–58, 61, 85–86 LXX with Ps 103:19–22). This psalm relates the earthly and the celestial praise of God to his restitutional action in the forgiveness of sins. In the historical context of the Additions to Daniel, this psalm can only be understood as a further text announcing God's gracious forgiveness of Israel's sins after the time of judgment and his return to his temple as the place that he had left and abandoned to the heathen idols in his wrath.

tory over the perils of Seleucid idolatry and the oppression of Judaism by Babylonian force. At the same time, Daniel's expectation that God would triumphantly establish his kingdom in Jerusalem forever is transformed by the cultic experience of God's everlasting presence in his temple and among his people Israel. Daniel's prophecy of God's eschatological coming at the end of history is celebrated as a cultic truth. Its eschatological character is sustained, however, by the image of creation at peace—which also relates to a certain period of history, namely, the time of Simon. Finally, there is Daniel himself, who as a prophet had foretold God's victory over the power of Babylon, but who now steps forth as a priest to confirm Israel's new integrity thereby the truth of what he had foretold.

So far the story of Susanna, the most prominent tale contained in the Additions to Daniel, has been left aside. Externally, the story may not appear to belong to the cycle of the other Additions, since it does not deal with the question of Israel's cult. In the prophetic tradition, however, the question of lawlessness and perversion of justice, which is the focus of the story, is always tied to the problem of Israel leaving its God. A people practicing idolatry has lost its cultic integrity and thus has become a lawless nation. This is clearly revealed by the prophetic texts that form the background of the story of Susanna, the hermeneutical flow of thought being in keeping with that of the other Additions. Again, the introductory sentence of the story as it is transmitted by the LXX guides the reader toward a proper understanding of the plot. In the introduction the author, before he opens the curtain and has the protagonists step on stage, directs the reader's attention toward the lawlessness of Israel's authorities by referring to Jer 29:23 and 23:15: "Concerning those, of whom the Lord has spoken: 'Lawlessness has gone out from Babylon, from elder-judges, who seemed to guide the people'" (Sus 5 LXX).[36]

Since, in the commentaries on Susanna, interpreters have restricted themselves to dealing with the quoted verses from Jeremiah as they stand, especially with Jer 29:23,[37] it should be stressed again that the meaning of the scriptural

---

36. Translation according to Engel, *Die Susanna-Erzählung*, *3. The question whether the quoted verse is the beginning of the text of the lxx, or whether the original introduction to the tale has been lost, is still controversial. See Engel, *Die Susanna-Erzählung*, 12–15, 177–78. Since in this study the Additions have been proven to reread the prophetic Scriptures in the light of a changed historical situation, it is highly probable that the verse Sus 5 LXX, which refers to the book of Jeremiah, is the original introduction to the story.

37. Although the allusion to Jer 23:15 in Sus 5 LXX is clear, since it explicitly refers to the problem of adultery, most commentators pass over this verse as being of minor importance for understanding the text, because it refers to the prophets and priests in *Jerusalem* (cf. Jer 12:11). This seems to contradict the content of the story of Susanna, which, most evident in θ, focuses on Babylon. If Jer 23:15 gets mentioned at all, then it is only as the result of complicated textual associations; cf. Steussy, *Gardens in*

background of the Additions can only be grasped if the *context* of all scriptural allusions is taken into consideration. Otherwise, one would have to assume that the author of the Susanna story referred only by chance to a text that also forms the background of Dan 9. This text is Jeremiah's letter containing the famous prophecy of Jerusalem lying in ruins for seventy years before being raised up by God again. This prophecy exerted a major influence on the apocalyptic expectations of the book of Daniel, as they deal with the ending of the period of the destruction of Jerusalem. In the book of Jeremiah, however, the prophecy of the seventy years is framed by the motif of Israel having been seduced by the nation's authorities, who therefore bear responsibility for what has befallen the people. So what happens to Susanna in the Daniel story appears as a paradigm of juridical perversion in times of Babylonian (i.e., Seleucid) affliction. The fact that Susanna is the victim not of prophets, which one might have expected from Jer 23:15 (cf. Jer 29:15), but of the nation's elders, implies that the situation is even worse than in Jeremiah's time, because 29:1 puts the elders above the priests and the prophets as Israel's representatives and highest authorities. In this context, it is of major importance to remember that under Antiochus IV it was with the help of the Jewish authorities, including the priests, that Jerusalem was transformed into a Hellenistic city and the temple turned into a place of idolatry.

Idolatry is often pictured as adultery in the tradition, the most famous example of this being Hos 4:9–15, a passage to which the story of Susanna also alludes[38] by building up a contrast between the daughters of Israel and Judah (Hos 4:15)[39] and in which adultery represents Israel's cultic aberration. Yet Hosea is very clear in stating that, since the law comes from God, cultic aberration leads to the breakdown of law and order (Hos 4:6). Lawlessness is but the other side of idolatry. Therefore, against the background of overall national

---

*Babylon*, 147, 150–52. One of the major problems of the interpretation of the Additions remains the failure to recognize that the *identification* of Jerusalem with Babel was the hermeneutical key that helped to cope with the religious crisis under Antiochus IV and the consequences it had for the Jewish people. Since, under the Seleucids and with the help of Jerusalem's religious authorities, Babylon and her gods had moved into Jerusalem and the holy temple, Babylon and Jerusalem are seen as one and are typologically interchangeable. For the history of interpretation, see Engel, *Die Susanna-Erzählung*, 67–77.

38. Most commentators use only Hos 4:12–15 as a reference text for the interpretation of the story. Cf. José R. Busto Saiz, "La interpretación del relato de Susana," EstEcl 57 (1982): 421–28, who understands the story of Susanna as a midrash to Hos 4:12–15. This point of view is too narrow with respect to the reception of the prophetic books as a whole, which in the case of the story of Susanna includes not only the book of Hosea but also the book of Habakkuk.

39. This is the antithesis in θ. In the LXX, the tension between Judah and Israel is heightened by calling the Israelites Sidonites, who, according to Gen 10:15, are the direct descendants of Canaan, which makes them exemplary idolaters.

decay, Susanna is to be seen as representing all of Israel. She is the "daughter of Zion" who yields to heathen influence.[40] Closely connected to this image is the unveiling of Susanna (Sus 32,) which, according to Jer 13:26–27, serves to uncover secret idolatry (cf. Hos 2:4–5; Ezek 16:37–39). Since, however, Susanna is falsely accused of having sinned, the act of unveiling becomes the proof of Israel's cultic integrity, which only became a historical reality again at the rededication of the temple in 164 B.C.E. Susanna's rescue through Daniel's intervention is the sign of Israel having overcome the crisis.

But there are still more textual allusions to consider. Susanna gets rescued because God hears her prayer. This represents the fulfillment of the prophecy in the letter of Jeremiah that Babylon's destruction will be the result of Israel praying to God and of God hearing these prayers (Jer 29:12; Sus 35–35a.) In the historical context, as has been outlined here, this is the sign that the downfall of law and order has finally been overcome. Again it becomes evident how much the people's political and religious situation has changed, and how intensive the search was for a theological confirmation of this historical development.

Enough has been said about the role of Scripture in this hermeneutical process. The confirmation that the story of Susanna thematically belongs with the other Additions to Daniel is finally given by the book of Habakkuk, which, in its opening verses, programmatically points to the close connection between lawlessness penetrating Israel and Israel's seduction by heathen idols: "This is the oracle of God which Habakkuk the prophet saw: ... destruction and violence are before me.... Therefore the law becomes slack and justice never goes forth. For the wicked surround the righteous, so justice goes forth perverted" (Hab 1:1–4). One can almost see the lecherous men surrounding Susanna! Because of the extended reception of Habakkuk in the Additions, it may safely be stated that these verses gave the impulse[41] for taking the motif of adultery out of its cultic context in Jeremiah and Hosea and transposing it to a juridical setting. Here it became the symbol not only of Israel's cultic aberration but also of Jewish life as a whole in danger of being destroyed by evil influence. The thread connecting the story of Susanna with the rest of the Additions to Daniel comes full circle

---

40. It is noteworthy that in Sus 22 LXX Susanna is called ἡ Ἰουδαία, a term that is otherwise used only for the land of Judah. With this title, Susanna appears as the personification of the Jewish nation. In the book of Judith, this personification is made clear from the beginning through the heroine's name, "Judith," i.e., "the Jewess." Cf. Mittmann-Richert, "Einführung," 89, 94–95.

41. Perhaps in connection with Dan 9:12: "God has confirmed his word, which he spoke against us and against our judges who ruled us, by bringing upon us a great calamity; for under the whole heaven there has not been done the like of what has been done against Jerusalem." It becomes evident that the Babylon typology in the Additions to Daniel is based on the identification of Jerusalem with Babylon. See n. 37.

in the LXX version with the punishment of the lawless by fire (Sus 60–62 LXX). The fiery death of the lawless is the counterpoint of Israel's deliverance from the flames of the furnace, as well as a symbol of God's judgment and the reversal of the fate that Israel had to suffer under heathen rule. The picture now is complete: together with the other pieces of the Daniel material, the story of Susanna bears testimony to a scriptural rereading of Daniel taking place at a time when the perils of Seleucid oppression, although gone, had to be both reflected and explained on the basis of Scripture.[42]

### 3. Summary

At the end of this overview of the Additions to Daniel, looking back to the beginning, it should be noted that the answer to the urgent question of unfulfilled prophecy was not given carelessly. On the contrary, in coping with history by letting Scripture speak for itself, the authors of the Additions reach a very high level of reflection and engage in a double-sided hermeneutical process. However, the function of the Additions, as they reread the book of Daniel in the light of the words of the earlier prophets, is not to correct the book of Daniel but, on the contrary, to preserve it and establish its authority as a prophetic book.[43] With the help of the Additions, Daniel, as he is paralleled with Jeremiah and Habakkuk, reaches the rank of a prophet of old. Daniel was not only found worthy of knowing Israel's fate, but was also destined, as the priest and judge of his people, to personally preserve the nation from being destroyed by heathen forces.

What makes these additions to the book of Daniel unique is that, although the *form* is consciously not based on the apocalyptic second half

---

42. This theological frame of the story of Susanna confirms that the LXX version is the primary one, although many scholars adhere to the Theodotion version because of its narrative superiority. In contrast to θ, however, the LXX deals with the problem of the perversion of the cult and of the abuse of the law in a fundamental way, whereas in θ the focus is on Susanna as a person, and the story is remodeled into an edifying, even piquant narrative. This remodeling of the tale results in the abandonment of the historical and theological problems with which the story had once dealt, while the individual piety and fate of Susanna as a paradigm of Jewish life becomes the focus of interest. In the Theodotion version, therefore, the whole plot is changed and the fact that the slanderous elders themselves, despite the crime they have committed, still serve as the appointed judges of the Jewish people (Sus 29, 34 LXX) is suppressed. Instead, justice is administered by an independent group of people (Sus 28, 34, 41 θ). Thus, with respect to the political authorities, the story loses its critical function.

43. The prophetic rank of Daniel is also documented by the fact that the book of Daniel is numbered among the prophets in the Greek tradition. In the texts from Qumran, Daniel is also called a prophet; see 4QFlor (4Q174) II 3; 4Q 178 I 1; 11QMelch (11Q13) II 18.

of Daniel, but rather upon the court tales in Dan 1–6, they are *theologically* grounded in the visions of the prophets in Dan 7–12. So it is in these Additions, therefore, that Daniel fulfills all the prophecies proclaiming the victory of Israel over heathen Babylon.

Finally, as a reflection of their historical period, the Additions to the book of Daniel should not be looked at as a direct but rather as an indirect source of history, and one of great value. These Additions not only document the theological discussion about the religious persecution under Antiochus IV but reflect, especially in the poetical sections, a feeling of joy and thankfulness for the newly granted situation of outward freedom and internal justice. They show how the authors of the Hasmonean period turned "the present" into a time in which joy and thankfulness prevailed over sorrow and grief and in which the cultic integrity confirmed the validity of the Jewish law.[44] The Additions to Daniel certainly deserve more appreciation and attention than they presently get, as they attest to an indissoluble connection between historical experience and scriptural interpretation, which is grounded on the firm conviction that God is the true ruler of history.

---

44. Presumably the programmatic ending of the story of Susanna in the LXX, which alludes to the generation "of the young people" (Sus 63 LXX), is a hint about a religious movement after the Maccabean crisis and about the formation of a group whose pious model was Daniel. The existence of such a group may also be deduced from Dan 11:33–35.

# Part 3:
# The Textual Tradition of the Hebrew and Greek Bible

# READING DEUTERONOMY IN THE SECOND TEMPLE PERIOD

*Sidnie White Crawford*

## 1. INTRODUCTION

The book of Deuteronomy was one of the most popular religious texts in the Second Temple period. The finds from the Judean Desert present us with a wealth of manuscripts of Deuteronomy from the late Second Temple period, and the literature of Second Temple Judaism attests to the importance of Deuteronomy in Jewish thought in the period, quoting, alluding, and reusing the text in numerous ways. In this paper I will present at least some of the evidence for the popularity of Deuteronomy through a look at some of the texts found in the caves at Qumran. I will begin with manuscripts of Deuteronomy itself, next I will turn to a group of texts that uses portions of Deuteronomy for liturgical or study purposes (including the phylacteries and the mezuzot), and finally I will examine two texts from the category "Rewritten Bible" that utilize Deuteronomy, 4QReworked Pentateuch and the *Temple Scroll*.

## 2. THE POPULARITY OF DEUTERONOMY

Deuteronomy is well represented in the Qumran caves, second only to the book of Psalms in the number of copies. The total number of Hebrew Deuteronomy manuscripts from the Qumran caves is twenty-nine, a number that includes four excerpted texts to be discussed below. There is also one Greek Deuteronomy manuscript from Cave 7.[1] This exceptionally high number of preserved manuscripts witnesses to the importance of Deuteronomy in the life and thought of the Qumran community.

---

1. One Deuteronomy manuscript from Wadi Murabba'at, one from Naḥal Ḥever/Wadi Seiyal, and one from Masada were also recovered. Émile Puech has recently identified two previously unidentified Cave 4 fragments as a possible thirtieth copy of Deuteronomy from Qumran. Émile Puech, "Identification de Nouveaux Manuscrits Bibliques: *Deutéronome* et *Proverbes* dans les Débris de la Grotte 4," *RevQ* 20 (2001): 121–28.

From a text-critical viewpoint, Deuteronomy exhibits a well-preserved textual tradition. The major witnesses to the text of Deuteronomy in the Second Temple period are the proto-Masoretic text, the proto-Samaritan text, and the Septuagint text. Some of the Qumran manuscripts align with one of these major witnesses. For example, 4QDeut$^g$ does not deviate from the proto-Masoretic text in its preserved fragments, and Julie Duncan suggests that 4QDeut$^j$, 4QDeut$^h$, and 4QDeut$^q$ witness to the Hebrew *Vorlage* of the Septuagint.[2] The majority of Qumran manuscripts, however, are too fragmentary to place with certainty within any textual tradition.

The chief observation regarding the text of Deuteronomy in the Second Temple period is that it is expansionistic. This is not surprising given the repetitive nature of Deuteronomic prose. Duncan notes that the proto-Masoretic witness is the least expansionistic, followed by the proto-Samaritan and the Qumran manuscripts as a group. She argues that the Septuagint group is the most expansionistic.[3] However, it should be noted that most of the variants preserved in the textual tradition are minor and the result of scribal error rather than deliberate intervention into the text. Deuteronomy does not exist in two variant literary traditions, as does, for example, Jeremiah.

### 3. Deuteronomy as a Study Text and Basis for Liturgical Practice

We can best observe the expansionistic tendency of the textual tradition of Deuteronomy in the excerpted texts used for liturgical or study purposes, including the phylacteries and the mezuzot. The recovery of this type of text from the Qumran caves demonstrates the importance of Deuteronomy as a study text and a basis for liturgical practice in the late Second Temple period. Four manuscripts have been identified as excerpted texts or "special-use" manuscripts: 4QDeut$^j$, 4QDeut$^{k1}$, 4QDeut$^n$, and 4QDeut$^q$. These manuscripts, distinguished by their small size, collect several passages from Deuteronomy, sometimes interspersed with passages from the book of Exodus. 4QDeut$^j$ probably included (when complete) Deut 5:1–6:3; 8:5–10; 10:12–11:21; Exod 12:43–13:16; and Deut 32:1–9. 4QDeut$^{k1}$ contains Deut 5:28–32; 11:6–13; 32:17–18, 22–23, and 25–27. 4QDeut$^n$, an almost complete manuscript, preserves Deut 8:5–10 and 5:1–6:1, in that order. 4QDeut$^q$ appears to have contained only the Song of Moses, Deut 32:1–43. A pattern emerges for the passages preserved: three manuscripts preserve portions of chapters 5

---

2. Julie A. Duncan, "Deuteronomy, Book of," in *The Encyclopedia of the Dead Sea Scrolls* (ed. L. H. Schiffman and J. C. VanderKam; 2 vols.; New York: Oxford University Press, 2000), 1:199.
3. Ibid.

and 6, containing the Decalogue and the beginning of the Shema. According to *m. Tamid* 5:1, the Decalogue was recited daily in the temple along with the Shema; thus these study texts may be concerned with temple liturgy. Two manuscripts contain 8:5–10, which becomes the rabbinic basis for grace after meals;[4] two manuscripts preserve portions of chapters 10–11, which also include part of the Shema; two contain parts of the Song of Moses (Deut 32:1–43);[5] and one contains the passage from Exodus concerning the wearing of tefillin and the use of mezuzot. In these four manuscripts we have a collection of passages that we know from other evidence were used in worship.

In addition, 4QDeut[n], an expansive, harmonistic text, supplements the fourth commandment of the Decalogue, Deut 5:12–15, with the parallel passage from Exodus, 20:8–11. Thus:

9) שמור /////// את יום השבת לקדשו כאשר צוך יהוה
10) אלוהיך ששת ימים תעבוד ועשית את כול מלאכתך
11) וביום השביעי שבת ליהוה אלוהיך לוא תעשה בו כל מלאכה
12) אתה בנך בתך עבדך ואמתך שורך וחמורך
1) ובהמתך גריך אשר בשעריך //// למען ינוח עבדך ואמתך
2) כמוך וזכרתה כי עבד היית /////// בארץ מצרים ויציאך
3) יהוה אלוהיך משם ביד //////////// חזקה ובזרוע נטויה
4) על כן צוך יהוה אלוהיך /////// לשמור את יום השבת
5) לקדשו כי ששת ימים עשה יהוה את השמים ואת הארץ
6) את הים וכול אשר בם וינוח ביום השביעי על כן ברך יהוה
7) את יום השבת לקדשו

Observe the sabbath day to sanctify it, according as the LORD your God commanded you. Six days you shall labor and do all your work, but the seventh day is a sabbath to the LORD your God. You shall not do in it any work; you, your son, your daughter, your male slave or your female slave, your ox or your ass or your beast, your sojourner who is within your gates, in order that your male slave and your female slave may rest like you. And remember that you were a slave in the land of Egypt, and the LORD your God brought you out from there with a mighty hand and an outstretched arm; therefore the LORD your God commanded you to observe the sabbath day to sanctify it. For six days the LORD made the heavens and the earth, the sea and everything which

---

4. Moshe Weinfeld, "Grace after Meals at Qumran," *JBL* 111 (1992): 427–40. Weinfeld considers 4QDeut[j] and 4QDeut[n] to be liturgical texts.

5. The Song of Moses was recited in the temple on the Sabbath (*b. B. Ros. Has.* 31a; *y. Meg.* 3:6, 74b) and at the service of Ma'madot (ibid.).

is in them, and he rested on the seventh day; therefore the Lord blessed the seventh day to sanctify it.[6]

From the way in which the expansion appears, we can note the deliberate work of the scribe. The word לקדשו serves as a linking word at the beginning and end of the expansion (lines 5, 7). It is likely that the scribe wished to harmonize the two Decalogue versions for his special-use copy.

With the exception of Deut 8:5–10, all the passages found in the special-use manuscripts are also found in the phylacteries and mezuzot found at Qumran. Twenty-two phylacteries and six mezuzot were recovered at Qumran. These exemplars preserve a wider range of texts than the four mandated in rabbinic practice. The four rabbinic passages are Exod 13:1–10; 13:11–16; Deut 6:4–9; and 11:13–21. The phylacteries from Qumran contain all of these passages, but they contain other passages as well. According to Milik, the "maximum choice" for phylactery texts is Deut 5:1–6:9; 10:12–11:21; and Exod 12:43–13:16.[7] 4QPhyl$^N$ also contains Deut 32, so that passage must also be added to the repertoire. In addition to a wider range of pericopes included in the phylacteries, the texts of these pericopes tend to be highly expansive and often produce harmonizations.[8] For example, the Decalogue in 4QPhyl G contains elements from both Deuteronomy and Exodus, although Deuteronomy appears to be the controlling text.[9] Further, the Deuteronomy passages always appear first, attesting to Deuteronomy's priority, at least at Qumran.[10] While some have labeled these phylacteries "sectarian" because of their differences from rabbinic practice and their scribal patterns,[11] I think it is more likely that the texts deemed suitable for use in phylacteries had not stabilized prior to the Bar Kokhba period. The examples from Qumran most likely represent the various Second Temple types. From the special-use manuscripts, the phylacteries, and mezuzot found at Qumran, it is clear that by this period Deuteronomy had become a central text in Judaism, and certain passages had become almost standardized for worship and study.

---

6. Sidnie White Crawford, "41. 4QDeut$^n$," in Eugene Ulrich et al., *Qumran Cave 4.IX: Deuteronomy, Joshua, Judges, Kings* (DJD 14; Oxford: Clarendon, 1995), 124–25.

7. As quoted by Julie Duncan, "37. 4QDeut$^j$," in Ulrich et al., DJD 14, 79.

8. Józef Tadeusz Milik, "II. Tefillin, Mezuzot et Targums (4Q128–4Q157)," in Roland de Vaux and Józef Tadeusz Milik, *Qumrân Grotte 4.II* (DJD 6; Oxford: Clarendon, 1977), 33–89.

9. Innocent Himbaza, "Le Décalogue du Papyrus Nash, Philon, 4Qphyl G, 8Qphyl 3 et 4Qmez A," *RevQ* 20 (2002): 414–16, 424–25; George Brooke, "Deuteronomy 5–6 in the Phylacteries from Qumran Cave 4," in *Emanuel: Studies in the Hebrew Bible, Septuagint, and Dead Sea Scrolls in Honor of Emanuel Tov* (ed. S. M. Paul et al.; VTSup 94; Leiden: Brill, 2003), 60.

10. Milik, "Tefillin, Mezuzot et Targums," 38.

11. Lawrence Schiffman, "Phylacteries and Mezuzot," in Schiffman and VanderKam, *Encyclopedia of the Dead Sea Scrolls*, 2:676.

## 4. Harmonizations in the Scriptural Text

We have noted that several of these liturgical or special-use manuscripts that include passages from Deuteronomy contain harmonistic or expanded texts. This phenomenon also occurs in the so-called "proto-Samaritan" group of texts, named as such because they exhibit the type of scribal intervention most fully evident in the Samaritan Pentateuch. The history of the text of the Samaritan Pentateuch has become clearer since the discoveries in the Judean Desert. It is now accepted that the Samaritan community selected as their canonical scripture a text of the Pentateuch that was in general circulation in Palestine in the Second Temple period. They then subjected this text to a thin veneer of sectarian editing.[12] Once we remove this veneer of sectarian editing a text of the Pentateuch characterized by harmonizations remains. The importation of an element from one part of the text into another in order to remove contradictions from the two passages in question serves as an example of this harmonization. In the proto-Samaritan text harmonization is particularly noticeable in the importation of elements from Deut 1–9, Moses' speech on the plains of Moab reciting the wilderness history, into the parallel passages in Exodus and Numbers. Sometimes the opposite process occurred; material from Exodus or Numbers was imported into the text of Deuteronomy. For example, in Deut 2:1–8 Moses recalls that the Israelites avoided the territory of Edom, following God's command. However, in the parallel account in Num 20, Moses sends messengers to the king of Edom asking permission to cross his territory, permission that is refused. The Samaritan Pentateuch's text of Deuteronomy inserts Moses' request from Numbers into his account after 2:7, bringing the two accounts into harmony. The presence of this change in 4QReworked Pentateuch[b] (4Q364), a manuscript related to the proto-Samaritan group, demonstrates its nonsectarian nature. We observed this phenomenon of harmonization by importing elements of Exodus into the controlling Deuteronomy text in one of the Deuteronomy manuscripts classified as a liturgical or study text, 4QDeut[n], as well as the phylactery text 4QPhyl G. Thus harmonization is not a practice limited to a single *stemma* of biblical texts but is a more widespread phenomenon, better characterized as producing a "group."

This proto-Samaritan group is also characterized by what Emanuel Tov has termed "content editing," sometimes loosely referred to as "expansion."[13]

---

12. The two sectarian changes introduced by the Samaritans involve the addition to the Decalogue of a commandment to build an altar on Mount Gerizim and changing the formulaic statement in Deuteronomy, "the place which the Lord will choose [יבחר]" to "the place which the Lord has chosen [בחר]."

13. Emanuel Tov, "Rewritten Bible Compositions and Biblical Manuscripts, with Special Attention to the Samaritan Pentateuch," *DSD* 5 (1998): 334–54.

"Content editing," as used by Tov, means scribal intervention into the text in order to smooth out inconsistencies in the authoritative text. An example of this involves the fulfillment of commandments or the giving of commandments later fulfilled. A good example from Deuteronomy occurs in 4Q158, a manuscript related to the proto-Samaritan group.[14] In 4Q158, which contains Deut 5:30–31, God tells Moses to command the Israelites to return to their tents (5:30). In all other known texts of Deuteronomy it is not mentioned whether or not the Israelites obeyed. 4Q158 makes clear that they did by adding the phrase "and the people returned, each man to his tent."

The fact that we have noted at least two manuscripts from the proto-Samaritan group, 4QDeut$^n$ and 4Q158, that contain scribal editorial changes not duplicated elsewhere in the tradition indicates that we are not dealing with exact copies of a certain manuscript stem but with a wider tradition of scribal intervention for harmonization and content editing. The details of this intervention may differ from witness to witness (although there is much overlap). What makes these manuscripts a group is their common scribal tradition.

This group of texts was no less authoritative in Second Temple Palestine than the shorter, more "pristine" texts of the proto-Masoretic family. This is obvious by the use of these longer texts in phylacteries, mezuzot, and liturgical/study texts. The Samaritans also selected one member of this group as the base text of their Pentateuch. So the authoritative status of these longer texts prior to the fall of the Second Temple should not be in doubt.

### 5. A Reworked Pentateuch or a Rewritten Bible?

The authoritative nature of the next group of texts I wish to examine is open to question. This group of texts, the Reworked Pentateuch, has often been placed in the category "Rewritten Bible." Others dispute that designation, arguing that the manuscripts found in the Reworked Pentateuch group are simply manuscripts of the Pentateuch and should be classified as such.[15] Two of the manuscripts, 4Q364 and 4Q365, complicate the question. They appear to have been, when whole, complete manuscripts of the Torah. 4Q158, 4Q366, and 4Q367 were probably much more limited in scope, although their exact nature has yet to be determined.[16]

---

14. As first demonstrated by John Strugnell, "Notes en marge du volume V des 'Discoveries in the Judaean Desert of Jordan,'" *RevQ* 7 (1969–70): 172.

15. E.g., Michael Segal, "4QReworked Pentateuch or 4QPentateuch?" in *The Dead Sea Scrolls Fifty Years after Their Discovery, 1947–1997* (ed. L. H. Schiffman et al.; Jerusalem: Israel Exploration Society, 2000), 391–99.

16. The characterization given here differs from that in the DJD edition of 4Q364–367, where Tov and I referred to these manuscripts as copies of one composition: Emanuel Tov and

Further, these manuscripts reflect the same scribal techniques of harmonization and content editing found in the proto-Samaritan group. These manuscripts can be grouped together under the same rubric and differentiated from the proto-Samaritan group because, in addition to the scribal techniques of harmonization and content editing described above, these manuscripts exhibit a further scribal phenomenon: the addition of completely new material into the text.

Since the manuscripts of Reworked Pentateuch are not copies of a single composition, but different exemplars of the same scribal technique, we will consider each separately.

### 5.1. 4QReworked Pentateuch[b]

4Q364 is a late Hasmonean manuscript that preserves portions of Genesis, Exodus, Numbers, and Deuteronomy. Fragments of Deut 1–14 are extant. As Tov and I have shown elsewhere, 4Q364's base text is a member of the proto-Samaritan group, agreeing with the Samaritan Pentateuch in two major instances of harmonization at Gen 30:36 and Deut 2:8, and not disagreeing with the Samaritan Pentateuch in any major details.[17] Most of the Deuteronomy fragments of 4Q364 simply contain a running text of what we know as Deuteronomy; however, several of the fragments contain additions that illustrate the expansive scribal technique behind Reworked Pentateuch.

The best example of this technique is found in frag. 26b, e, col. ii. Line 3 of the fragment contains Deut 10:1, "And the Lord said to me, carve out for yourself two tablets of stone…" continuing on through verse 4. Lines 1 and 2 contain text that has parallels to 9:21 and 25 (the episode of the golden calf) but is really new material inserted before 10:1. The extant text reads:

(1 [ ואשליך את ר[לעפ]
(2 [ ואתפלל לפני :יהוה ארבעים

1) [to dus]t, and I threw [
2) And I prayed before the Lord forty [[18]

---

Sidnie White, "Reworked Pentateuch," in H. Attridge et al., *Qumran Cave 4.VIII: Parabiblical Texts, Part 1* (DJD 13; Oxford: Clarendon, 1994), 188–91. I no longer believe that these manuscripts are copies of the same composition; rather, they are separate exemplars of the same scribal technique.

17. Ibid., 193.
18. Ibid., 239–40.

Although this new text does not occur in any of the known witnesses, it is an expansion of the base text that fits the context perfectly well. It has no discernible exegetical *Tendenz*, only repeating elements from the preceding verses, which provide a context for Moses' next foray up the mountain.

### 5.2. 4QReworked Pentateuch<sup>c</sup>

4Q365, another late Hasmonean manuscript, preserves fragments of all five books of the Torah. Tov and I also placed 4Q365 in the proto-Samaritan group, although the evidence for 4Q365 is less clear-cut than it is for 4Q364.[19] 4Q365 only preserves two fragments from Deuteronomy. Still, one of those fragments, frag. 37, gives an excellent illustration of the scribal technique found in Reworked Pentateuch. The four readable lines of the fragment are as follows:

(2 [וכול העם המלחמה]
(3 [מנחל ארנון ויחנו]
(4 [יו ויחנו באר]נון
(5 [מים עד בית]

2. ]and all the warriors [
3. ]from the river Arnon, and they camped [
4. ]and they camped at Ar[non
5. ]water (?) until Beth (?) [[20]

The subject matter of this fragment relates to Moses' speech in Deut 2, which narrates the Israelites' journey through Transjordan. Verses 24 and 36 of chapter 2 mention the river Arnon. This material in frag. 37 is unparalleled elsewhere; it appears to be an expansion of the narrative in chapter 2. Again, we find no theological *Tendenz* in this addition. Since the manuscript is fragmentary we cannot place the passage in any more than a general context.

### 5.3. 4QReworked Pentateuch<sup>d</sup>

4Q366, unlike 4Q364 and 365, was probably not a complete manuscript of the Pentateuch, but may have been a thematic collection of passages from the Torah.[21] It preserves two fragments of Deuteronomy. One, frag. 5, contains Deut 14:13–21 with no significant variants. The other, frag. 4, col. i, has an illustra-

---

19. Ibid., 194.
20. Ibid., 311.
21. Segal, "4QReworked Pentateuch or 4QPentateuch?" 395–98.

tion of the Reworked Pentateuch scribal technique. Numbers 29:32–30:1 and Deut 16:13–14, two texts concerning the festival of Sukkoth, are juxtaposed.

1) [וביום השביעי פרים שבעה אילם ש[נ]י[]ם כבש]ים בני שנה ארבעה עשר תמימם[
2) [ומנחתם ונסכהם לפרים לאילם ולכבשי]ם במספר]ם כמשפט(ם) ושע]יר חטאת אחד מלבד
3) עולת התמיד מנחתה ונסכה vac[at
4) [(ו)ביום השמיני עצרת תהיה לכם כל מלאכת ע]בודה לא תעשו והקרבתם עולה ליהוה
5) [אשר ריחה ניחח פר אחד איל אחד כבשים בני שנ]ה שבעה תמימם ומנחתם ונסכיהם
6) [לפר לאיל ולכבשים במספרם כמשפט ושעיר ח]טאת אחד מלבד עולת התמיד מנחתה
7) [ונסכה אלה תעשו ליהוה במועדיכם לבד מנד]ריכם ונדבותיכם לעלתיכם ולמנחתיכם
8) [ולנסכיכם ולשלמיכם vacat ויאמר משה [אל בני ישראל ככל אשר צוה יהוה
9) [את משה vac[at
10) [חג הסכות תעשה לך שבעת ימים באספך מגרנ]ך ומיקבך ושמחת בחגך אתה ובנך

1) [And on the seventh day; seven bulls, t]w[o] ram[s, fourteen male lambs without blemish,]
2) [and their grain offering and their drink offering for the bulls, for the rams and for the lamb]s according to [the commandment of their] number; [and] one [male go]at for a sin offering, besides
3) [the daily burnt offering, its grain offering, and its drink offering.]
4) [(And) on the eighth day you shall have solemn assembly;] you will not do [any work of la]bor. And you shall offer a burnt offering to the Lord,
5) [which is a pleasant odor: one bull, one ram,] seven y[ear old male lambs] without blemish, and their grain offering and their drink offerings
6) [for the bull, for the ram, and for the lambs according to the commandment of their number; and] one [male goat for a s]in offering, as well as the daily burnt offering and its grain offering
7) [and its drink offering. These you shall offer to the Lord at your festivals, as well as] your [votive] offerings and your freewill offerings, for your burnt offerings and for your grain offerings
8) [and for your drink offerings and for your offerings of well-being. And Moses spoke] to the children of Israel according to all which the Lord commanded
9) [Moses.]

10) [You shall keep the festival of Sukkot for seven days, when you have gathered from] your [threshing floor] and from your wine press. And you shall rejoice during your festival, you and your son...[22]

Although we have placed this fragment following frag. 3, which contains Num 29:14–25, it is not clear where this fragment actually belonged in the manuscript, or what the context for the juxtaposition was (the contents of col. ii have not been identified). We seem to have a harmonization similar to those found in the proto-Samaritan group, but in a legal passage, which does not occur in the proto-Samaritan group (with the exception of the Decalogue). This example pushes the bounds of the scribal technique beyond that of the proto-Samaritan group; however, we still cannot identify a particular theological *Tendenz* behind the application of the scribal technique.

The question of the authoritative nature of the texts in the Reworked Pentateuch group remains unresolved. We know, of course, that the Torah, including Deuteronomy, was authoritative in the Second Temple period. According to the evidence from Qumran, we can add to that statement that various text forms of Deuteronomy existed, from short (proto-MT) to expansive (proto-Samaritan group), and even translated (LXXDeut), but that the text form did not matter for the book's authority. Yet even if the form of the text did not matter for the book's authority, the fact that the various forms are consistently preserved indicates that the differences were recognized by the scribes. Thus it is possible that some differentiation between the text forms was made.

If Reworked Pentateuch, especially 4Q364 and 365 as complete Torah scrolls, were simply viewed as two more copies of the Pentateuch, then we can assume they were authoritative.[23] The manuscripts certainly present themselves as Torah scrolls, indicating that the scribes responsible for their production wished them to be considered authoritative. The addition of new material, which we find in Reworked Pentateuch but not in the proto-Samaritan group, may have pushed the boundaries of the text beyond the acceptable limit. If this were the case, then they may not have had the same authority as other forms of the same biblical text.[24] Reworked Pentateuch takes us into a gray area with

---

22. Tov and White, "Reworked Pentateuch," 341.
23. Eugene Ulrich, "The Qumran Scrolls and the Biblical Text," in Schiffman et al., *Dead Sea Scrolls*, 57.
24. One important criterion for determining a text's authoritative status is its use by another text. It is possible, but not absolutely certain, that the additional material in 4Q365, frag. 23, regarding the festivals of wood and fresh oil, is reused in the *Temple Scroll*. Frag. 23's most important similarity with the *Temple Scroll* occurs in 11QTemple[a], col. 24, where the order of the days of the tribal offerings for wood is given: first day Levi and Judah, second day Benjamin and Joseph, third day Reuben and Simeon, fourth day Issachar and Zebulun, fifth day Gad and Asher, and

fluid boundaries between "biblical" and "rewritten." Lacking definitive evidence, the question must remain unresolved.

### 6. The Use of Deuteronomy in the Temple Scroll

Finally, I wish to examine the reuse of the book of Deuteronomy in the Temple Scroll, found in three, possibly four copies at Qumran.[25] The oldest copy, 4Q524, dates to approximately 150 B.C.E.[26] The last section of the *Temple Scroll*, cols. 51–66 (according to the most complete manuscript, 11QTemple$^a$), is based on large chunks of Deuteronomy and is variously called Expanded Deuteronomy or the Deuteronomic Paraphrase. Embedded within this section is the Law of the King (cols. 57–59), which originally was a separate document and now functions as a long exegetical appendix to the Deuteronomic Law of the King (Deut 17:14–20).

The Deuteronomy section of the *Temple Scroll* is a collection of laws for life in the towns of the land, following the instructions for the ideal temple (cols. 3–13, 30–47), the Festival Calendar (cols. 13–30), and a collection of purity regulations (cols. 48–51). The redactor/composer of the Deuteronomic Paraphrase takes Deuteronomy as his base text but interweaves material from other parts of the Torah, other parts of what later became the Jewish canon, and other sources, such as the Law of the King, in addition to his own exegetical comments. This produces a paraphrase of Deuteronomy, with a particular, identifiable exegetical perspective. This perspective accords in basic outline, although not always in detail, with other major documents from the Qumran collection, such as the *Damascus Document*.

---

the sixth day Dan and Naphtali. This appears to be the same order called for by 4Q365, frag. 23, which preserves Levi on the first day and Reuben and Simeon on the third day. But as I have shown elsewhere, the two texts are not identical, so it may be that they are depending on a common tradition (Sidnie White Crawford, "Three Fragments from Qumran Cave 4 and Their Relationship to the Temple Scroll," *JQR* 85 [1994]: 261–65). In the absence of a clear quotation of any of the additional material found in 4QReworked Pentateuch as scripture, the authoritative nature of the Reworked Pentateuch remains uncertain. However, we can say that at this point that frag. 23 of 4QReworked Pentateuch$^c$ gives evidence of a particular exegetical stance, an understanding of the proper practice of ritual law, that is also reflected in the *Temple Scroll*. This is the only instance of an identifiable *Tendenz* in the "reworked" portions of 4QReworked Pentateuch.

25. I do not believe that 4Q365a, labeled 4QTemple? in the *editio princeps*, is a copy of the *Temple Scroll*, but it contains material that may have been a source for the *Temple Scroll*. See Sidnie White Crawford, *The Temple Scroll and Related Texts* (Sheffield: Sheffield Academic Press, 2000), 15.

26. Émile Puech, "524. 4QRouleau du Temple," in idem, *Qumrân Grotte 4.XVIII: Textes hébreux (4Q521–4Q528, 4Q576–4Q579)* (DJD 25; Oxford: Clarendon, 1998), 85–88.

The opening segment makes the redactor/composer's method for the reuse of Deuteronomy evident. The Deuteronomic Paraphrase begins in col. 51:11–18 (after an "open paragraph") with a discussion of just judges. In accordance with the fiction of the *Temple Scroll*, God speaks in the first person.

11) שופטים ושוטרים תתן לכה בכול שעריכה ושפטו את העם
12) משפט צדק ולוא יכירו פנים במשפט ולוא יקחו שוחד ולוא
13) יטו משפט כי השוחד מטה משפט ומסלף דברי הצדק ומעור
14) עיני חכמים ועושה אשמה גדולה ומטמא הבית בעוון
15) החטאה צדק צדק תרדוף למען תחיה ובאתה וירשתה
16) את הארץ אשר אנוכי נותן לכמה לרשתה כול הימים והאיש
17) אשר יקח שוחד ויטה משפט צדק יומת ולוא תגורו ממנו
18) להמיתו

11) You shall appoint judges and officers in all your towns, and they shall judge the people
12) with righteous judgment. And they shall not show partiality in justice, and they shall not take a bribe, and they shall not
13) pervert justice, for the bribe perverts justice, and subverts the cause of the righteous, and blinds
14) the eyes of the wise, and causes great guilt, and defiles the house with the sin of
15) iniquity. Justice, justice you shall pursue in order that you may live and come and inherit
16) the land which I am giving you as a possession forever. And the man
17) who takes a bribe and perverts righteous justice shall be put to death; you should not be afraid of him
18) to put him to death.[27]

The segment begins with Deut 16:18; the redactor omits the phrase יהוה אלהיך נתן לך לשבטיך. It continues with 16:19 but weaves in part of Deut 1:17, converts the second-person verbs to third person, changes the order of the clauses, and adds the phrase כי השוחד מטה משפט, "for the bribe perverts justice," to emphasize the point of the verse. Before the quotation from Deuteronomy continues in line 15 with צדק צדק (16:20), the redactor adds several phrases punctuating the consequences of perverting justice, the climax of which is defilement of the temple (הבית). Deuteronomy 16:20 is quoted nearly verbatim, although the text is expanded beyond the MT text and the fiction that God is speaking is maintained. Lines 17–18 draw on both Deut 1:17 and 18:22

---

27. Yigael Yadin, *The Temple Scroll* (rev. ed.; 3 vols.; Jerusalem: Israel Exploration Society, 1983), 2:227–29.

("you shall not be afraid"); like the false prophet in 18:20, the unjust judge is to die, because his actions have polluted the land.[28] This punishment is not biblical but follows naturally for the redactor from his theological stance against impurity, both moral and ritual.[29] Thus the point of this whole introductory section is the importance of צדק, righteousness, in the land which is God's gift. If Deuteronomy functions as a "second law" in the Torah, both a recap of Exodus, Leviticus, and Numbers and an enlargement of their law codes to emphasize life in the land, then the *Temple Scroll* is a kind of "third law," meant to recap and expand Deuteronomy by the exegetical techniques and legal interpretation of the priestly circles in which the *Temple Scroll* originated. It is not meant to replace the Torah (including Deuteronomy) but to stand alongside it as an equally authoritative representation of God's revelation to Moses on Sinai (illustrated throughout the scroll by God speaking in the first person). This makes the Temple Scroll an excellent exemplar of the category "Rewritten Bible."

Another example of this exegetical technique is found at the end of 11QTempleª, col. 66:8–11.

8) כי יפתה איש נערה
9) בתולה אשר לוא אורשה והיא רויה לו מן החוק ושכב עמה
10) ונמצא ונתן האיש השוכב עמה לאבי הנערה חמשים כסף ולוא
11) תהיה לאשה תחת אשר ענה לוא יוכל לשלחה כול ימיו

8) If a man seduces a young woman
9) who is not betrothed, and she is fit for him according to the law, and he lies with her
10) and it is discovered; the man who lay with her shall give to the young woman's father fifty silver shekels, and
11) she shall be his wife, because he has violated her; he shall not be able to divorce her all his days.[30]

Lines 8–11 contain Deut 22:28–29. However, the redactor/composer added a clause in line 9, והיא רויה לו מן החוק, "and she is fit for him according to the law," which changes the rule according to the redactor's concern for proper, ritually pure marriages. Even in the case of the sexual seduction of a virgin, marriage within acceptable bounds is the paramount concern. A similar ruling occurs in the *Damascus Document* (4Q270 5 16, 4Q271 3 9–10), which warns

---

28. Ibid., 1:381, 2:227–29.
29. Eyal Regev, "Abominated Temple and a Holy Community: The Formation of the Notions of Purity and Impurity in Qumran," *DSD* 10 (2003): 261.
30. Yadin, *Temple Scroll,* 2:298–99, with modifications.

a father not to marry his daughter to an unfit partner. The admonition is based on exegesis of an earlier pericope in Deuteronomy, 22:9–11, and Lev 19:19, which contain the prohibitions against "mixing" (כלאים). 4QMMT B 75–82 also likens improper marital unions between priests and laity as כלאים. Thus we have a constellation of texts with the same concern for "proper" marriages, all basing their ruling on exegesis of the same Deuteronomy passage. In these texts we can observe the legal interests of the redactor/composer and his circle through the exegetical techniques he applies in his reuse of Deuteronomy. The exact relationship between the *Temple Scroll*, 4QMMT, and the *Damascus Document* is as yet undetermined, but the fact that they have the same legal concerns proves their relationship: they are products of the same movement within Judaism.

## 7. Conclusion

I have presented several examples of manuscripts from the Qumran collection that testify to the importance and popularity of the book of Deuteronomy in the Second Temple period. Deuteronomy was an authoritative text in and of itself, an important book in the creation of texts for study purposes and/or liturgical use, and was used as a base text in the exegetical creation of Rewritten Bible works with claims to their own authority. Deuteronomy may be termed the "second law" but clearly had attained first place in Second Temple Judaism.

# BUILDING THE ALTAR AND READING THE LAW: THE JOURNEYS OF JOSHUA 8:30–35

*Kristin De Troyer*

1. INTRODUCTION

For the past five years I have worked on the critical edition of the Schøyen papyrus 2648.[1] This Greek papyrus from around 215 C.E. contains Josh 9:27–11:3.[2] In my opinion, the papyrus is a witness to a pre-Masoretic text of Joshua.[3] The absence of the location Gilgal as Joshua's headquarters in 10:15 and 43 has been problematic since the study of the Old Greek text began. I also found a difference between the OG and the MT with regard to the report of the precise execution of commands given by God or Joshua. In the MT there is a more precise repetition of the execution of the commands in the report than in the OG. Orders given by important people seem to have been followed to the letter. The MT has further developed the importance of the orders by repeating them in the execution line. Both differences can be considered as pluses of the MT, not as minuses of the OG. While working on the differences between the OG and the MT, I also studied the 4Q Joshua fragments, more specifically 4QJosh<sup>a</sup>, edited by Eugene Ulrich.[4] My interest in 4QJosh<sup>a</sup> grew when I noticed similarities and differences between 4QJosh<sup>a</sup> and the MT and the OG. For my edition,

---

1. Kristin De Troyer, *Joshua* (Papyri Graece Schøyen. PSchøyen 1; Papyrologica Florentina 35; Manuscripts in the Schøyen Collection 5; Firenze: Edizioni Gonnelli, 2005), 79–159 + pls. xvi–xxvii.

2. Its Rahlfs's Verzeichnis number is 816.

3. See the following contributions on this topic: Kristin De Troyer, "Did Joshua Have a Crystal Ball? The Old Greek and the MT of Joshua 10:15, 17 and 43," in *Emanuel: Studies in the Hebrew Bible, Septuagint, and Dead Sea Scrolls in Honour of Emanuel Tov* (ed. S. M. Paul et al.; VTSup 94; Leiden: Brill, 2003), 571–89; idem, "Reconstructing the Old Greek of Joshua," in *The Septuagint in Ancient Judaism and Early Christianity* (ed. W. Kraus and G. Wooden; SBLSCS 35; Atlanta: Society of Biblical Literature, forthcoming).

4. Eugene Ulrich, "4QJosh<sup>a</sup>," in E. Ulrich et al., *Qumran Cave 4.IX: Deuteronomy, Joshua, Judges, Kings* (DJD 14; Oxford: Clarendon, 1995), 143–52.

I focused on Josh 9:27–11:3, the story about the sun standing still and the fight against the five kings. I, however, also studied other pieces of the book of Joshua as they related to the text of the papyrus and encountered some interesting problems, one of which I choose to present in this contribution: the problem of the location of the passage regarding the building of the altar and the reading of the law.

In this contribution, I will focus on three differences among the MT, the OG, and the Qumran texts. First, I will study the importance of Moses. Then I will discuss the reinterpretation of Deut 27 in the book of Joshua. Finally, I will give some attention to the location of the altar built by Joshua. This means that I will tackle the famous "reading of the law and building of the altar" section: MT 8:30–35, or should I say, the section in the OG "post 9:2" or the section in 4QJosh$^a$ post chapter 4? It is my thesis that the location of the section is an example of how the Qumranites read Scripture as a way of interpreting their present.

## 2. The Texts

### 2.1. Deuteronomy 27:2–8[5]

2 והיה ביום אשר תעברו את־הירדן אל־הארץ אשר־יהוה
אלהיך נתן לך והקמת לך אבנים גדלות ושדת אתם בשיד:
3 וכתבת עליהן את־כל־דברי התורה הזאת בעברך למען
אשר תבא אל־הארץ אשר־יהוה אלהיך נתן לך ארץ זבת חלב
ודבש כאשר דבר יהוה אלהי־אבתיך לך: 4 והיה בעברכם
את־הירדן תקימו את־האבנים האלה אשר אנכי מצוה אתכם
היום בהר עיבל ושדת אותם בשיד: 5 ובנית שם מזבח ליהוה
אלהיך מזבח אבנים לא־תניף עליהם ברזל: 6 אבנים שלמות
תבנה את־מזבח יהוה אלהיך והעלית עליו עולת ליהוה אלהיך:
7 וזבחת שלמים ואכלת שם ושמחת לפני יהוה אלהיך: 8 וכתבת
על־האבנים את־כל־דברי התורה הזאת באר היטב:

2 On the day that you cross over the Jordan into the land that the Lord your God is giving you, you shall set up large stones and cover them with plaster. 3 You shall write on them all the words of this law when you have crossed over, to enter the land that the Lord your God is giving you, a land flowing with milk.... 4 So, when you have crossed over the Jordan, you shall set up these stones, about which I am commanding you today, on Mount Ebal, and you shall cover them with plaster. 5 And you shall build an altar there to the Lord

---

5. The Hebrew text for nos. 1 and 3 is from *Biblia Hebraica Stuttgartensia* (Stuttgart: Deutsche Bibelgesellschaft, 1983). The English translation is the New Revised Standard Version.

your God, an altar of stones on which you have not used an iron tool. 6 You must build the altar of the Lord your God of unhewn stones. Then offer up burnt offerings on it.... 7 Make sacrifices.... 8 You shall write on the stones all the words of this law very clearly.

2.2. 4QJosh<sup>a</sup>, FRAGS. 1–2 (JOSH 4:34–35; 5:X; 5:2–3)[6]

[בספר] התורה 35 לא היה דבר מכל צוה משה] את יה[ושוע
אשר לא קרא יהשע נגד כל [ישראל בעברו ]את הירד[ן]
והנשים והטף והג[ר] ההולך בקרבם 5:X אחר אשר נתקו[ן ]
[ ל] [את ספר התורה אחר בן ] [ל נושאי הארון] [ 5:2
בעת ]ההיא אמר יהוה אליהש[ע ע]ש[ה לך חרבות צרים]
[ושוב מל את בני ישראל 5:3 ויעש ]לו י[הושע ח]רבות
צ[ר]ים וימל את בני ישראל אל] [גבעת הערלות 5:4 וזה
הדבר אשר מל יהושע כ]ל[ ]העם היצ]א ממצרים הזכרים כל[

34 [After this he read all the words of the law, the blessing and the curse, just as it is written in the book of ] the [l]aw. 35 There was not a word of all Moses commanded [Jo]shua which Joshua did not read before all […] the Jorda[n, and] the women and children, and the stra[ngers] living among them. 5X After they had removed [their feet from the Jordan, …] the book of the law. After that, the ark-bearers [.... 5:2 At t]hat [time] the Lord said to Josh[ua, "Ma]k[e yourselves flint knives, and again circumcise the children of Israel." 3 So Jo]shua [made flint] kn[ives] for [himself, and circumcised the children of Israel at the hill of the foreskins. 4 And this is the reason why Joshua had them circumcised: a]ll [the people who had come out of Egypt, all the males of military age, had died in the desert along the way, after leaving] E[g]ypt.

2.3. MT JOSHUA 8:30–35

30 אז יבנה יהושע מזבח ליהוה אלהי ישראל בהר עיבל:
31 כאשר צוה משה עבד־יהוה את־בני ישראל ככתוב בספר
תורת משה מזבח אבנים שלמות אשר לא־הניף עליהן ברזל
ויעלו עליו עלות ליהוה ויזבחו שלמים: 32 ויכתב־שם על־האבנים
את משנה תורת משה אשר כתב לפני בני ישראל: 33 וכל־ישראל
וזקני ושטרים ושפטיו עמדים מזה ומזה לארון נגד הכהנים

---

6. The text is taken from Ulrich, "4QJosha," 143–52. The English translation comes from Martin Abegg Jr. et al., *The Dead Sea Scrolls Bible: The Oldest Bible Translated for the First Time in English* (San Francisco: HarperCollins, 1999).

הלוים נשאי ארון ברית־יהוה כגר כאזרה חציו אל־מול הר־
גרזים והחציו אל־מול הר־עיבל כאשר צוה משה עבד־יהוה
לברך את־העם ישראל בראשנה: 34 ואחרי־כן קרא את־כל־דברי
התורה הברכה והקללה ככל־הכתוב בספר התורה: 35 לא־היה
דבר מכל אשר־צוה משה אשר לא־קרא יהושע נגד כל־קהל
ישראל והנשים והטף והגר ההלך בקרבם:

30 Then Joshua built on Mount Ebal an altar to the Lord, the God of Israel, 31 just as Moses the servant of the Lord had commanded the Israelites, as it is written in the book of the law of Moses, "an altar of unhewn stones, on which no iron tool has been used"; and they offered on it burnt offerings to the Lord, and sacrificed offerings of well-being. 32 And there, in the presence of the Israelites, Joshua wrote on the stones a copy of the law of Moses, which he had written. 33 All Israel, alien as well as citizen, with their elders and officers and judges, stood on opposite sides of the ark in front of the levitical priests who carried the ark of the covenant of the Lord, half of them in front of Mount Gerizim and half of them in front of Mount Ebal, as Moses the servant of the Lord had commanded at the first, that they should bless. 34 And afterward he read all the words of the law, blessings and curses, according to all that is written in the book of the law of the people of Israel. 35 There was not a word of all that Moses commanded that Joshua did not read before all the assembly of Israel, and the women, and the little ones, and the aliens who resided among them.

2.4. OG JOSHUA 9:2 ("8:30–35")[7]

9:2a [8:30] Τότε ᾠκοδόμησεν Ἰησοῦς Θυσιαστήριον κυρίῳ τῷ θεῷ Ισραηλ ἐν ὄρει Γαιβαλ, 2b.[31] καθότι ἐνετείλατο Μωυσῆς ὁ θεράπων κυρίου τοῖς υἱοῖς Ισραηλ, καθὰ γέγραπται ἐν τῷ νόμῳ Μωυσῆ, θυσιαστήριον λίθων ὁλοκλήρων, ἐφ' οὓς οὐκ ἐπεβλήθη σίδηρος, καὶ ἀνεβίβασεν ἐκεῖ ὁλοκαυτώματα κυρίῳ καὶ θυσίαν σωτηρίου. 2c.[32] καὶ ἔγραψεν Ἰησοῦς ἐπὶ τῶν λίθων τὸ δευτερονόμιον, νόμον Μωυσῆ, ὃν ἔγραψεν ἐνώπιον υἱῶν Ισραηλ. 2d.[33] καὶ πᾶς Ισραηλ καὶ οἱ πρεσβύτεροι αὐτῶν καὶ οἱ δικασταὶ καὶ οἱ γραμματεῖς αὐτῶν παρεπορεύοντο ἔνθεν καὶ ἔνθεν τῆς κιβωτοῦ ἀπέναντι, καὶ οἱ ἱερεῖς καὶ οἱ Λευῖται ἦραν τὴν κιβωτὸν τῆς διαθήκης κυρίου, καὶ ὁ προσήλυτος καὶ ὁ αὐτόχθων, οἳ ἦσαν ἥμισυ πλησίον ὄρους Γαριζιν, καὶ οἳ ἦσαν ἥμισυ πλησίον ὄρους Γαιβαλ, καθότι ἐνετείλατο Μωυσῆς ὁ θεράπων κυρίου εὐλογῆσαι τὸν λαὸν ἐν

---

7. The Greek text is taken from A. Rahlfs, *Septuaginta: Id est Vetus Testamentum graece iuxta LXX interpretes* (Stuttgart: Deutsche Bibelgesellschaft, 1979), the English translation from Charles Lee Brenton, *The Septuagint Version of the Old Testament and Apocrypha with an English Translation and with Various Readings and Critical Notes* (Grand Rapids: Zondervan, 1978).

πρώτοις. 2e.[34] καὶ μετὰ ταῦτα οὕτως ἀνέγνω 'Ιησοῦς πάντα τὰ ῥήματα τοῦ νόμου τούτου, τὰς εὐλογίας καὶ τὰς κατάρας, κατὰ πάντα τὰ γεγραμμένα ἐν τῷ νόμῳ Μωυσῆ· 2f.[35] οὐκ ἦν ῥῆμα ἀπὸ πάντων, ὧν ἐνετείλατο Μωυσῆς τῷ Ἰησοῖ, ὃ οὐκ ἀνέγνω 'Ιησοῦς εἰς τὰ ὦτα πάσης ἐκκλησίας υἱῶν Ἰσραηλ, τοῖς ἀνδράσιν καὶ ταῖς γυναιξὶν καὶ τοῖς παιδίοις καὶ τοῖς προσηλύτοις τοῖς προσπορευομένοις τῷ Ἰσραηλ.

> "30" Then Joshua built an altar to the Lord God of Israel in mount Gaebal, "31" as Moses the servant of the Lord commanded the children of Israel, as it is written in the law of Moses, an altar of unhewn stones, on which iron had not been lifted up; and he offered there whole-burnt-offerings to the Lord, and a peace-offering. "32" And Joshua wrote upon the stones a copy of the law, *even* the law of Moses, before the children of Israel. "33" And all Israel, and their elders, and their judges, and their scribes, passed on one side and on the other before the ark; and the priests and the Levites took up the ark of the covenant of the Lord; and the stranger and the native *were there,* who were half of them near mount Garizin, and half near mount Gaebal, as Moses the servant of the Lord commanded at first, to bless the people. "34" And afterwards Joshua read accordingly all the words of this law, the blessings and the curses, according to all things written in the law of Moses. "35" There was not a word of all that Moses charged Joshua, which Joshua read not in the ears of all the assembly of the children of Israel, the men, and the women, and the children, and the strangers that joined themselves to Israel.

### 3. Ulrich's theory

In his critical edition of 4QJosh[a], Ulrich states that the "sequence in 𝔐𝔊 is puzzling."[8] Indeed, the sequence of the narrative in 4QJosh[a] seems more logical than the ones of the MT and the OG. The structure and the contents of the passage in 4QJosh[a], fragment 1 and 2, look as follows: (1) 8:34(end)–35, the reading of the law; (2) a transitional temporal clause, called 5:X; (3) the text of 5:2, the circumcision account. In 4QJosh[a] the Israelites cross the Jordan at Gilgal in chapter 4, and immediately after, Joshua builds the altar. Joshua does not wait for another couple of chapters, namely, until chapter 8 in the MT or chapter 9 in the OG, to fulfill the command given in Deut 27:2–3:

> On the day that you cross over the Jordan into the land that the LORD your God is giving you, you shall set up large stones and cover them with plaster.

---

8. Ulrich, "4QJosh[a]," 145.

You shall write on them all the words of this law when you have crossed over, to enter the land that the LORD your God is giving you, a land flowing with milk.

Ulrich correctly states that, "in as far as the present arrangement is correct, the sequence of the narrative in this manuscript would place the building of the first altar in the newly entered land immediately after the crossing of the Jordan at Gilgal." He also notes that, "although the first two lines of frg .1 correspond to Josh 8:34–35 (the reading of the Torah), it is not certain that 8:30–31 (the building of the altar) preceded."[9] Ulrich, however, argues for the sequence entering the land, building the altar, and, finally, reading the law as the more original sequence of the Joshua narrative. The assumption that the sequence of 4QJosh[a] is thus less puzzling than the one in the MT and the OG is based on the presumption that the altar was built immediately upon entering the land and that the building of the altar preceded the reading of the law.[10] This sequence is in conformity with the commandment given in Deut 27, where the altar is required to be built upon crossing the Jordan and the reading of the law closely follows the building of the altar.[11] Indeed, following the section on the erection of the altar in Deut 27:2–8 stands a section on reading the law (27:9–10).

Ulrich not only studied 4QJosh[a] but also took into account the Samaritan text of Deut 27 and Josephus's paraphrase of the book of Joshua. At this point in the discussion, Deut 27:4 enters the scene as the verse in which it is commanded that "these stones should be set up" on Mount Ebal. Later on it is said that on these stones the law is written (27:8).

> 4 So, when you have crossed over the Jordan, you shall set up these stones, about which I am commanding you today, on Mount Ebal, and you shall cover them with plaster. 5 And you shall build an altar there to the Lord your God, an altar of stones on which you have not used an iron tool. 6 You must build the altar of the Lord your God of unhewn stones. Then offer up burnt offerings on it.... 7. Make sacrifices.... 8 You shall write on the stones all the words of this law very clearly. (NRSV)

Mount Ebal, however, is a rather late, or at least a secondary, "invention," for it was not mentioned in the first stage of the history of the text, represented by

---

9. Ibid.

10. For a summary of Ulrich's theory, see Heinz-Josef Fabry, "Der Altarbau der Samaritaner—Ein Produkt der Text- und Literaturgeschichte?" in *Die Textfunde vom Toten Meer und der Text der Hebräischen Bibel* (ed. C. Dahmen et al.; Neukirchen-Vluyn: Neukirchener, 2000), 35–52, esp. 41–44.

11. It is also based on the order of the text of frag. 1 and the relation between frags.1 and 3; see Ulrich, "4QJosh[a]," 145.

4QJosh{a} and Josephus. According to Ulrich, there are three stages in the textual history of the altar building and reading the law section:

> First, 4QJosh{a} and Josephus present an early form of the narrative which places the building of the altar at Gilgal at the end of chapter 4, in accord with the command as read in Deut 27:2–3 and Deut 27:4 without the insertion of a place-name. Secondly, the Samaritan tradition includes bahar Gerizin at Deut 27:4, constituting a Samaritan claim. A tertiary sequence in preserved in 𝔐 𝔊, with bahar Ebal in 𝔐 at Deut 27:4 as a Judaean counterclaim to bahar Gerizin. According to this hypothesis then, the narrative about the building of the altar, which originally followed the crossing of the Jordan and preceded the circumcision account, was subsequently transposed in accordance with Moses' revised command in 𝔐 to its present, curious position at Josh 8:30–35.[12]

## 4. A Threefold Analysis of the Texts

As I will argue that the text of 4QJosh{a} is an example of how the Qumranites read scripture in order to interpret their present, I need to evaluate the reconstruction of the history of the text, especially the location of the erecting of the altar and the reading the law section. In order to solve the problem of the location of MT 8:30–35, I focus on three elements: (1) The issue of who is giving a command; (2) The interpretation of Deut 27; and (3) The location of the altar. I will address these three issues by analyzing and comparing the MT, the OG, and 4QJosh{a}.

### 4.1. Who Commands Whom?

*4.1.1. MT*

In the Masoretic Text of the book of Joshua, more precisely in 4:1, 15; 5:2; 6:2; 8:1, 18; and then in chapter 10 and following, it is Yhwh who commands Joshua. In two sections, however, Moses pops up, namely, in 8:30–35 as well as in the Gibeonites' story in 9:3–27.

In 8:31 Joshua builds an altar, "just as Moses, the servant of the Lord had commanded the Israelites, as it is written in the book of the law of Moses" (followed by a quotation of the Deuteronomy text). The text of 8:32 reads: "And there, in the presence of the Israelites, he [Joshua] wrote on the stones a copy of the law of Moses, which he had written." The next line, 8:33, mentions the position of the people during Joshua's activities and ends again with a reference

---

12. Ibid., 146.

to Moses: "as Moses the servant of the Lord had commanded at the first, that they should bless the people of Israel." In verse 35 Joshua seems to follow Moses precisely, for it is written: "There was not a word of all that Moses commanded that Joshua did not read before all the assembly of Israel." In chapter 9, more precisely from verse 3 onward, the Gibeonites turn to Moses. Their story also ends with a reference to Moses, for in verse 24 they answer the following to Joshua: "Because it was told to your servants for a certainty that the LORD your God had commanded his servant Moses to give you all the land and to destroy all the inhabitants of the land before you."

*4.1.2. OG*

Since the critical edition of the book of Joshua, as prepared by Udo Quast of the *Septuaginta Unternehmen,* has not yet been published,[13] I rely on the old Ralfhs and thus especially on Codex Vaticanus—although I strongly believe that even Codex Vaticanus already contains prehexaplaric corrections toward the MT. The OG keeps the same line of command in Josh 4–8 and 10. The section about the altar building and the reading of the law is positioned after 9:2, just before the Gibeonites' story. In the account of the Gibeonites story, I notice the following minor differences from its MT parallel. In the parallel verse to 8:31, Moses is mentioned in the following expression. It is not "as it is written in the book of the law of Moses," but "as it is written in the law of Moses"—not in his *book*. This is also the case in verse 34. There is thus no "book of the law of Moses" in the OG. In verse 35, the OG has a minor plus. Instead of stating "There was not a word of all that Moses commanded," the OG reads, "There was not a word of all that Moses commanded to Joshua." Joshua is explicitly mentioned as the one receiving direct orders from Moses. In the Gibeonites narrative also, Moses is mentioned. Hence, Moses is mentioned in two stories that follow precisely one after the other: the altar building and reading of the law story and the Gibeonites' story.

*4.1.3. 4QJosh^a*

Unfortunately, most of the verses just mentioned do not appear in 4QJosh^a. The only parallel verse that is extant is 5:2, and there Adonai commands Joshua. The parallel text to MT 8:30–35, more precisely the end of 34 and 35, reveals, however, the following remarkable elements. In verse 34 Ulrich reconstructs at the end of the verse "the book" before the word "(of) the law." Even with the element "the book" reconstructed, the text of 4QJosh^a seems to be like the MT

---

13. Udo Quast, *Liber Iosue* (Septuaginta Vetus Testamentum Graecum Auctoritate Academiae Scientiarum Gottingensis editum; Göttingen, Vandenhoeck & Ruprecht, forthcoming).

and unlike the OG, which reads "the law of Moses." The verse parallel to 8:35 follows the MT again. That the reconstruction of "the book of the law" is very plausible is obvious when studying the piece of text labeled 5:X. There reference is made to "the book of the law." The text of 4QJosh[a] seems to side with the MT. However, in the parallel text to 8:35, 4QJosh[a] has the plus of the OG, namely, the explicit mention of Moses commanding Joshua. The position of 4QJosh[a], especially its relation with both the MT and the OG, is thus not entirely clear. It has one characteristic reading in the MT and one in the OG. The location of the text—precisely after the crossing of the Jordan—however, is unlike both the MT and the OG.

## 4.2. The Interpretation of Deuteronomy 27

*4.2.1. MT Deuteronomy 27*

The text of Deut 27 is a curious text. Focusing on the stones and the altar and omitting all the rest, the text reads as follows:

2. On the day that you cross over the Jordan ... you shall set up large stones....
3. You shall write on them all the words of this law....
4. So, when you have crossed over the Jordan, you shall set up these stones ... Mount Ebal....
5. And you shall build an altar there..., an altar of stones on which you have not used an iron tool.
6. You must build the altar ... of unhewn stones. Then offer up burnt offerings on it....
7. Make sacrifices...
8. You shall write on the stones all the words of this law very clearly.

Verses 2 and 3 give the command to set up the stones and write the words of the law on them. Verse 4 repeats the command to set up the stones but specifies that it must happen on Mount Ebal. Verses 5 and 6a deal with the building of an altar of unhewn stones. Verses 6b and 7 deal with the sacrifices, then verse 8 again deals with the stones on which the words of the law must be written. It stipulates that the words must be written "very clearly."

According to Fabry, there are a series of problems with Deut 27, especially with regard to the place of the altar and the place of the stones.[14] The altar is set up at Mount Ebal, the stones at the border of the Jordan. Moreover, looking at

---

14. Fabry, "Altarbau der Samaritaner," 35.

and comparing with the book of Joshua, the altar and the stones keep moving around: the altar moves from Gilgal to Shechem, the stones from Gilgal to Mount Ebal. Finally, the mountains themselves keep moving: Are they located at Shechem or at Gilgal?

With regard to Deut 27, Fabry distinguishes between the following layers. There is a "Grundschicht" in 27:1*–3, 11, 16–25. The text deals with the crossing of the Jordan, the stones, the plastering of the stones, and the curses. It is composed as a counterpart to Deut 5. Then a group of "kultisch interessierten Leviten" added 27:5–8, 14, 15, and 26. The location of the stones is still the Jordan area. A second round of editing was done to specify the location of the altar; so 27:4, 12, and 13 were added. This is how Mount Ebal entered the text.[15] Moreover, at this point the editors inserted the division of the Israelites into two groups, one to utter curses on Mount Ebal, the other for blessings on Mount Gerizim. At this very point in the textual history, Deut 11:29 was also created. Finally, a third redactor added 27:9–10 to tie the text within its context of Deut 26 and 28.

In my opinion also, the text of Deut 27 deals with two separate issues. First, the text deals with setting up large stones and writing the law on these stones (27:2, 3, 4, and 8). Second, the text speaks about building an altar (27:5–6a), and the first offerings (27:6b-7). Moreover, 27:4 repeats 27:2, adding, however, an element: the stones must be erected on Mount Ebal; and 27:8 repeats the content of 27:3 and then adds an additional element: they must be written "very clearly." It is precisely the mention of Mount Ebal that leads the reader to interpret the stones mentioned in verse 2 as belonging to the altar that is being dealt with in verses 5–7. I, however, argue that the text of Deut 27 originally dealt with stones (27:2) and a command to write on these stones the words of the law (27:3). Moreover, the text specified where the stones needed to be erected, namely, on Mount Ebal (27:4). The text also states that on these stones the words of the law needed to be written very clearly (27:8). Then an editor connected the stones with the altar by inserting 27:5–7.[16] The stones of 27:1 and 4 thus could be regarded as the "cornerstones" of the altar.[17] Schematically, the text grew as follows:

---

15. See below, however, for a further description of how Mount Ebal came into the text.

16. Michael Fishbane argues that Deut 27:5–6 is a rearticulation of Exod 20:22. Both prescriptions deal with the construction of an outdoor slaughter site made of natural blocks of stone. Deut 27:5–6, in his opinion, "reflects the old Shechemite stratum of the Book of Deuteronomy, and has links with the ritual erection of stones at Gilgal (Josh. 4:19–24; cf. 24:25–6)." In his book Fishbane discusses the reinterpretation of Deut 27:5–6 within the context of 1 Kgs 6:7. See Michael Fishbane, *Biblical Interpretation in Ancient Israel* (New York: Oxford University Press, 1985), 160.

17. Fishbane considers verses 5–6 to be an interpolation: "vv. 5–6 are drawn from Exod. 20:22 and have been interpolated into their present context" (ibid., 161).

27:2–3 and 4, 8
   Plus: 27:5–7

One could also argue that the editor who inserted 27:5–7 needed to use the technique of *Wiederaufnahme* to continue the narrative.[18] In the latter case, verse 4a–b ("so, when you have crossed over the Jordan you shall set up these stones) and verse 8a–b ("you shall write on the stones all the words of this law") can be credited to the editor who inserted verses 5–7. The "additional" information of verse 4c ("on Mount Ebal"[19]) and 8c ("very clearly") then becomes part of the original narrative—a narrative that has been spliced by the editor who inserted verses 5–7. The revised schema would look as follows:

Verses 2–3 and 4c, and 8c
   + verses 5–7
      + verse 4a–b
         + verse 8a–b

Structurally, the text now looks as follows:

27:2:                        continued in 27:4
            27:5–7           interpolated
27:3:                        continued in 27:8

Verse 4 is thus the *Wiederaufnahme* and continuation of verse 2. Similarly, 27:8 picks up and continues 27:3. Verses 5 to 7 are inserted between the two verses that deal with the stones, namely, 27:2, 4 and 27:8. The purpose of the insertion of the verses is to connect the stones with the stones of the altar on which the words of the law needed to be written. In the original narrative—that

---

18. With thanks to Bernard M. Levinson for this suggestion. Similarly, Fishbane points to the recapitulation of verse 3 in verse 8, "and therewith brackets the secondary (or parenthetical) material" (ibid., 162).

19. According to Fabry, the original reading of Deut 27:4 was Mount Gerizim. Fabry argues that the Samaritans must have been admonished to build an altar on Gerizim. After their separation from the Jewish community, a redactor changed Gerizim into Ebal, turning the mountain of blessings into a mountain of curses. This redactor also relocates the mountains to Gilgal instead of Shechem, "so daß sie nirgendwo liegen" (Fabry, "Altarbau der Samaritaner," 38). Fabry also follows Tov's main textual argument that the Giessen Papyrus witnesses to an Old Greek text that also reads *hargarizim* (as does the Samaritan Pentateuch and the Old Latin), and not Ebal (as in the MT and in the Septuagint). See Fabry, "Altarbau der Samaritaner," 37–38, with reference to Emanuel Tov, "Pap.Giessen 13,19,22,26: A Revision of the LXX?" *RB* 78 (1971): 355–83.

is the narrative without the insertion of 27:5–7, the law was written on the large stones that were erected (and plastered).

Fishbane draws the conclusion that "the words of this Torah" were to be written solely on the altar stones mentioned in 27:5–6, not on the free-standing stelae, as suggested by 27:2–4."[20] I would argue that originally the words were written on the larger stones mentioned in 27:2–4. Only by inserting 27:5–7 did it become possible to read that the words of the law were written on the stones of the altar. Fishbane, then, continues and remarks: "indeed, this latter is precisely how the text was understood in Josh. 8:31–2."[21] These remarks lead me to the text of Joshua.

### 4.2.2. MT *Joshua 8:30–35*

In Josh 8:30 Joshua builds the altar on Mount Ebal. Verse 31 refers to the text of Deut 27, more precisely to the "altar of unhewn stones." Then, as in Deut 27, Josh 8:31b records the burnt offerings that are offered. Moreover, in 8:32, as commanded in Deut 27, Joshua writes on the stones a copy of the law (of Moses). In 8:33 the location of the people is specified (again, as commanded in Deut 27). In 8:34 Joshua reads the law, and, finally, there is the note that Joshua did not forget anything that Moses commanded. Joshua 8:30–35 presents itself as an execution of the command given in Deut 27.[22] It interprets the two separate issues from Deut 27—the stones and the altar—as belonging to one and the same piece: the altar. The stones on which the law is written are the stones of the altar. The law is thus written on the stones of the altar. Therefore, Fishbane is entirely correct in saying that according to Josh 8:31–31 the words of the law are written on the stones of the altar.[23]

When I look at the structure of the book of Joshua, I notice that the section about the altar and the reading of the law is located right after the report on the events with the city of Ai and before the remark in 9:1–2. The structure of the book of Joshua looks as follows:[24]

I. Introduction
    1:1–9: report on the installation of Joshua, the new leader
    1:10–15: report on Joshua's first commands
    1:16–18: report on acceptance of Joshua's leadership

---

20. Fishbane, *Biblical Interpretation in Ancient Israel*, 162.
21. Ibid.
22. As Fabry puts it, Josh 8:30–35 "zeigt eindeutig das Bestreben, das Geschehen als Ausführung der Anweisungen von Dtn 27,1–8 darzustellen" (Fabry, "Altarbau der Samaritaner," 39).
23. Fishbane, *Biblical Interpretation in Ancient Israel*, 162.
24. See Kristin De Troyer, *Rewriting the Sacred Text: What the Old Greek Texts Tell Us about the Literary Growth of the Bible* (SBLTCS 4; Atlanta: Society of Biblical Literature; Leiden: Brill, 2003), 40–41.

II. Israel crosses the Jordan and marks the event
    2:1–24: story about the spies and Rahab
    3:1–4:24: report on Israel's preparation for, actual crossing of, and ritually marking of their crossing of the Jordan
    5:1–8: report on circumcision
    5:9: comment on location
    5:10–12: report on Passover celebration
    5:13–15: report on Joshua's brief encounter with God
III. Examples of how to live in the land
    6:1–27: the Jericho story
    7:1–8:29: report on the first and second attempt on taking Ai
    8:30–35: report on the building of an altar
IV. Conquering the land
    9:1–10:43: report on the first round of battle against the kings of the land
    11:1–12:24: report on the second round of battle against the kings of the land
V. Conquering the land, phase two
    13:1–22:34: report on how the Israelites took possession and divided the land
VI. Conclusions
    23:1–16: first concluding chapter of the book of Joshua
    24:1–33: second concluding chapter

In my opinion, 9:1–2 functions as the opening statement of the conquering of the land by a fight, which starts with all the kings rising up and gathering to fight Joshua (9:1–12:24 and 13:1–22:34). Joshua 8:30–35 provides the closing story of a section that I have entitled "Examples of how to live in the land" (6:1–8:35).[25] It deals with what the people do once they have entered the land. The erection of the altar and the reading of the law are not a part of the section that I labeled "Israel crosses the Jordan and marks the event" (2:1–5:15).

Whereas Joshua is the key person in the first sections ("Introduction," 1:1–18, and "Israel crosses the Jordan and marks the events," 2:1–5:15), Moses is the key figure at the end of the section "Examples of how to live in the land" (8:31, 35) and at the beginning of the section on conquering the land. More precisely, Moses appears at the beginning and ending of the Gibeonites' story (9:3, 24). It

---

25. I agree with Fabry that setting up an altar right after all the inhabitants of Ai and its king have been slaughtered does not throw a good light on the building of an altar—after all, one does not build an altar next to a heap of corpses. See Fabry, "Altarbau der Samaritaner," 44.

seems as if Moses needs to be near Joshua whenever a new stage in the history of Israel opens or closes.

### 4.2.3. OG Joshua "post 9:2"

The Old Greek of Joshua has the same interpretation of Deut 27: the stones on which a copy of the law of Moses is written are the stones of the altar. The OG of Joshua, thus, seems to be in line with the interpretation of Deut 27 in the MT of Joshua.

The structure of the LXX of Joshua also resembles the one of the MT. There are, however, some pluses and minuses. There is also the relocation of the section on erecting the altar and reading the law. Indeed, the section on erecting the altar and reading the law comes after 9:2, hence the title "post 9:2."[26] The structure is as follows:[27]

I. Introduction
    1:1–9: report on the installation of Joshua, the new leader
    1:10–15: report on Joshua's first commands
    1:16–18: report on acceptance of Joshua's leadership

II. Israel crosses the Jordan and marks the event
    2:1–24: story about the spies and Rahab
    3:1–4:24: report on Israel's preparation for, actual crossing of, and ritually marking of their crossing of the Jordan
    5:1–8: report on circumcision
    5:9: comment on location
    5:10–12: report on Passover celebration
    5:13–15: report on Joshua's brief encounter with God

III. Examples of how to live in the land
    6:1–27: the Jericho story
    7:1–8:29: report on the first and second attempt to take Ai

IV. Conquering the land
    9:1–2: introduction to the first round of battle
    9:2* additional verses: report on the building of an altar (par. to MT: 8:30–35)
    9:3–10:43: report on the first round of battle against the kings of the land
    11:1–12:24: report on the second round of battle against the kings of the land

---

26. Note that when analyzing the verses of the Old Greek of Joshua, I refer to the numbering of the MT so as to make comparison easier.

27. De Troyer, *Rewriting the Sacred Text*, 45–46.

V. Conquering the land, phase two
        13:1–22:34: report on how the Israelites took possession
                and divided the land
        (omission of 20:4–5: the verses on fugitives)
        (additional sections in 21:42 regarding Joshua's acquiring
           of Thamnasachar )

VI. Conclusions
        23:1–16: first concluding chapter of the book of Joshua
        24:1–33: second concluding chapter
        (additional section in 24:30: Joshua is buried in Thamnasachar).

The context of the erection of the altar and reading of the law section is, however, different in the MT. As remarked earlier, the section about the altar and the reading of the law follows the introductory remark about the kings gathering to fight Joshua and precedes the Gibeonites' story.

As a consequence, the two differences of the OG with the MT that I discussed earlier—the reference to the law of Moses (8:31) and the explicit statement in 8:35 that Moses commanded Joshua—must be seen in this new context. In the OG, a reference to Moses is made at the beginning of the Gibeonites narrative and at its end. Moreover, it is located in the long section on conquering the land (9:1–12:24 and 13:1–22:34). It is not a part of the section entitled "Examples of how to live in the land" (6:1–8:35), nor does it belong to the section that deals with Israel crossing the Jordan and marking the event (2:1–5:15).

*4.2.4. 4QJosh*[a][28]

Ulrich presumes that 4QJosh[a] interprets Deut 27. 4QJosha thus, like the OG and the MT, seems to associate the stones on which the law must be written with the stones of the altar.

The context of the section, however, is very different from the ones in the OG and the MT.[29] In 4QJosh[a], the context is more logical and coherent.[30] The Israelites just crossed the Jordan. Moreover, twelve men representing the twelve tribes just picked up large stones from the Jordan. Verse 7 says that the stones are "a memorial forever to the Israelites." The Israelites do precisely as Joshua

---

28. Again, I refer to the MT verse numbering when analyzing the Qumran Joshua frag. 1 from Cave 4.

29. As we do not have a lot of the material of the book of Joshua in 4QJosh[a], I refrain from offering a structure. The description of the contents and structure of the material is based on the reconstruction of the fragments and the location of "8:34–35" and following.

30. Paraphrasing Ulrich, "4QJosh[a]," 145.

commanded them. They cross the river, pick up the stones, and then camp for the night at Gilgal. In Gilgal, Joshua sets up the stones. The stones will remind the Israelites that they crossed over the Jordan there on dry ground. If, now, the placing of the frag. 1 is correct—and I believe it is, for not only the section on the reading of the law is present, but also 5:2 and 3 are present in the same fragment—then the stones picked out from the Jordan are still the subject in the next section. Hence, these stones are used for the building of the altar, and on these the law is written and read. I agree with Ulrich that the sequence crossing and picking up the stones, building the altar, reading the law, and then the circumcision of the Israelites is more logical and coherent than its sequence and logic in MT or OG.

The problem with Ulrich's reasoning is not the sequence of the narrative, but the sequence of the history of the text. Before I turn to this point, however, I will study the different texts with regard to the location of the altar. The question is where and when the altar is built. Was it built right after crossing the Jordan? Or was it built somewhere after the events that happened in Ai? Or could it have been built right before Joshua starts conquering the land in 9:3?

### 4.3. The Location of the Altar

*4.3.1. MT Joshua 8*

In MT Josh 8 it is obvious where the altar was built: on Mount Ebal. That the altar was built on Mount Ebal might seem strange. After all, Mount Ebal has been associated with the curses that the Israelites uttered at the event of the covenant-renewal ceremony of Deut 11:29 (see also Deut 27:13). The text, however, clearly states that the altar was indeed built on Mount Ebal. That the altar was built on Mount Ebal points also to the fact that the author of the book of Joshua—or at least, the editor who composed this section—had a (proto-)MT Deuteronomy in front of him, that is, Deut 27:4, with a reference to Mount Ebal.

The question now is where Mount Ebal and Mount Gerizim are located: Shechem or Gilgal? In Josh 8, the mountains seem to be located near Gilgal.

One could now ask the question whether or not this geographical location is possible in Josh 8. In chapter 8 Joshua deals with the city of Ai. The precise location of Ai is not known. In chapter 9 one can read that Joshua's military camp is in Gilgal. In 9:6 it is Gilgal where the Gibeonites turn to in order to find Joshua. Joshua does not build the altar in Gilgal. He and his army are only stationed in Gilgal. Gilgal only plays a role in the religious history of Israel during the time of Samuel (1Sam 7:16) and Saul (1 Sam 10:8; 11:14–15);[31] later on it

---

31. Angels too seem to be coming from Gilgal in Judg 2:1.

is associated with worshiping other gods (Hos 9:15; 12:11; Amos 4:4; 5:5; etc.). Hence, Gilgal would not be considered a religious center in later times. Joshua, however, builds his altar on Mount Ebal and camps at Gilgal. There seems to be a clear distinction between Mount Ebal, on which Joshua built his altar, and Gilgal, where Joshua has stationed his people.

MT Joshua seems to differentiate between Gilgal (Josh 8) and Shechem (Josh 24), which seems to imply that there were or two Ebals and Gerizims or that the author of the MT had not taken a class in geography or that he or she intentionally created this confusion.

*4.3.2. OG Joshua 8*

In the OG, too, Joshua also builds his altar on Mount Ebal. Again, there seems to be a distinction between Mount Ebal and Ai—wherever Ai might be. The altar has moved a bit closer to the place of the Gibeonites and thus is a bit further from Shechem, from Gilgal, and from the Jordan. At this point, it needs to be said that Gilgal plays a lesser role in the OG than in the MT.[32]

*4.3.3. 4QJosh$^a$*

In 4QJosh$^a$ the altar is built—or at least the reading of the book of the law associated with the building of the altar—happens at Gilgal. Just after crossing the Jordan and locating the people at Gilgal, Joshua—presumably, for the fragment does not contain this part of the text—builds his altar in Gilgal. In 4QJosha, Deut 27 follows more precisely. As specified in Deut 27, the building of the altar happens right after crossing the Jordan. Unfortunately, however, we do not have the part of the text that is supposed to deal with the erection of the altar. There is thus no way of checking whether or not the altar was built at Gilgal. Moreover, it is impossible to verify whether or not 4QJosh$^a$ has kept the reference to Mount Ebal in its reinterpretation of the quotation of Deut 27:2–4. By locating, however, the section of the building of the altar and the reading of the law to the beginning of Josh 5 (or the end of Josh 4), 4QJosh$^a$ has clarified that the altar was built conform to the prescription of Deut 27, that is, precisely after crossing the Jordan. Or, as Fabry states it, Josh 8:30–35 was "an seiner Position für falsch gehalten" and therefore "zieht (4QJosh$^a$, insertion by KDT) … den Text nach vorne."[33]

---

32. See De Troyer, *Rewriting the Sacred Text*, 48–53; idem, "Did Joshua Have a Crystal Ball?" 580–82.

33. Fabry, "Altarbau der Samaritaner," 46.

## 5. The Textual History

In my opinion, the textual history runs differently from the one proposed by Ulrich. Using the three analyses—the commandments given by Moses, the interpretation of Deut 27, and the location of the altar—I have come to the following reconstruction of the history of the texts.

The OG of Joshua interprets the stones in Deut 27 as the stones of the altar on which the law of Moses must be written. According to the OG, building the altar and reading the law happen in the context of the conquering of the land, more precisely when the conquering starts. After it is said that all the kings gather to fight Joshua, Joshua builds the altar, gathers his people, and prepares them by reading the law. Both at the beginning and at the ending of the Gibeonites' story there is now a reference to the law of Moses and to the fact that people—both the Israelites and the Gibeonites—follow the orders given by Moses. The building of the altar happens on Mount Ebal, not in Gilgal—Joshua gets to Gilgal only in 9:6. As the text of Joshua is the "first" text to interpret Deut 27, it might have been possible that the negative connotations associated with Mount Ebal did not yet exist and that, thus, building an altar on Mount Ebal was not yet so problematic. Finally, it looks as though the OG stressed that Moses commanded Joshua directly, and hence it is said in the verse parallel to 8:35 that Moses commanded Joshua.

In the MT, the text of Deuteronomy and its interpretation remain pivotal. The reading of the law and the building of the altar are bound tightly together. The author of the MT, however, makes sure that it is not the law of Moses that Joshua follows but the book of the law of Moses. That the author was not entirely consistent can be seen from verse 32, where a reference to the law of Moses is kept, without changing it to the book of the law of Moses.[34] The MT relocates the text to chapter 8, namely, 8:30–35, its current position. In my opinion, on the one hand it makes a location on Mount Ebal more plausible, and, on the other hand, it dissociates Mount Ebal further from Gilgal, where Joshua happens to be in 9:6. In my opinion, the MT distinguishes between Mount Ebal and Gilgal, the latter being the military campground and the former a religious center, a center that by this time might have become problematic.

Finally, there is the text of 4QJosh[a]. I agree with Ulrich that the text about the reading of the law was most likely preceded by the one regarding the building of the altar. Moreover, Ulrich is right in pointing to the importance of Deut 27 for the text of 4QJosh[a].[35] Like the MT, 4QJosh[a] keeps the reference to the book of law of Moses, albeit in the section called 5:X. Unfortunately, the verses

---

34. I acknowledge that changing the text here would have been difficult.
35. Ulrich, "4QJosh[a]," 145–46.

parallel to 8:31 and (most of the part of) 34 are not extant, leaving no possibility to check the text. 4QJosh$^a$ does keep the reference to Joshua in the parallel text to 8:35: it is Moses who commanded Joshua. But the text parallel to 8:30–35 is now relocated to the beginning of Josh 5, resulting in a loss of an inclusion at the beginning and the ending of the Gibeonites story, namely, the reference to both Moses and Joshua. The new position of the text, right after the crossing of the Jordan, is, however, more logical and more consistent with Deut 27. The Qumranites—or whoever wrote 4QJosh$^a$—kept stressing the importance of the place where the Israelites crossed the Jordan. The reading of the law happened at Gilgal. That there was an altar in Gilgal cannot be concluded from the text—the Israelites crossed the Jordan opposite Jericho (MT 3:16), then they camped in Gilgal on the east border of Jericho (MT 4:19), and finally Joshua set up the stones at Gilgal (MT 4:20)—it cannot be presumed, but it is possible.[36] That the altar was not built on Mount Ebal, however, is to be expected. First, the law of Deuteronomy needed to be followed. Second, Mount Ebal was no longer the place to be for a religious community that devoted itself to the God of Israel.

So far, one could reconstruct the textual history as follows: first, there was the Hebrew *Vorlage* of the OG, then the MT, and finally the text of 4QJosh$^a$. The reference to Joshua in the verse parallel to 8:35, however, seems to point to some influence of the *Vorlage* of the OG on the text of Qumran. Maybe 4QJosh$^a$ presumes the existence of two independent versions of the text of Joshua at Qumran: both the *Vorlage* of the OG and the MT. I remain undecided as to the precise textual history of the narrative of the building of the altar and the reading of the text. The three texts may witness to a linear and chronological development of the text of the book of Joshua, or they may witness to a plurality of texts.

## 6. How Scripture, in the Opinion of the Qumranites, Interpreted Their Experience

Whether or not 4QJosh$^a$ witnesses to a linear development of the text of the book of Joshua or to a plurality of Joshua texts at Qumran, it is clear that with the text of 4QJosh$^a$ the Qumranites interpreted their present situation. For the members of Qumran, it was evident that the fight to conquer the land started right after they camped outside of Jerusalem. Their religious quest and yearning for a clean and new Jerusalem started from the desert. I think the Qumranites saw and realized the importance of what I label the second Gilgal and the second conquering. Gilgal might have been "relocated" in Modein, the place to

---

36. This statement does not say that Gilgal was a religious center during the Maccabean period.

which Mattathias withdrew and out of which a new uprising began. Modein and the hill country behind it thus became the new headquarters of the second conquering of the land—a conquering of the land not under Joshua but under Mattathias the Maccabee.[37]

There are many other similarities between the actions of Joshua and the actions of the Maccabees. Joshua gathers an army around him. He circumcises the new generation of people that came out of Egypt—the children of those who actually left Egypt. Joshua encounters an envoy from God. On his command, he marches against Jericho and conquers it (in a very special way). Joshua also has to plead with God when things get bad and have the one responsible killed (stoned to death). In the next battle, Joshua and his men are following God's advice and Ai is taken and burned—the battle against Ai symbolizes the rest of the conquest. After these exemplary events, the conquest and cleansing of the land start.

Mattathias starts a revolt against the Hellenistic kings and their ideology of unifying all the people under one regime and one law.[38] Mattathias leaves Jerusalem and takes refuge in Modein (1 Macc 2:1–14). After a confrontation with the delegates of the king and their request to Mattathias to bring offers to the (Greek) gods (2:15–27), Mattathias and his sons withdraw to the mountains (2:27). They are joined by the Hasidim, strong men from Israel who are fervent fighters for the law (2:42), and by fugitives (2:43). Together they form an army. They set out to destroy altars (2:45). They circumcise children (2:46). They destroy those who oppose the law (2:47). Before Mattathias dies, he orders his sons to rally all those who are fighting to uphold the law and go after revenge for the entire people (2: 67–68). Son Judas continues the job of his father. He is the one who conquers and cleanses the land. In his first assault, Judas has his men sound the trumpets (4:13). Like Joshua, he counts on God to do or help with the fighting (see, e.g., 4:30). He cleanses the temple and has an altar built of unhewn stones. Finally, he rededicates the altar, makes sacrifices on the altar, and installs a new feast in memory of the rededication of the temple. Both Mattathias and Judas continue work done by Joshua. They both walk in his footsteps. Modein thus could have functioned as a new Gilgal.

What is striking, however, is that the second conquest—at least as recounted in 1 Maccabees—does not have the cleansing of the temple as its first event; to

---

37. See De Troyer, *Rewriting the Sacred Text*, 39–58.
38. The precise reason for the revolt is still debated. See V. Tcherikover, *Hellenistic Civilization and the Jews* (Peabody, Mass.: Hendrickson, 1999); and Elias Bickerman, *Der Gott der Makkabäer: Untersuchungen über Sinn und Ursprung der makkabäischen Erhebung* (Berlin: Schocken/Jüdischer Buchverlag, 1937); idem, *The Jews in the Greek Age* (Cambridge, Mass.: Harvard University Press, 1988).

the contrary, only with Judas does the temple come into play again. That the temple did not come first might have been an all too Hasmonean characteristic. And precisely that is what distinguishes the Qumranites from the Hasmoneans. It is also no surprise that 2 Maccabees starts with a letter from the inhabitants of Jerusalem and Judea to the Jews of Egypt regarding the festivities of the purification and the rededication of the temple—it too criticizes the Hasmoneans!

Moreover, the Qumranites considered themselves members of a new covenant. Entering the community of Qumran covenanters was marked and annually renewed in a ceremony in which they reaffirmed their adherence to the law. Following the law was crucial. A new community could only be a real new community if it built an altar right after emerging from the waters. The relocation of the text to the section after the crossing of the Jordan shows that at least the command of Deut 27 was followed: right after the crossing, Joshua built the altar, or at least he read the law at Gilgal. The relocation of the text, to its Qumran position after the crossing of the Jordan, makes at least the presence of the large stones more acceptable. Not only is the law written on large stones, namely, the stones of the altar; the law is written on the twelve large stones that represent Israel. As the members of the Qumran community considered themselves the true Israel, they read the twelve stones as referring to themselves, and thus, they identified themselves with the Israel that emerged from the waters of the Jordan. A copy of the book of Moses was written on themselves. They literally incorporated the law of Moses. Finally, by relocating the passage they not only followed the law to the letter, but they could also omit the reference to building an altar on Mount Ebal. The ceremony of covenant renewal is described in the *Rule of the Community* (1QS 1–2). In this ceremony the priests bless all the men of God's lot (II 1–2) and the Levites curse all the men of the lot of Belial (II 4).[39] As Esther Chazon remarks: "Unlike the biblical model, the sectarian blessings are extended only to the Qumran Covenanters (i.e., God's lot) while the curses automatically attach to their opponents (Beliah's lot)."[40] The ceremony of covenant renewal, indeed, has been modified. There is no way of allowing the Covenanters to be on Mount Ebal, the mountain of the curses, let alone build an altar on it. Relocating the text, the community of Qumran used scripture to interpret their experience of being the true Israelites.

---

39. See Florentino García Martínez and Eibert J.C. Tigchelaar, *The Dead Sea Scrolls: Study Edition* (2 vols.; Leiden: Brill; Grand Rapids: Eerdmans, 1997), 1:70–73.

40. Esther G. Chazon, "Hymns and Prayers in the Dead Sea Scrolls," in *The Dead Sea Scrolls after Fifty Years: A Comprehensive Assessment* (ed. P. W. Flint and J. C. Vanderkam; 2 vols.; Leiden: Brill, 1998–99), 1:244–70, esp. 261.

## 7. Summary of Conclusions

The threefold analysis of the four texts has led me to accept the OG as the oldest stratum of the text of the book of Joshua. The central camping ground "Gilgal" is a characteristic of the MT; Gilgal as Joshua's military headquarters was not yet present in the pre-Masoretic text.[41] This noninterest in Gilgal as military headquarters is reflected in the OG. The focus on Gilgal appeared late in time, say in the second century B.C.E. It appeared in the Masoretic Text. This (proto-)Masoretic text could have been available to the Qumranites.[42] Now, the Qumranites could accept an MT with Joshua having a military headquarter in Gilgal, headquarters similar to the headquarters of the Maccabean revolt. They could not, however, accept a crossing of the Jordan without an immediate erecting of an altar and reading the law, and thus MT needed to be reorganized. Moreover, by reorganizing the text, the Qumranites avoided mentioning an altar built on Mount Ebal.

4QJosh$^a$ is thus not only a witness to a later text than the MT; it also gives an idea of how the Qumranites read their present using biblical text.

---

41. Ibid.

42. I leave open the possibility that both texts, namely the proto-Masoretic text (i.e., the consonantal text of the Hebrew Bible) and the pre-Masoretic text (as witnessed by the Old Greek) were available in the late second and first century B.C.E.

# Part 4:
# Authoritative Literature in Ancient Israel and Judah

# INTERPRETING THE EXILE: THE EXPERIENCE OF THE DESTRUCTION OF THE TEMPLE AND DEVASTATION OF THE LAND AS REFLECTED WITHIN THE NONPENTATEUCHAL BIBLICAL ABRAHAM TRADITION

BEATE EGO

What hermeneutics did the ancients use to interpret their own reality through scriptural exegesis with respect to existing traditions? In the main stream of authoritative literature, this question poses a challenge. Generally, only the relationship between traditions and their actualized version is studied, but here we must also consider a third factor; we have to look at the experience or the contemporary situation of the people as they interpreted their own traditions.

This case confronts us not only with problems connected with innerbiblical exegesis but also with the problem that narratives, and other forms of tradition, do not normally tell us explicitly about their function and the concrete situation of their actualization. Although it seems self-evident that particular experiences lead to changes within already existing traditions ("the traditum") and therefore to new traditions ("traditio"),[1] it appears very difficult for the exegete to grasp the contemporary situation of a given tradition. Usually, exegetes try to reconstruct the experiences and contemporary situations implied within the text. However, there are appreciable difficulties attached to this process; consider for instance, the differences among scholars in determining the dates of biblical texts.

With regard to the already mentioned problem of hermeneutics, the nonpentateuchal, biblical Abraham traditions supply an appropriate paradigm for the process of dealing with traditions within the light of new experiences. Even if we are in most cases not able to define the shape of the "traditum" of these passages, these texts hint in a rather clear way as to the experiences of the narrating communities in which they were used as well as to their function in this context.[2] Within this paper, in order to paradigmatically elucidate the relationship between tradition and experience, I will first analyze Ezek 33:23–34 and then turn to Isa 51:1–3; 63:15–16; and Neh 9:7–8. These texts are of special

---

1. Concerning the differentiation between "traditum" and "traditio," see Michael Fishbane, *Biblical Interpretation in Ancient Israel* (Oxford: Clarendon, 1985), 6–16.
2. Cf. Christof Hardmeier, "Erzählen–Erzählung–Erzählgemeinschaft: Zur Rezeption der Abrahamserzählungen in der Exilsprophetie," *Wort und Dienst* NS 16 (1981) 27–47, here 27ff.

interest for the question posed above, since they all reflect a current experience of exile by changing and developing already existing traditions.

### 1. Ezekiel 33:23–24: Abraham as Symbol for the Hope of the Possession of the Land

In order to gain an understanding of how, in exilic times, the Abraham tradition was connected to the contemporary situation of the people, let us first turn to a passage from the book of Ezekiel. In Ezek 33:23–24 we read:

> [23] Then the word of the Lord came to me: "Son of man, the people living in those ruins in the land of Israel are saying: 'Abraham was only one man, yet he possessed [ויירש] the land. [24] But we are many; surely this has been given to us as our possession [מורשה].' "[3]

In this passage the current situation of the people, who here relate to the Abraham tradition, is evident. The situation is that of the remnant of the people of Israel, who not being exiled either in 597 or 587 B.C.E. by the Babylonians, remained in the devastated ruins of Jerusalem or in the ruins of other towns and villages in the Land of Israel (cf. 2 Kgs 24:10–18; 25:11–12, 18–21).[4] For those who stayed in the land, the question arose as to who should now be the legitimate owner of the abandoned lands.[5] In terms of who possessed the land we know that after the destruction of Jerusalem in 587 B.C.E., the Babylonians appointed Gedaliah ben Ahikam as governor (Jer 40:7), therefore giving Judah the opportunity to establish its own governmental structures under Babylonian dominance within the abandoned areas of Israel. Gedaliah erected his own residence in Mizpah within the Benjaminite borders north of

---

3. All biblical quotations come from the New International Version.

4. Concerning the exact dating of Ezek 33:21–23, different proposals exist. According to Walther Zimmerli, *Ezechiel* (2nd ed.; 2 vols.; BK 13; Neukirchen-Vluyn: Neukirchener, 1979), 2:818, the dating of the saying that describes the people of the land as "living in those ruins" cannot be dated before 587 B.C.E. However, according to Thomas Krüger this saying should be dated to the years before 587 B.C.E.; see Thomas Krüger, *Geschichtskonzepte im Ezechielbuch* (BZAW 180; Berlin: de Gruyter, 1989), 323.

5. This same problem is to be found in Ezek 11:14–15. Here the argument is based on ideology concerning the temple in Jerusalem and the assumption that Zion is the place of God's presence on earth. Thus, those living in Jerusalem and near to the sanctuary on Mount Zion were believed to be close to God, whereas those living in the Babylonian exile were regarded as being distant from God. Concerning this issue, see Andreas Ruwe, "Die Veränderung tempeltheologischer Konzepte in Ez 8–11," in *Gemeinde ohne Tempel: Zur Substituierung und Transformation des Jerusalemer Tempels und seines Kults im Alten Testament, antiken Judentum und frühen Christentum* (ed. B. Ego et al.; WUNT 118; Tübingen: Mohr Siebeck, 1999), 8–9.

Jerusalem (40:6, 8). In Jer 40:9–12 the reasons for Gedaliah's politics become plain. Here we read:

> 9 Gedaliah, son of Ahikam, the son of Shaphan, took an oath to reassure them and their men (i.e., the men, women and children who were the poorest in the land and who had not been carried into exile to Babylon). "Do not be afraid to serve the Babylonians," he said. "Settle down in the land and serve the king of Babylon, and it will go well with you. 10 I myself will stay in Mizpah to represent you before the Babylonians who come to us, but you are to harvest the wine, summer fruit and oil, and put them in your storage jars, and live in the towns you have taken over. 11 When all the Judeans[6] in Moab, Ammon, Edom and all the other countries heard that the king of Babylon had left a remnant in Judah and had appointed Gedaliah son of Ahikam, the son of Shaphan, as governor over them, 12 they all came back to the land of Judah, to Gedaliah at Mizpah, from all the countries where they had been scattered. And they harvested in abundance of wine and of summer fruit.

From this passage it becomes evident that Gedaliah accommodated himself with the Babylonians. He encouraged the poor people to work in the fields and to harvest the fruits of the land. Thus, it is reasonable to assume that under the leadership of Gedaliah a new partitioning and distribution of land took place. Gedaliah also acknowledged the taking of possession of deserted settlements by Israelite refugees who were returning to Judah from neighboring countries.[7]

According to Ezek 33:21–23, the Israelites remaining in Judah related to the Abraham tradition as a means of legitimating their claims to the land. They claimed that, "Abraham was only one man, yet he possessed the land. But we are many; surely the land has been given to us as our possession." These sentences contain *a fortiori* argument: if Abraham, as a single person, possessed the land,[8] how much more so for the large group of his descendants.[9] Those Israelites living

---

6. NIV reads "the Jews."

7. Concerning this issue, see Rainer Albertz, *Die Exilszeit (6. Jahrhundert)* (Biblische Enzyklopädie 7; Stuttgart: Kohlhammer 2001), 81–83; translated as *Israel in Exile: The History and Literature of the Sixth Century B.C.E.* (trans. D. Green; SBLSBL 3; Atlanta: Society of Biblical Literature, 2003), 90–93.

8. According to Bernard Gosse, in emphasizing that Abraham was one, Ezek 33:24 alludes to Gen 13:6; cf. B. Gosse, "Les traditions sur Abraham et sur le jardin d'Éden en rapport avec Is 51,2–3 et avec le livre d'Ézéchiel," in *Studies in the Book of Genesis: Literature, Redaction and History* (ed. A. Wénin, BETL 155; Leuven: Leuven University Press/Peeters, 1999), 421–22.

9. That Abraham is not titled here as "father" seems, to Thomas Römer, to imply that Abraham had not yet begun his career as the father of Israel. See Thomas Römer, *Israels Väter: Untersuchungen zur Väterthematik im Deuteronomium und in der Deuteronomistischen Redaktion* (OBO 99; Fribourg: Universitätsverlag; Göttingen: Vandenhoeck & Ruprecht, 1990), 517. This

in exile, however, also regarded themselves as descendants of Abraham. Therefore, it was of great importance for those living in the land that they should be seen as representing the majority of the people of Israel—indeed, this fact was crucial for their reference to the Abraham tradition.[10]

Even if the argument used within this passage seems obvious, it is quite difficult to say upon which particular traditions this saying is based. The word מורשה is frequently used in the book of Ezekiel.[11] Apart from this, it is only used within the context of the land of Israel in Exod 6:8, which belongs to P$^g$. The verb ירש, however, belongs to Deuteronomic-Deuteronomistic language. In the narratives of the patriarchs we find the verb ירש used within the context of the land in Gen 15:7, 8, as well as in such passages as Gen 22:17 and 28:4. It is remarkable that, according to the sayings of those Israelites who remained in Israel, Abraham already possessed the land. That is to say, the Lord's promise to Abraham of giving him the land was regarded as already having been fulfilled in the time of Abraham himself. A similar idea seems to be present in the priestly passage of Gen 28:4, which states: "May he give you and your descendants the blessing given to Abraham, so that you may take possession of the land where you now live as an alien, the land God gave to Abraham."

Based solely on these different connections and allusions, parts of which belong to very late layers of the patriarchal narrative, it is difficult to find out to which particular tradition Ezekiel refers. It seems plausible to say that he borrowed from still-fluctuating traditions.[12] Here, however, is not the time or place to enter into the very complicated discussion of pentateuchal criticism. If we assume that during the times of monarchic Israel at least the basics of the Abraham-Lot and Abraham-Sarah compositions (Gen 13*; 18–19*), as well as the basics of the stories of Jacob and Joseph, existed,[13] it becomes evident that the retelling and respective rereading of these stories emphasized the aspect of the land. The reference to Abraham's multiplying within this text acts as a motif through which the majority of the people of Israel, who stayed in the land, could regard themselves as the legitimate inheritors of Abraham and the promises given to their father.

---

hypothesis is problematic in that without the presupposition of the validity of Abraham as the father of Israel, the whole argument within this passage becomes un-understandable.

10. Cf. Ezek 28:25; 37:25, where reference to the patriarch Jacob is made.

11. See Ezek 11:15, 25:4, 10; 36:2, 3, 5; see Gosse, "Les traditions sur Abraham," 423.

12. See, e.g., Römer, *Israels Väter,* 517.

13. See, e.g., Erhard Blum, *Die Komposition der Vätergeschichte* (WMANT 57; Neukirchen-Vluyn: Neukirchener, 1984) 273–97; Irmtraut Fischer, *Die Erzeltern Israels* (BZAW 222; Berlin: de Gruyter, 1994), 339–43; Albertz, *Exilszeit,* 191–97, esp. 195; idem, *Israel in Exile,* 246–57, with further references to recent research on pentateuchal criticism.

This attempt to legitimize the ownership of the land by referring to Abraham was not accepted by the Israelites living in the Babylonian exile. According to Ezek 33:25–29, it becomes clear that sins such as eating meat containing blood, idolatry, bloodshed, murder, the doing of detestable things, and adultery disqualified the people's claim to the land and led to the wrath of God and the complete devastation of the land.[14]

### 2. Isaiah 51:1–3: Abraham and Sarah as Symbols of Fertility

In other contexts, the figure of Abraham becomes crucial when dealing with the problems connected with the destruction of the temple and the desolation of the land. This becomes clear when reading Isa 51:1–3:

1 Listen to me, you who pursue righteousness
and who seek the Lord:
Look to the rock [צור] from which you were cut [נקר]
and to the cistern [מקבת בור][15]
from which you were hewn [חצב];
2 look to Abraham your father,
and to Sarah, who gave you birth.
When I called him he was but one [כי אחד קראתיו],
and I blessed him [ואברכהו] and made him many [וארבהו].
3 The Lord will surely comfort Zion
and will look with compassion on all her ruins;
He will make her deserts like the garden of the Lord.
Joy and gladness will be found in her,
thanksgiving and the song of singing.

In this text, which is part of a larger composition,[16] the actual situation appears to be obvious. According to Rainer Albertz and other scholars, Isa 51:1–3 belongs to the second edition of the book of Deutero-Isaiah, which dates from the end of the sixth or the beginning of the fifth century B.C.E. Since in this layer of Deutero-Isaiah we find a distinct emphasis concerning Zion, Albertz

---

14. Concerning the issue of ethics in the book of Ezekiel see Andrew Mein, *Ezekiel and the Ethics of Exile* (Oxford Theological Monographs; Oxford: Oxford University Press, 2001).

15. NIV reads "quarry."

16. Cf. Odil Hannes Steck, "Zions Tröstung: Beobachtungen und Fragen zu Jes 51:1–11," in *Die Hebräische Bibel und ihre zweifache Nachgeschichte: Festschrift für Rolf Rendtorff zum 65. Geburtstag* (ed. E. Blum et al.; Neukirchen-Vluyn: Neukirchener, 1990), 257–76.

assumed that this text was written in Jerusalem.[17] Since "Zion is in ruins," I hypothesize that this text was written before 515 B.C.E., the time of the rebuilding of the Temple. If those who are "longing for justice and salvation" (Isa 51:1) and who are "reproached of men and terrified by their insults" (Isa 51:7) are comforted, we may infer that the listeners to the "prophet" were in a desolate spiritual state.[18] The old promises of God, i.e., the eternal kingdom of the house of David, the shelter of the holy temple, and the possession of the land, were seriously questioned. The people who were struck by the destruction of the temple and the devastation of the land and the exile, found themselves therefore—according to the words of Odil Hannes Steck—in a "heilsgeschichtslosen Raum," that is to say, an existence without salvation history.[19]

In this situation of loss and despair the prophet encourages his listeners by referring to their "parents," Abraham and Sarah.[20] In Isa 51:2 we find a paraphrase of the Abraham narrative. Using only three terms the prophet summarizes the story of Israel's father as a story of God's blessing, calling, and multiplying of Abraham. This short representation makes it clear that the things the prophet describes are already known. However, as with the previous example, it is difficult to pin down the exact form of the original source. In the paraphrase of Deutero-Isaiah we see first of all the parallel to Gen 12:1–3, where we are told:

> The Lord had said to Abraham,
> "Leave your country, your people and your father's household
> and go to the land I will show you.

---

17. Albertz, *Exilszeit*, 320–21; idem, *Israel in Exile*, 429–31.

18. Cf. also the complaining of the Israelites, that "their way is hidden from the Lord" (Isa 40:27) or that "the Lord has forsaken and forgotten Zion" (Isa 49:14).

19. Odil Hannes Steck, "Deuterojesaja als theologischer Denker," in *Wahrnehmungen Gottes im Alten Testament: Gesammelte Studien* (TB 70; Munich: Kaiser, 1972), 210.

20. Verse 1b uses mythological metaphors. Based on the parallel structure between v. 1b and v. 2a, one might get the impression that Abraham is implicitly compared to a rock, whereas for Sarah the metaphor of a cistern is used. These metaphors are without parallels in Old Testament literature. According to Nico Adriaan van Uchelen, the image of the rock has its roots in the symbolism of a grave stone and should be understood as a representative of the father; see N. A. van Uchelen, "Abraham als Felsen (Jes 51,1)," *ZAW* 80 (1968): 183–91. The connection between Sarah and a cistern could be explained by the fact that a cistern is associated with water, which represents life and fertility. However, Steck points out that the words נקר and חצב are always used with a pejorative meaning; therefore, they should be linked to the exile of the people, whereas "rock" and "quarry" can be understood as references to Zion; see Steck, "Zions Tröstung," 269. This solution is striking, since it explains the metaphors used here in terms of the background of biblical images of Jerusalem (cf. Zion as a rock [e.g., Pss 27:5; 61:3; Isa 30:19] and the waters of the sanctuary [e.g., Pss 46:5; 65:110; 87:7; Ezek 47; Joel 4:18]); see also J. Gerald Janzen, "Rivers in the Desert of Abraham and Sarah and Zion (Isaiah 51:1–3)," *HAR* 10 (1986): 139–55.

I will make you into a great nation [ואעשך];
and I will bless you [ואברכך];
I will make your name great [ואגדלה שמך]."

It is difficult, however, to describe the exact relationship between these texts. According to traditional pentateuchal criticism, Gen 12:1–3 belongs to J, which dates from the early or middle monarchic time.[21] On this assumption, Isa 51:1–3 can be regarded as an example of innerbiblical exegesis. However, new research suggests that Gen 12:1–3 belongs to the late pre-Priestly parts of the Pentateuch.[22] If this is the case, then we can conclude that Gen 12:1–3 and Deutero-Isaiah's references to the Abraham figure in Isa 51:1–3 were formed at the same time, and Deutero-Isaiah refers to a still-fluctuating narrative tradition, whose specific form is no longer known to us.[23] More important than the complicated and wide-ranging discussion about the dating of Gen 12:1–3[24] is the connection that we find between the Abraham tradition and the hope of the restitution of Zion in Isa 51:1–3. This feature found here in Isaiah is unparalleled in the pentateuchal Abraham. Apart from the lack of the motif of Abraham's calling in patriarchal narratives,[25] what is important for our context is the connection between the Abraham tradition and the hope of the restitution of Zion. As the line of argumentation in this passage clearly shows, the traditum telling about God's revival of life in the past functions as a paradigm showing God's might in general and that God can arouse new life in the land. As in Ezek 33:21–23, the motif of Abraham's wonderful multiplying is, in this text, subordinated to the motif of the land and its revival. Therefore, the tradition relating to Abraham and Sarah as found in Isa 51:1–3 focuses on a very distinct aspect of the aforementioned traditum, namely, God's wonderful might to create new life.

---

21. See, e.g., Claus Westermann, *Genesis* (2nd ed.; 3 vols.; BKAT 1; Neukirchen-Vluyn: Neukirchener, 1989), 2:163–84; Hartmut Gese, "Zur Komposition der Abrahamserzählung," in idem, *Alttestamentliche Studien* (Tübingen: Mohr Siebeck, 1991), 31–32; Horst Seebass, *Genesis* (3 vols. in 4; Neukirchen-Vluyn: Neukirchener, 1996–2000), 2/1:17; with references to earlier literature.

22. Cf. Matthias Köckert, *Vätergott und Väterverheißungen: Eine Auseinandersetzung mit Albrecht Alt und seinen Erben* (FRLANT 142; Göttingen: Vandenhoeck & Ruprecht, 1988), 248–99; John Van Seters, *Abraham in History and Tradition* (New Haven: Yale University Press, 1975), 272; Blum, *Komposition der Vätergeschichte*, 297–301, 349–59; Fischer, *Erzeltern Israels*, 340; Albertz, *Exilszeit*, 193–94; idem, *Israel in Exile*, 248–51.

23. See Blum, *Komposition der Vätergeschichte*, 358; Hardmeier, "Erzählen–Erzählung–Erzählgemeinschaft," 32ff. Concerning the shape of the preexilic patriarchal narrative, see n. 12 above.

24. Cf. the argument in Seebass, *Vätergeschichte*, 16.

25. Concerning קרא in prophetic traditions, see Hos 11:1 and Isa 41:8–9.

### 3. Isaiah 63:15–16: The Rejection of the Hope Connected with the Abraham Tradition

A further paradigm reflecting the Abraham tradition in the face of the experience of the destruction of the temple and the exile is the prayer of lamentation in Isa 63:7–64:11. According to Rainer Albertz and other scholars, this prayer dates to late exilic times (between 530 and 520 B.C.E.).[26] We read in verses 15–16:

> 15 Look down from heaven and see
> from your lofty throne, holy and glorious.
> Where are your zeal and your might?
> Your tenderness and compassion are withheld from us.
> 16 But you are our Father [כי־אתה אבינו],
> though Abraham does not know us [כי אברהם לא ידענו]
> or Israel acknowledge us [וישראל לא יכירנו];
> you, O Lord, are our Father [אתה יהוה אבינו],
> our Redeemer from of old is your name.

We know that the destruction of the temple served as Israel's background in this lament, since verse 18 states: "Our enemies have trampled down your sanctuary." Furthermore, in Isa 64:10–11 we hear: "Your sacred cities have become a desert; even Zion is a desert; Jerusalem a desolation. Our holy temple, where our fathers praised you, has been burned with fire, and all that we treasured lies in ruins." According to the writer of this psalm, God has become "the enemy of his people, because they rebelled against him" (v. 10); now, because of the impurity of the people, he has hidden his face (vv. 5–7). Although these sentences are based on Deuteronomic-Deuteronomistic theology, this psalm appears to be influenced by the idea that God himself hardened the hearts of the people and let them wander from his ways (Isa 64:17; cf. 6:9–10).

In this situation of experiencing sin and powerlessness, the people have only the one hope that God, addressed here as their father, will turn toward them with his might and redeem them. Within this context, the importance of Abraham in relation to the salvation of the people is rejected. In regard to the opposition between Abraham, "who does not know his people," and God as Israel's real

---

26. See Albertz, *Exilszeit*, 121; idem, *Israel in Exile*, 146–47, with references to further literature. Concerning differing datings, see now Johannes Goldenstein, *Das Gebet der Gottesknechte: Jes 63,7–64,11 im Jesajabuch* (WMANT 92; Neukirchen-Vluyn: Neukirchener, 2001), 232–47. However, even if this prayer dates from a later time, one assumes that an experience of war and destruction existed.

father and redeemer, we may draw the conclusion that some held the opinion that the reference to Abraham could also bring salvation to the afflicted ones.

Within this context ידע means "to care about."²⁷ However, there are difficulties in identifying what is meant exactly by the whole sentence כי אברהם לא ידענו. In the past it was assumed that the term ידע in this context was connected to the biblical ידענים; thus this formula referred to ancestor worship and necromancy (cf. Lev 19:31a; Isa 8:19).²⁸ Other scholars have been inclined to interpret this passage as a reflection of the beginning of popular belief in the patriarchs as angelic guardians, a belief explicitly attested to in rabbinic literature. Abraham and Jacob, therefore, according to this passage, were guilty of neglecting their charges. A further attempt at interpretation tries to show that ידע has to be understood in a juridical context. Within this framework "not knowing" was perceived in the sense of a juridical formula of separation, including the end of the promises of the blessing.²⁹ Johannes Goldenstein, in his recently published dissertation, however, rejects all these hypotheses in favor of an "intertextual" solution. According to Goldenstein, the phrase אברהם לא ידענו should be understood in opposition to Isa 41:8 and 51:1–8.³⁰ His proposal implies that the term "Abraham" functions here as an "abbreviation," hinting at the promises given by God to the fathers of Israel. Thus, the whole formulation "Abraham does not know us" is understood as a relinquishing of the belief in the promises to the patriarchs:

> Jes. 63,16 verläßt sich nicht auf die von den Vätern gegebenen Verheißungen, sondern appelliert an jenen Vater, der sich in der Geschichte als Retter (מושיע 43,3) und Erlöser (גאל 43,14) erwiesen hat und der die Rückkehr der Söhne und Töchter nach Zion bewirkt (43,6): an Jahwe.³¹

In the context of rejecting the Abraham tradition, a different conception comes to light and is emphasized, the idea of God as Father who is also the mighty Creator of humans (Isa 64:7).

---

27. Cf. Willy Schottroff, "ידע," THAT, 691.
28. Concerning the concept of necromantics generally, see Joseph Tropper, *Nekromantie: Totenbefragung im Alten Orient und im Alten Testament* (AOAT 223; Kevelaer: Butzon & Bercker; Neukirchen-Vluyn: Neukirchener, 1989).
29. See the summary in Johannes Goldenstein, *Gebet der Gottesknechte*, 92–93.
30. Ibid., 93–96; see also O. H. Steck, "Die letzte Jesajaredaktion in Tritojesaja," in idem, *Studien zu Tritojesaja* (BZAW 203; Berlin: de Gruyter, 1991), 240 n. 72.
31. Goldenstein, *Gebet der Gottesknechte*, 95.

## 4. Nehemiah 9:7–8: Abraham as a Figure of God's Grace and Ideal for Doing Righteousness

As a last paradigm for the nonpentateuchal Abraham tradition, let us look at Neh 9:7–8. It may come as a surprise that I mention this passage here, in the context of the destruction of the temple and the experience of the exile. However, although the postexilic penitential[32] prayer of Neh 9:37 dates from the fourth century B.C.E.,[33] it is still connected to the experience of the exile in a very significant manner. This becomes clear when we note that at the end of the prayer in Neh 9:36–37 the people regard themselves as being slaves in their own land, since foreign kings now control the gifts of the land that their ancestors enjoyed, including its produce. The situation described here may refer to the Persians as well as to the Hellenistic rulers, since Judea was already bound to pay high taxes under the Persian government.[34] As such, we may speak of a definite concept related to the exile. According to the author of this prayer, the exilic situation did not come to an end with the return from Babylon and the building of the Second Temple but in fact remained even until this very day.[35] According to Deuteronomic-Deuteronomistic ideology, this situation of inner exile can be explained by the fact that people had sinned since the days of the desert and since the epochs of the judges (vv. 16–18, 26, 29). Not only this, but later their kings, their princes, and their forefathers did not keep the law nor heed the commandments and the warnings which God gave them (v. 34). Hinting at the sins of the people emphasizes that God, who acted throughout history gracefully and compassionately, is righteous in the punishment that he has brought upon them (v. 33).[36]

We see that within the context of Neh 9:36–37 the figure of Abraham plays a crucial role, since at the beginning of this penitential prayer we read:

> 7 You are the Lord God who chose Abram and brought him out of Ur of the Chaldeans and named him Abraham. 8 You found his heart faithful to you [ומצאת את לבבו נאמן לפניך], and you made a covenant with him to his

---

32. Concerning Neh 9:6–37 as a penitential prayer, see Rodney Alan Werline, *Penitential Prayer in Second Temple Judaism: The Development of a Religious Institution* (SBLEJL 13; Atlanta: Scholars Press, 1998), 56; Mark J. Boda, *Praying the Tradition: The Origin and Use of Tradition in Neh 9* (BZAW 277; Berlin: de Gruyter, 1999), 26–41.

33. Concerning the dating of Neh 9:6–37, see Volker Pröbstl, *Nehemia 9, Psalm 106 und Psalm 136 und die Rezeption des Pentateuchs* (Göttingen: Cuvilliers, 1997), 103–5; Boda, *Praying the Tradition*, 193–95; Dietmar Mathias, "Nachexilische Geschichtsrezeption am Beispiel von Neh 9,6–31," *Mitteilungen und Beiträge 9* (1995): 3–25.

34. Cf. Mathias, "Nachexilische Geschichtsrezeption," 10–11.

35. Cf. Tob 14:4–5.

36. See, e.g., Neh 9:9–15, 17b, 19–25, 27–28, 30–31.

descendants the land of the Canaanites, Hittites, Amorites, Perizzites, Jebusites and Girgashites. You have kept your promise because you are righteous [כי צדיק אתה].

In these verses we find a short paraphrase of the Abraham narrative, which makes it interesting in a number of ways. Four incidents in Abraham's life are alluded to in verses 7–8. First I shall refer to those incidents, which are recognizable at a glance by the distinctive vocabulary used in Neh 9:7–8. Whereas "God who chose Abram and brought him out of Ur of the Chaldeans" hints at Gen 11:28, 31; 12:1–5, the changing of Abram's name has its source in Gen 17:5. God's covenant with Abraham and his promise concerning the land of the Canaanites and of other peoples alludes to Gen 15:17–21.[37] What appears ambiguous, however, is the source of the phrase ומצאת את לבבו נאמן לפניך "you found his heart faithful before you" in Neh 9:8a. At first glance, the source of this clause seems to lie in the wording of Gen 15:6, where it is stated והאמן ביהוה ויחשבה לו לצדקה "and (Abraham) trusted in God and he was found as righteous before him."[38] Yet when comparing this phrase to later Second Temple interpretations of the Abraham tradition, the reference seems to point more to Gen 22, where we see Abraham obediently moving to sacrifice his son when God tests him. We also read, for example, in Sir 44:20: "God established the covenant in his flesh, and when he was tested, he was found faithful" (καὶ ἐν πειρασμῷ εὑρέθη πιστός). A very similar phrase is to be found in 1 Macc 2:52, which states: "Was not Abraham found faithful when tested, and it was reckoned to him as righteousness" (Αβρααμ οὐχὶ ἐν πειρασμῷ εὑρέθη πιστός, καὶ ἐλογίσθη αὐτῷ εἰς δικαιοσύνην). In both cases the wording πειρασμός hints clearly to Gen 22:1. Some scholars, such as Manfred Oeming and Judith Newman, regard the phrase concerning Abraham's righteousness in Neh 9:8a as a reference to the Akedah.[39] However, since we find Abraham's righteousness being directly connected to God's covenant with Abraham only in Neh 9:8a and Gen 15:6, 17–21, it seems more plausible to regard the clause ומצאת את לבבו נאמן לפניך as referring primarily to Gen 15:6.[40] This does not imply

---

37. However, there exist several differences between the lists of the nations in Gen 15:19–21 and Neh 9:7, 8; see Tomoo Ishida, "The Structure and Historical Implications of the List of Pre-Israelite Nations," *Bib* 60 (1979): 461–90.

38. See Pröbstl, *Nehemia 9*, 50–55.

39. Manfred Oeming, "Der Glaube Abrahams. Zur Rezeptionsgeschichte von Gen 15,6 in der Zeit des zweiten Tempels," *ZAW* 110 (1998): 24; Judith K. Newman, *Praying by the Book: The Scripturalization of Prayer in Second Temple Judaism* (SBLEJL 14; Atlanta: Scholars Press, 1999), 70, 74.

40. See also Wilhelm Rudolph, *Esra und Nehemia* (HAT; Tübingen: Mohr Siebeck, 1949), 158: "Die Namensänderung Abrahams (Gen 17,5) wird erwähnt, weil sie mit Verheißungen verbunden war, von denen die wesentlichste, die Zusage des Landbesitzes (Gen 17,7f.), zitiert wird;

that within this context we have to exclude an allusion to the Akedah altogether. Regarding the late dating of the penitential prayer of Neh 9:6–37, which presupposes the existence of the Pentateuch,[41] we have to take into account that the intention of the author of this prayer was to actualize the whole Abraham tradition. Thus, as Newman suggests, it is possible to regard Neh 9:7, 8 as being a preliminary to the later tradition of Abraham's ten trials, first explicitly attested to in the book of *Jubilees*.[42]

Whatever the case may be, when considering the perception of the Abraham tradition in Neh 9:7, 8 different aspects seem to be crucial: (1) The figure of Abraham is depicted as the object and recipient of God's grace and working. Thus, as Judith Newman states, "These two verses emphasize the divine agency guiding Abraham's life. God is the subject of all verbs in Neh 9:7–8, not Abraham."[43] In the biblical depiction of the figure of Abraham we find no parallels to the status afforded Abraham by the author of this prayer. In his first clause the author speaks about God's choice of Abraham and by this gives a distinctive edge to the tradition of Abraham to be found in Gen 11:28, 31; 12:1–5:[44]

> Because the divine choice refers normally to David or Jerusalem, the semantic range of this verb adds regal standing to the status of Abraham. Perhaps also the association with the eternal choice of the Davidic dynasty and Jerusalem suggests immutability of the divine promise made to Abraham and his descendants.[45]

Accordingly we are informed that Abraham did not leave Ur of the Chaldeans on his own volition; rather, it was God who brought him out of Ur. As

---

doch zeigt der Hinweis auf Abrahams Bewährung (נאמן) und die Aufzählung der einzelnen Völkerschaften Palästinas, daß dem Dichter bei der Formulierung nicht Gen 17 (P), sondern der Bundesschluß von Gen 15 (J) vorgeschwebt hat (15,6 והאמין; 15,18–21)"; see also the short reference to Gen 15 given by Jacob M. Myers, *Ezra-Nehemiah* (AB 14; Garden City, N.Y.: Doubleday 1979), 167; and Mathias, "Nachexilische Geschichtsrezeption," 17.

41. See, e.g., Pröbstl, *Nehemia 9*, 86; Newman, *Praying by the Book*, 103; Boda, *Praying the Tradition*, 195–96.

42. Cf. Newman, *Praying by the Book*, 74. Concerning the tradition of Abraham's ten trials, see Beate Ego and Armin Lange, "'Und es ward ihm zur Gerechtigkeit angerechnet' (4QPsJubᵃ 2 I 8)—Gen 15,6 im Pseudo-Jubiläentext von Qumran und in der antik-jüdischen Literatur," in *Der Mensch vor Gott: Forschungen zum Menschenbild in Bibel, antikem Judentum und Koran. Festschrift für Hermann Lichtenberger zum 60. Geburtstag* (ed. U. Mittmann-Richert et al; Neukirchen-Vluyn: Neukirchener, 2003), 183–87.

43. Newman, *Praying by the Book*, 71.

44. Concerning the use of the term בחר in biblical tradition, see Newman, *Praying by the Book*, 71.

45. Ibid., 73.

in the last reference to the pentateuchal Abraham tradition, the wording of this first clause is not actually found in Gen 11:28, 31; 12:1–5:

> At the beginning of Gen 12, God simply commands Abraham to leave, and Abraham gathers his family and obeys. Though Neh 9:7 refers to the events of Gen 12, the actual word in the clause 7c "והוצאתו מאור כשדים" shares the language of Gen 15:7a. In Gen 15, the phrase appears as part of God's self identification of Abram, "I am the Lord who brought you out of Ur of the Chaldaens…" In Neh 9:7 the phrase occurs in the second person; the prayer identifies God as the one who brought Abram out of Ur.[46]

(2) Apart from this emphasis on God's acting, the author also stresses Abraham's righteousness.

(3) In the context of this passage, God's promise concerning the land may be regarded as a result of Abraham's righteousness. As a reaction to the patriarch's integrity, God gives Abraham and his descendants the covenant and promises the possession of the land. Therefore, the crux of the argument in this passage is found in the connection between the righteousness of Abraham, who was chosen by God, and the promise of the land as God's reaction.

Seen against the background of the whole prayer, the figure of Abraham plays a double role: On the one hand, Abraham is perceived as a symbol for the people of Israel, since he first received God's grace, a grace which was also given to the people of Israel at later times in their history.[47] On the other hand, we can detect a great contrast between the patriarch and his people, since his piety characterizes an anti-typos to Israel as a sinning nation. Furthermore, in God's repeating of his promise concerning the land,[48] it becomes clear that God has not changed. Israel, however, has to change and to behave like Abraham to regain the promised land. In this way Abraham functions as a kind of model, hinting to Israel how it should behave to be worthy of living in the land as a free people. The patriarch becomes not only a symbol of hope but also a symbol of adoration and admonition.

## 5. Conclusions

The nonpentateuchal parts of the Abraham tradition are particularly fitting for inquiring about the relationship between contemporary experience and tradition. In opposition to the narrative passages of the Abraham story in the book

---

46. Ibid., 71.
47. Concerning the idea of Abraham as "principium" of salvation history, see Gese's distinguished article "Zur Komposition der Abrahamserzählung," 29, 48.
48. Cf. Neh 9:15a, 22b–24a, 35–36.

of Genesis, we find here references not only to the actual situation of the community in which the story was narrated but also to the motives of telling.[49]

The referential character of the prophetic texts hints to the fact that at the time of writing traditions relating to Abraham (traditum) already existed. However, during the time of the exile, these traditions referring to the patriarchs were still fluctuating. What is clear is that the traditum was greatly shortened by its interpreters who limited themselves to giving only the most important facts in relation to the situation in question.

This makes it impossible to know how exactly the traditum in the time of the exile was changed and interpreted. Only later traditions, for example Neh 9:5–37, that a completed Pentateuch text presupposes, make answering this question possible. Although even in this text we cannot detect a distinct "scripture consciousness," as is later in Qumran pesharim.[50]

Decisive for the relationship between experience and tradition is the fact that the tradition concerning Abraham's increasing was recited within differing contexts in exilic times. For example, on the one hand, according to Ezek 33:23–24, this tradition was used by those Israelites still living in Israel for themselves, in order to support their claim to the land. In so doing their aim was to overcome, in a positive way, their experience of uncertainty, shortness, and poverty. On the other hand, Isa 51:1–3 points to the miracle of the increase of Abraham and Sarah and uses it as a metaphor of hope. The author does this to stabilize their troubled state of mind and overcome their experience of hopelessness.

What stands out in these passages is that two differing groups are relating to similar traditions but are laying claim to them in different ways.

> Each tradition can be regarded as a self-contained body of experience…. when someone recites one of these traditions, he enables his listeners to have part in those experiences told of. However, what the listener or reader of that told hears or reads, depends entirely on his experience and situation at the time of hearing.[51]

Thus, a particular tradition opens differing possibilities of identification and makes possible much play in its interpretation.

---

49. Hardmeier, "Erzählen–Erzählung–Erzählgemeinschaft," 27.
50. See Newman, *Praying by the Book*, 104.
51. Regarding this aspect, see Hardmeier, "Erzählen–Erzählung–Erzählgemeinschaft," 37; concerning the connection between tradition and experience, see also the contribution of Christine Helmer in this volume.

Ezekiel 33:23–28 shows clearly that the laying claim to such traditions was not always accepted. Particularly at that point, where traditions were used to verify and justify claims, it appears that other controls were necessary in order to prove their legitimacy.

Finally, Isa 63:15 makes clear that the abilities of single traditions to help their hearers overcome problems in concrete situations are limited. Thus we see that older traditions become implausible and are superseded by other traditions that, through becoming accentuated, release their potential for the overcoming of problematic situations. In our case, for example, the conceptions of God as redeemer and creator arise, and become crucial and dominant for Israel in their dealing with their time in exile.

In closing, when dealing with traditions in order to perceive the present it soon becomes clear that the processes involved within this are dynamic and exciting in their nature.

# READING THE DECLINE OF PROPHECY*

*Armin Lange*

The Qumran pesharim are among the earliest preserved commentaries in Israelite-Jewish literature.[1] They employ special interpretative and hermeneutical techniques also found in ancient Near Eastern omen interpretations and in later Petirah midrashim.[2] Using the example of Jer 23:33–40, in this article I will compare the hermeneutics of the pesharim to the way earlier literary prophecy interprets prophetic oracles. I will show that the pesher hermeneutics allow for a better understanding of how the prophetic redactors understood and perceived their own reality in light of authoritative literature. With regard to Jer 23:33–40, I will thus inquire how the redactor responsible for this passage understood the postexilic marginalization of aural prophecy by applying pesher hermeneutics to an earlier prophetic utterance preserved in Jer 23:33. But before the hermeneutics of Jer 23:33–40 can be compared with the hermeneutics of the Qumran pesharim, we must consider the postexilic attitude toward prophecy.

## 1. THE MARGINALIZATION OF PROPHECY IN PERSIAN TIMES

In several episodes the Hebrew Bible provides stories of crime and passion. One of these stories is Neh 6:1–14. When Nehemiah rebuilt the wall around Jerusalem in the middle of the fifth century B.C.E., he met fierce opposition. Among other things, the book of Nehemiah refers to intrigues spun by Sanballat, the governor of Samaria. Because of Nehemiah's mission, Sanballat was about to lose a significant part of his province. Thus, in Neh 6:6–7, Sanballat accuses Nehemiah of using prophets to further his own political goal of becoming king. Not only had Nehemiah fortified Jerusalem for the purposes of an

---

* I am indebted to my former UNC colleague Randall Styers for improving the English of this article.

1. The only other known ancient Jewish composition that might be described as exegetical is the work of Aristobulus.

2. See below, 186–89.

anti-Persian rebellion, but he had even sought prophetic endorsement for his claim to kingship.³ Sanballat writes to Nehemiah:

> It is reported among the nations ... that you and the Jews intend to rebel; that is why you are building the wall; and according to this report you wish to become their king. You have also set up prophets to proclaim in Jerusalem concerning you, "There is a king in Judah!" And now it will be reported to the king according to these words. (Neh 6:6–7)⁴

Regardless of whether Nehemiah really asked prophets to proclaim him as king, that Sanballat accuses Nehemiah of such a plot is interesting. For Sanballat, there seems to be no doubt that prophets are willing to be used for the purposes of political intrigue. For the author of Neh 6:1–14, a prophet communicates not the word of God but the word of whoever pays him. The prophetic message is for sale.

Just as Sanballat accused Nehemiah of using prophets for political intrigue, the book of Nehemiah accuses Sanballat of the same thing. According to Neh 6:10–14, when all other measures failed, Sanballat hired a Jerusalem prophet to lure Nehemiah into the inner court of the temple:

> One day when I went into the house of Shemaiah son of Delaiah son of Mehetabel, who was confined to this house, he said: "Let us meet together in the house of God, within the temple, and let us close the doors of the temple, for they are coming to kill you; indeed, tonight they are coming to kill you." But I said, "Should a man like me run away? Would a man like me go into the temple to save his life? I will not go in!" Then I perceived and saw that God had not sent him at all, but he had pronounced the prophecy against me because Tobiah and Sanballat had hired him. He was hired for this purpose, to intimidate me and make me sin by acting in this way, and so they could give me a bad name, in order to taunt me. Remember Tobiah and Sanballat, O my God, according to these things they did, and also the prophetess Noadiah and the rest of the prophets who wanted to make me afraid. (Neh 6:10–14)

As before, prophecy is for hire. In this case, a paid prophet tries to lure Nehemiah into the inner court of the temple reserved for priests. According to Num 18:7, any nonpriest who entered this part of the temple was threatened with capital punishment—including Nehemiah. To frighten Nehemiah into

---

3. For prophetic endorsements of kings in the Iron Age, see 1 Sam 9–10; 1 Kgs 1:32–40; 2 Kgs 9:1–13.

4. If not indicated otherwise, translations of biblical references are taken from the New Revised Standard Version.

this part of the Jerusalem temple would be a murder plot. In this way, a hired prophet participated in a plot to kill Nehemiah.[5]

If Neh 6:1–14 is in any way representative of the attitude toward prophecy in Persian times, we can see that prophecy was not held in high regard. But comparable accusations had been made before. The idea that prophecy is for hire echoes Mic 3:5, 11:

> Thus says the LORD concerning the prophets who led my people astray, who cry "Peace" when they have something to eat, but declare war against those who put nothing into their mouths…. Its rulers give judgment for a bribe, its priests teach for a price, its prophets give oracles for money, yet they lean upon the Lord and say, "Surely the Lord is with us! No harm shall come upon us."

Unlike the time of Micah, the postexilic Jewish literature testimony of aural prophecy is very sparse. Instead, we find an increasing activity of reworking and rewriting prophetic texts. Examples are the late redactions of Jeremiah, Trito-Isaiah, Deutero- and Trito-Zechariah, Mic 4–7, and the book of Joel. Thus to a great extent prophecies composed in postexilic times seem to have been attributed to prophets of the past. In other words, aural prophecy was largely a phenomenon of the past.

The degree to which aural prophecy was disregarded in this period can also be seen in Zech 13:2–6. As part of the eschatological purification, God will not only remove idols and unclean spirits but also prophets:

> On that day, says the Lord of hosts, I will cut off the names of the idols from the land, so that they shall be remembered no more; and also I will remove from the land the prophets and the unclean spirit. (Zech 13:2).

In this eschatological time, even the parents of a prophet will condemn him to death:

> And if any prophets appear again, their fathers and their mothers who bore them will say to them, "You shall not live, for you speak lies in the name of the Lord"; and their fathers and their mothers who bore them shall pierce them through when they prophecy. (Zech 13:3).

---

5. For this interpretation, see H. G. M. Williamson, *Ezra, Nehemiah* (WBC 16; Waco, Tex.: Word, 1985), 258–59 and Joseph Blenkinsopp, *Ezra-Nehemiah: A Commentary* (OTL; Philadelphia: Westminster, 1988), 271.

The latter verse equates prophecy with idolatry and impure demons.[6] The author of Zech 13:2–6 longs for the eschatological eradication of prophecy. In the blessed times of the eschaton, even the parents of a prophet will condemn him to death (Zech 13:3). Without any distinction between true and false prophets, Zech 13:3 claims that prophets speak lies and therefore should be killed. Prophecy seems to be totally condemned. But in contradistinction to its condemnation of prophecy, Zech 13:2–6 contains the highest density of quotations and allusion to prophetic writings in Zech 12–14. Only aural prophecy is condemned in Zech 13:2–6, while written prophecy is highly valued.[7]

To summarize, unlike Iron Age Israel and Judah, in postexilic Judaism aural prophecy is despised and becomes increasingly marginal. Prophecy and prophets are for hire and can be used in political intrigue or for other nefarious purposes. It is not the word of God that is communicated by the prophets of the Persian era but the message of the prophet's employer. Yet unlike the despised aural prophecy, prophetic literature from exilic and preexilic times is highly regarded in the Persian period.

How can this change in the esteem of aural prophecy be understood? Why has God spoken through his prophets in the past but not in Persian times? Why are aural prophets despised in Persian times? These are the questions that a late redactor of the book of Jeremiah tries to answer in Jer 23:33–40.

## 2. Reading Jeremiah in Jeremiah 23:33–40

Jeremiah 23:33–40 is an extension to the collection of Jeremiah's utterances against his prophetic opponents. In Jer 23:33 the redactor responsible for this extension quotes an original word of the prophet Jeremiah: "When this people, or the prophet or a priest ask you, 'What is the burden of the Lord?' you shall say to them, 'you are the burden of the Lord,[8] and I will cast you off, says the

---

6. For the "unclean spirit" of Zech 13:2 as a designation of a demon, see A. Lange, "Considerations Concerning the 'Spirit of Impurity' in Zech 13:2," in *Die Dämonen/Demons: Die Dämonologie der israelitisch-jüdischen und frühchristlichen Literatur im Kontext ihrer Umwelt/The Demonology of Israelite-Jewish and Early Christian Literature in the Context of their Environment* (ed. A. Lange et al.; Tübingen: Mohr Siebeck, 2003), 254–68.

7. For this interpretation of Zech 13:2–6 and the allusions to prophetic literature in this passage, see A. Lange, *Vom prophetischen Wort zur prophetischen Tradition: Studien zur Traditions- und Redaktionsgeschichte innerprophetischer Konflikte in der Hebräischen Bibel* (FAT 34; Tübingen: Mohr Siebeck, 2002), 291–306.

8. את מה משא יהוה is a copying error. The text originally read אתמה משא יהוה. Thus first B. Duhm, *Das Buch Jeremia* (KHC 11; Tübingen: Mohr Siebeck, 1901), 194. Not knowing the special morphology of several biblical and nonbiblical Qumran manuscripts, Duhm proposed to read אתם המשא יהוה, but to read according to the Qumran morphology אתמה is

Lord.' " (Jer 23:33)[9]

Jeremiah's original utterance as well as the question of his opponents are puns playing with the two homonymous nouns משא I and משא II. Jeremiah's opponents play with the two nouns to attack the prophet. While משא II designates the utterance of a prophet, משא I means a burden. Asking Jeremiah what the משא of the Lord would be is thus a sarcastic attack against the very prophet who was forced to preach Judah's doom and utter destruction. To ask this prophet of doom what his burden would be ridicules thus the gist of Jeremiah's message. Jeremiah's answer gives an astounding testimony to his wit. Picking up on the pun of his opponents, he replies: "you are the burden of the Lord."[10]

A redactor of the Persian era[11] recontextualizes this fight between Jeremiah and his opponents with Jeremiah's words against his prophetic opponents. In this context, Jer 23:33 is not concerned with all of Jeremiah's enemies but only with his prophetic opponents. In 23:34–40 the redactor picks up just one element of 23:33, its negative attitude toward the phrase משא יהוה. The redactor is unambiguous: anyone who uses the phrase משא יהוה ("utterance of the Lord") is to be punished: "And as for the prophet, the priest, or the people who say, 'Utterance of the Lord,' I will punish them and their household" (Jer 23:34).

The redactor of the Persian era recommends a different attitude to the problem. Instead of saying "utterance of the Lord," you should ask, "what has the Lord answered?" (23:35) or "what has the Lord said?" (23:37). The phrase "utterance of the Lord" should be reserved for "the man of his word" (23:36) only, meaning the man of God's word. The past tense used in 23:35 and 37 is significant. Our Persian-era redactor does not recommend asking a prophet to inquire Yhwh's answer concerning the present. Apparently, Yhwh has already given his answer in the past.

It is thus not actual aural prophecy Jer 23:33–40 is recommending. On the contrary, one should ask only for prophetic words of old. What is earmarked by the phrase משא יהוה is not aural, but literary prophecy. The true word of

---

a grammatically more correct reading, as the construct משא is already determined by the proper noun יהוה and does not need to have an article prefixed.

9. For a detailed exegesis of Jer 23:33–40 according to the interpretation given here and an extensive discussion of the scholarly literature, see A. Lange, *Vom prophetischen Wort zur prophetischen Tradition*, 278–91.

10. For the homonymy, the different meanings of משא I and משא II, and this interpretation of Jer 23:33, see William McKane, "משא in Jeremiah 23 33–40," in *Prophecy: Essays Presented to Georg Fohrer on His Sixty-Fifth Birthday, 6 September 1980* (ed. J. A. Emerton; BZAW 150; Berlin: de Gruyter, 1980), 35–54, esp. 45–46, 53; and G. Wanke, *Jeremia 1,1–25,14* (vol. 1 of *Jeremia*; ZBK.AT 20.1; Zurich: Theologischer Verlag Zurich, 1995), 218–19.

11. For a Persian time date of Jer 23:33–40, see Lange, *Vom prophetischen Wort zur prophetischen Tradition*, 286–87.

God is to be found not in contemporary prophecy but in prophecy of the past transmitted in written form.

To summarize, Jer 23:34–40 interprets and expands Jer 23:33 by focusing on one aspect of Jeremiah's utterance, the negative attitude toward the phrase משא יהוה. Hermeneutically, this process can be described as atomization. This negative attitude towards the phrase משא יהוה is recontextualized within the collection of Jeremiah's words against his prophetic opponents. In this way, 23:33 acquires a new meaning. משא יהוה refers now to a prophetic "utterance of the Lord." To introduce any speech act with the phrase "utterance of the Lord" is forbidden. Saying "utterance of the Lord" stands thus *pars pro toto* for any act of aural prophecy. Thus aural prophecy as such is forbidden. Instead, one is supposed to seek for Yhwh's will in the prophecies of the past, meaning the written prophetic tradition of Judah.

But not only Jer 23:33 acquires new meaning by being placed into the collection of Jeremiah's word against the prophets. By placing Jer 23:33–40 at the end of this collection, the individual utterances against Jeremiah's prophetic opponents gain a new purpose. For example, Jeremiah's rejection of dream prophecy in Jer 23:25–32, which I believe was originally composed by the Dtr Jeremiah-redaction to attack the prophecies of Zechariah,[12] gains an appendix bolstering prophetic tradition as an appropriate alternative to Zechariah-type dream prophecy. With Jer 23:33–40 affixed at its end, the whole collection of Jeremiah's word against the prophets does not just condemn Jeremiah's prophetic opponents or even later recurrences of prophecy but argues now for the use of (written) prophetic tradition as opposed to aural prophecy.

### 3. Atomization and Recontextualization in the Qumran Pesharim and Ancient Near Eastern Omen Lists

The hermeneutics employed in Jer 23:33–40 are comparable to the hermeneutics of the Qumran pesharim. In Jer 23:33–40, the phrase אתמה משא יהוה "you are the burden of the Lord" is isolated and recontextualized within the context of prophetic conflict and the marginalization of prophecy. By way of this recontextualization, the text assumes a new meaning.

In the same way, the pesharim isolate items out of their biblical lemmata and recontextualize them into the life of the Essene movement.[13] A good

---

12. See Lange, *Vom Prophetischen Wort zur prophetischen Tradition*, 208–24, 261–68.

13. For the interpretative and hermeneutic strategies of the Qumran pesharim, see E. Osswald, "Zur Hermeneutik des Habakuk-Kommentar," *ZAW* 68 (1956): 243–256; Michael Fishbane, "The Qumran Pesher and Traits of Ancient Hermeneutics," in *Proceedings of the Sixth World Congress of Jewish Studies Held at the Hebrew University of Jerusalem 13–-19 August 1973 under the Auspices of*

example is 1QpHab III:2–6. *Pesher Habakkuk* quotes Hab 1:7: "It is dreadful and terrible; his judgment and his exaltation arise from himself." In order to interpret this rather cryptic verse, just one phrase is atomized out of it: "dreadful and terrible." These two words are recontextualized into pesherist's contemporary situation: "Its interpretation concerns the Kittim, the fear and dread of whom are on all the peoples; all their thoughts are premeditated to evil, and with cunning and treachery they behave towards all the nations" (1QpHab III:2–6).

In this context, "dreadful and terrible" refers now to the dread and fear experienced when ancient peoples encountered the Roman armies.[14] The appearance of the Romans heralded the judgment mentioned in the Habakkuk quote. And in the understanding of the pesherist this judgment was eschatological in character. The contemporary Essene situation was thus qualified as a time of eschatological judgment. In this way, atomization and recontextualization gave new meaning to both Hab 1:7 and the present context of the Essene community.

In the Qumran pesharim, this two-way process of reading was clearly inspired by ancient Near Eastern omen interpretation.[15] Even the key interpretative term פשר points in this direction. Besides the interpretation of authoritative literature, in Hebrew and Aramaic Israelite-Jewish literature the root פשר/פתר is used only in the context of the interpretation of dreams and the interpretation of other omina (see e.g., Gen 40:5, 8, 12, 16, 18, 22; 41:8, 11–13, 15).[16] This use of the root פשר/פתר agrees with the use of the

---

the *Israel Academy of Sciences and Humanities*, vol. 1: *Division A* (Jerusalem: World Union of Jewish Studies, 1977), 97–114, 98–100.

14. For "Kittim" as a cipher for the Romans in Qumran literature, see, e.g., T.H. Lim, "Kittim," in *Encyclopedia of the Dead Sea Scrolls* (ed. L. H. Schiffman and J. C. VanderKam; 2 vols.; Oxford: Oxford University Press, 2000), 1:469–71, 470.

15. For the pesharim and ancient Near Eastern omen interpretation, see L. H. Silbermann, "Unriddling the Riddle: A Study in the Scripture and Language of the Habakkuk Pesher" (1 Q p Hab)," *RevQ 3* (1961–62): 323–64, esp. 330–35; Asher Finkel, "The Pesher of Dreams and Scriptures," *RevQ 4* (1963–64) 357–70; I. Rabinowitz, "Pesher/Pittaron: Its Biblical Meaning and Its Significance in the Qumran Literature," *RevQ 8* (1972–75): 219–32, esp. 230–32; M. Fishbane, "Qumran Pesher," 97–114.

16. In Sir 38:14, a physician's diagnosis is called פשרה, but according to Sir 38:14 the success of a physician's diagnosis depends on a prayer. Therefore, in Sir 38:14 the use of פשרה links the diagnosis to God. In this way, Ben Sira makes pagan diagnostic medicine more acceptable for a Jewish audience (for the aim of Sir 38:1–15, see also Patrick W. Skehan and Alexander A. Di Lella, *The Wisdom of Ben Sira: A New Translation with Introduction* [AB 39; New York: Doubleday, 1987], 441–43). In Qoh 8:1 פשר is part of a gloss and carries the meaning "interpretation" (see A. Lauha, *Kohelet* [BKAT 19; Neukirchen-Vluyn: Neukirchener, 1978], 144.).

Akkadian lexeme *pašāru*, which also occurs in the context of dream interpretation (although it carries other meanings as well).[17]

In ancient Near Eastern omen interpretations we see the same hermeneutics of atomization and recontextualization that are applied in the Qumran pesharim.[18] A good example is a passage in the so-called Demotic Dream Interpretation (pap. XIV a 2–4).[19]

> When he drinks sweet beer, he becomes happy.
> When he drinks baker's beer, [he] becomes alive.
> When he drinks lager beer, [it means] salvation for him.

Typical for omen interpretation, each line consists of a protasis that summarizes the omen (e.g., "when he drinks sweet beer") and an apodosis that interprets the omen (e.g., "he becomes happy"). From the range of symbols provided by the dream, one symbol is picked (e.g., sweetness) and recontextualized into the life of the dreamer (e.g., "he becomes happy"). The actual act of omen interpretation thus happens when the omen is recontextualized within the life of the omen recipient.

---

17. For the meaning of *pašāru*, see A. L. Oppenheim, *The Interpretation of Dreams in the Ancient Near East: With a Translation of an Assyrian Dream-Book* (Transactions of the American Philosophical Society 46/3; Philadelphia: American Philosophical Society, 1956), 219.

18. To my knowledge, from the pre-Hellenistic ancient Near East only one commentary in the strict sense is preserved, i.e., Cyrus H. Gordon, *Smith College Tablets* (Smith College Studies in History 38; Northampton, Mass.: Department of History of Smith College, 1952), no. 110 (see A. Livingstone, *Mystical and Mythological Explanatory Works of Assyrian and Babylonian Scholars* [Oxford, Clarendon, 1986], 2; for text and translation of this commentary and a brief exposition, see 64–66). Regrettably, not enough text is preserved from this tablet to identify which text is commented upon and which hermeneutical techniques are employed. The Akkadian word *mu-bar-ru-ú* for "commentary" used in reverse line 4 of the tablet reminds of the words *bārû(m)* ("diviner") and *barû(m)* ("to see, to look"). Therefore, it appears possible that in Mesopotamian literature commentary hermeneutics were also related to omen interpretation. From Hellenistic Egypt another commentary called the Demotic Chronicle is preserved. Its interpretative techniques and hermeneutics are close to the pesharim. For the Demotic Chronicle, see W. Spiegelberg, *Die sogenannte Demotische Chronik: Pap. 215 der Bibliothèque Nationale zu Paris nebst den auf der Rückseite des Papyrus stehenden Texten* (Leipzig: Hinrichs, 1914); A. B. Lloyd, "Nationalist Propaganda in Ptolemaic Egypt," *Historia* 31 (1982): 33–55, esp. 41–45; F. Daumas, Littérature prophétique et exégétique égyptienne et commentaires esséniens, in *A la recontre de Dieu: Mémorial Albert Gélin* (ed. A. Baruq et al.; Bibliothèque de la Faculté Catholique de Théologie de Lyon 8; Le Puy: Mappus, 1961), 203–21, 203–11.

19. For the Demotic text and a German translation, see A. Volten, *Demotische Traumdeutung (Pap. Carlsberg XIII und XIV verso)* (Analecta Aegyptica 3; Kopenhagen: Munksgaard, 1942), 90–91. The English translation provided above is produced from the German translation of Volten's edition.

Not only the hermeneutics of atomization and recontextualization but also the structure of protasis and apodosis can be observed in the Qumran pesharim. In 1QpHab III:2–6, the quote of Hab 1:7 is analogous to the protasis of an omen list, while its interpretation corresponds to the omen list's apodosis. This close relation between ancient Near Eastern omen interpretation and pesher hermeneutics demonstrates that scriptural interpretation was an act of revelation for the pesherist.[20] This conclusion is even confirmed by the claim that God revealed the meaning of the prophetic books to the Teacher of Righteousness (see 1QpHab II:7–10; VII:3–4).

### 4. Reading the Present in Jeremiah 23:33–40

A comparison of the interpretative techniques and hermeneutics of Jer 23:33–40, 1QpHab III:2–6, and Pap. Carlsberg XIV a 2–4 shows that all three texts proceed in the same way. One element is isolated and then recontextualized to gain new meaning.

|  | Elements Isolated | New Context | Interpretation of the New Context |
|---|---|---|---|
| Pap. Carlsberg XIV a 2–4 | sweetness | life of dreamer | happiness |
| 1QpHab III:2–6 | dreadful and terrible | Roman threat | eschatological judgment is close |
| Jer 23:33–40 | utterance of the LORD | Jeremiah's word against his prophetic opponent | God commands use of Judah's prophetic tradition |

However, is the recontextualization of Jeremiah's prophetic utterance (Jer 23:33) into the context of Jeremiah's words against his prophetic opponents (Jer 23:9–32) the only recontextualization to be observed in Jer 23:33–40? In other words, is the interpretative interest of the Persian-era redactor responsible for Jer 23:33–40 directed only toward a better understanding of Jeremiah's prophecy? Or, as in the Qumran pesharim, is it also aimed at a better understanding of the redactor's own contemporary situation?

---

20. See A. Lange, "Interpretation als Offenbarung: Zum Verhältnis von Schriftauslegung und Offenbarung in apokalyptischer und nichtapokalyptischer Literatur" in *Wisdom and Apocalypticism in the Dead Sea Scrolls and in the Biblical Tradition* (ed. F. García Martínez; BETL 168; Leuven: Leuven University Press/Peeters, 2003), 17–33.

As argued above, in the Persian period we can observe a decline and marginalization of aural prophecy. Although there seem to be hints of later prophetic activities,[21] aural prophecy never recovered from this decline to its preexilic prominence. In Hellenistic times, 1 Macc 9:27 even refers to a distant past as "the days the prophets ceased to be seen among them." Regardless of how late the Persian-era redaction of Jer 23:33–40 is to be dated, marginalization and decline of aural prophecy were a part of the redactor's reality. According to the testimony of the redactions of prophetic books in the Hebrew Bible, the Persian-era redactor of Jer 23:33–40 would have encounter the phrase משא יהוה ("utterance of the Lord") repeatedly in the headings of prophetic collections (Isa 13:1; 15:1; 17:1; 19:1; 21:1, 11, 13; 22:1; 23:1; Nah 1:1; Hab 1:1; Zech 9:1; Mal 1:1). Most of these headings seem to have been added by postexilic redactors.

For the redactor of Jer 23:33–40, Jeremiah's rejection of his prophetic opponents and his rejection of the use of the phrase משא יהוה as well as the prominent function of the phrase משא יהוה in prophetic tradition explain the decline of aural prophecy and the reorientation toward older prophetic tradition in his own time. True, authoritative aural prophecy is a phenomenon of the past. The decline of aural prophecy is God's will. Those who wish to enquire concerning God's will need to study the prophetic traditions preserving past prophecies. Jer 23:33–40 attests to a dual process of atomization and recontextualization. משא יהוה is isolated not only from the original Jeremianic utterance but also from the contemporary reality of the redactor of Jer 23:33–40. And משא יהוה is recontextualized not only with the collection of Jeremiah's words against his prophetic opponents but also with the redactor's experience of prophecy. Alongside this dual process of atomization and recontextualization, a parallel process of interpretation is taking place. The redactor of Jer 23:33–40 interprets not only Jeremiah's utterance but also his own contemporary experience of the decline of prophecy. Just as in the pesharim, in this dialectic process both the redactor's contemporary situation and Jer 23:33–40 gain new meaning.

This creation of new meaning can be described as an act of prophecy in itself.[22] Since it is concerned with the understanding and enlargement of written prophetic tradition, this approach is described as literary prophecy ("Schriftprophetie").[23] The act of redactional enlargement of a prophetic book can thus be understood as an act of prophecy in its own right. This seems all the more

---

21. See, e.g., the hope for the coming of a prophet mentioned in 1 Macc 4:46 and 14:41.
22. See O. H. Steck, *Die Prophetenbücher und ihr theologisches Zeugnis: Wege der Nachfrage und Fährten zur Antwort* (Tübingen: Mohr Siebeck, 1996), 166–86.
23. See e.g., the book of Steck quoted in note 21.

appropriate, since the analysis above has shown that literary prophecy employs hermeneutical strategies developed in ancient Near Eastern omen interpretation.

## 5. Conclusions

A comparison of Jer 23:33–40 with the Qumran pesharim shows that the same hermeneutics are employed in Jer 23:33–40 and the pesharim. Hermeneutically speaking, what can be observed in Jer 23:33–40 is a double process of atomization and recontextualization. It is not only out of the prophetic utterance documented in Jer 23:33 that the Persian-era redactor isolates the phrase משא יהוה. He also isolates the phrase משא יהוה out of his own encounters of prophecy. In combining Jeremiah's utterance with the collection of Jeremiah's words against the prophets (Jer 23:9–32) and with the redactor's experience with his own contemporary experience (the use of משא יהוה in the headings of prophetic collections and the decline of prophecy), two interpretative processes are taking place. On the one hand, the redactor of Jer 23:33–40 attains a new understanding of 23:33 and a new understanding of the whole collection of Jeremiah's word against the prophets. On the other hand, he determines the meaning of the decline of prophecy in his own contemporary reality.

This case study has shown how pesher-hermeneutics were employed in a particular passage of the book of Jeremiah and how the understanding of pesher hermeneutics might illuminate the mechanisms of literary prophecy. But the limited scope of the present study urges for caution in generalizing its results. At best, the comparison between Jer 23:33–40 and the Qumran pesharim unearths one of many likely hermeneutical strategies at work in literary prophecy.

# CONCLUSIONS

# READING THE PAST, THE PRESENT, AND THE FUTURE IN THE HEBREW BIBLE AND THE DEAD SEA SCROLLS

*Kristin De Troyer*

How was the present interpreted by means of reading the (biblical) text? That was the question that we, Armin Lange and I, posed to the contributors to the Dead Sea Scrolls and Hebrew Bible Seminar at the International Meeting of the Society of Biblical Literature in Cambridge, 2003. We explained that we were not interested in an analysis of methods of biblical interpretation or applications thereof but in how the present was reread using authoritative literature.

The issue, we thought, would benefit from a hermeneutical introduction. And hence, we asked Christine Helmer (Harvard) to offer her thoughts on the possibility and issues related with reading the present.

Christine Helmer concluded her introductory contribution with a reference to the imagery of "eating a scroll" (Ezek 3). She wrote that "eating the scroll" transforms the prophet's present reality by making the scroll's contents its own "reality." The issue of transforming a biblical text immediately raised questions regarding the truth of the text and the academic ways of dealing with the text, which were sometimes in conflict with the Protestant doctrines on the inspiration of the text.

Helmer went on to historically describe the two claims, while at the same time systematically clarifying the conceptual problems related to the issue of truth. She showed how these claims, that regard the Bible as the "books of all books" or as any other book, can be rendered according to various ascriptions of truth and how the question "Is it true?" is related to the question "Is it true for me and for us?" Helmer turned first to the ascription to the Bible its historical truth value as the foundational document of particular religious traditions, then to the ascription to the Bible as text, its transparency both to an objective reality "behind" it that constitutes the religious tradition as such and to the subjective construals of that reality from diverse perspectives "in front of" the text. She concluded with the ascription to the Bible its spiritual value.

She, in the footsteps of Schleiermacher, convincingly argued that the religious significance of a biblical text can only be taken seriously if it is accompanied by a study of its historical embeddedness. Moreover, she showed that the transhistorical sense of the Bible leads to a dialogical engagement with other individuals who reread the text in light of their own experiences. Finally, she described how the biblical text engages the reader in a different sort of experience, namely one in which the Bible transforms the truth when physically embodied. In this context, Helmer systematically explored the predication of life to the divine word's agency and created a new conceptual paradigm for determining the relation between "word" and "life" using the concept of the eating of the scroll. The opening contribution by Helmer thus set the stage for a fruitful reflection on reading the present in the Hebrew Bible and the Dead Sea Scrolls by means of scriptural interpretation.

In her contribution, Jutta Jokiranta looked at pesharim in order to see how the authors of the pesharim perceived their reality and how Scripture colored their reality. Jokiranta also correctly pointed to the possible impossibility of the theme of this volume: how can one reconstruct using their texts the manner in which authors used Scripture to interpret their present if the texts are all we had to reconstruct the present of the author of the texts. This is precisely problematic in the case of the pesharim, for they are texts that aim at actualizing or applying (prophetic) texts. Focusing on the questions on who the enemies and the wicked figure are, Jokiranta stated that pesharim are a two-way mirror: they not only read the past as a report of community events but also offer a view on the identity of the community. *Pesher Habakkuk,* for instance, also creates by identifying the enemies and defining the traitors a positive reevaluation of the Qumran group, strengthening its social identity.

Schiffman, like Jokiranta, started his contribution with a statement about the prophetic texts, namely, that the words of the Hebrew Bible prophets were of direct relevance to the period of the later exegetes. He claimed that a similar phenomenon can be observed in legal, halakic exegesis.

Schiffman took the *Temple Scroll* as a first example and showed how the author used the tabernacle and desert camp texts to create a "modern" ideal plan for a Jewish temple. Schiffman not only demonstrated how the author used established ways of interpretation in combination with architectural data, but also how the plan of the ideal temple was brought "up to code," namely the halakic code of those days. The author smartly does so by differentiating between the different sorts of "camps" and by moving it from the Sinai Desert to the city of Jerusalem. The author also updates the appointment and job-description of the king.

In his second example, Schiffman tackled the *Damascus Document,* a text in which the contemporizing halakic exegesis occurs in a polemical context. Schiffman proves that in CD 4:12–17 the contemporizing aspect lies not so much in any outright allusions to the author's own period but in the selection of the halakic points of dispute and claims, true or false, by the Qumran text that render the author's interpretation of the law as necessarily correct. Schiffman then offered some examples from the *Damascus Document* that show how in a halakic dispute new arguments, even unfit ones, were selected to underline new rulings. It is precisely in this context that the categories of revealed and hidden law are used—the hidden law being only known to insiders. The system of supplementing the written Torah thus allowed the insiders to deviate from up until then divinely inspired biblical legal interpretation.

Lutz Doering studied the Diaspora letters allegedly issued by Jeremiah or Baruch, taking the correspondence of Jeremiah (MT Jer 29, OG 36) as a starting point. He wondered whether these letters viewed their implied addressees as living in an ongoing exile or at least in a situation analogous to it. He stated that the almost contradictory text of Jer 29, which on the one hand calls for a long exile and on the other hand promises a return after seventy years, asks for a long history of reception and rewriting. Doering then traced this history of reception and rewriting. He took the readers on a tour, visiting the Epistle of Jeremiah, *Targum Jonathan*, the Letter of Baruch, the *Paralipomena Jeremiae*, 4QApocryphon of Jeremiah C, and finally, the book of Baruch.

He showed how the Epistle of Jeremiah fleshes out how a long stay among the Babylonians would look like and how idolatry can be avoided—an issue that was indeed still at stake in third–second century B.C.E. Likewise, a letter by Jeremiah incorporated in *Targum Jonathan* on Jer 10:11 admonishes the readers to stay at God's side. Doering showed how in the Letter of Baruch the events of 70 C.E. are being read with the stories of the destruction of the temple in 587 B.C.E. in mind. According to Doering, the author integrated the addressees into the present of the exilic letter by carefully balancing imperfect and perfect tenses and using temporal markers. From his analysis of 4QApocryphon of Jeremiah C, recounting some form of written communication between Jeremiah from Egypt and the Babylonian Golah, it became clear that the circles responsible for this text indeed considered an ongoing exile as their predicament. The book of Baruch itself is significantly inspired by the Jeremianic communication between Jerusalem and Babylon.

All these texts thus show how different (groups of) people read their present in the Scriptures. The texts that dealt with the exilic situation were experienced as dealing with the present Golah situation of the readers of the texts.

George J. Brooke asked how people who joined the Qumran community justified their transition to themselves and to others. Brooke labeled the movement made to join the community of Qumran a "conversion." He then studied the process of conversion using the work of Lewis Rambo (*Understanding Reli-*

*gious Conversion*) and the seven-stage framework proposed by John Lofland and Rodney Stark ("Becoming a World-Saver"). According to the latter, "Converts must (1) experience enduring, acutely felt tensions (2) within a religious problem-solving perspective (3) that leads them to define themselves as religious seekers, (4) encountering the new group at a turning point in their lives, (5) wherein an affective bond is formed with one or more converts (6) where extracult attachments are absent or neutralized (7) and where, if they are to become deployable agents, they are exposed to intensive interaction"[1]

Brooke not only verified the theories of conversion but focused on the place of Scripture in all the stages of the conversion process. He definitively proved that for the members of the Qumran community, Scripture justified their deviant life(style) and "endorsed a particular reading of present experience."

The theme of this volume is also nicely dealt with by Loren T. Stuckenbruck, who looked at how sacred history has been turned into an eschatological future in the Animal Apocalypse. More precisely, he studied the predicament of the antediluvian patriarch Enoch and examined how it functioned as a parallel to the crisis years of the Maccabean revolt. Contrary to the antediluvian story, the Animal Apocalypse shows traces of a positive view on the future—one could say that divine intervention has already manifested itself in the present.

Stuckenbruck then explored a question that in a sense Jokiranta in her contribution also has raised "Which 'present' should be taken as a point of departure for our study?" With regard to the Animal Apocalypse, the answer to this question is rather complex, for the document itself already contains two "presents." There is the present of the young unmarried Enoch who narrates his visions and his reactions to them, and there is the present of the much older Enoch who briefs his son Methuselah on what he saw. Moreover, when it comes to identifying the "real" present of the author, Stuckenbruck analyzed *1 En.* 90:6–19 with its allusions to the activities of Judas Maccabeus. The author also offers a view on the present of the readers; more precisely, he points to the distinctions between the group of Judas and the author's present Enochic community.

In the opening section of her contribution, Ulrike Mittmann-Richert developed the hermeneutical problem, as posed by Christine Helmer, and applied it to the book of Daniel. She wondered why a most peaceful time like the one of Simon (142–135/4 B.C.E.) was not interpreted as the fulfillment of eschatological expectations. The subject of unfulfilled prophecy is a fascinating subject, given the fact that there is the religious credo that Scripture cannot be false. Mittmann-Richert analyzed the Additions to the book of Daniel. She demonstrated not only that the Additions thematically belong together but also

---

1. See the contribution of Brooke in this volume.

that they grew out of the transformation of the Daniel tradition. The author of the Additions transformed Daniel's prophecy by making Daniel part of the earlier prophecies, thus adding him to the past. At the same time, the author adapted the story to the present times using creation motifs. Daniel was not just saved by God but was also granted everlasting peace. This eschatological Daniel picture gave hope to Israel—an attitude most fitting in the peaceful times of Simon. Mittmann-Richert went on to make this eschatological picture more complete. She showed how the Additions to the book of Daniel reveal a renewed vision on the relationship between God and the Jewish people, culminating in a vision of God in the holy temple, and thus, how they justify and interpret the rededication of the temple by Judas Maccabeus.

Sidnie White Crawford took on the best-seller of the Qumran community: the book of Deuteronomy. Describing the Deuteronomy manuscripts from Qumran as well as their use in the liturgical scrolls and the study books, she first demonstrated that Deuteronomy was indeed a popular book and, thus, that this book served primarily for reading and interpreting the present of the members of the Qumran community. She added an important note on the two proto-Samaritan Deuteronomy texts, claiming that the authoritative character of even these texts in the period prior to the fall of the Second Temple should not be doubted.

Then Crawford turned to the texts that have rewritten (portions of) the book of Deuteronomy, namely, 4QReworked Pentateuch and the *Temple Scroll*. She wrote that the manuscripts of 4QReworked Pentateuch present themselves as Torah scrolls and, thus, that its author wanted the readers to consider this text as authoritative. Crawford, however, also pointed to the in comparison with Deuteronomy new material in 4QReworked Pentateuch as a possible source for questioning the authority of the text. In her analysis of the *Temple Scroll* she focused on the techniques that its author applied when reusing the book of Deuteronomy. Crawford labeled the author a "redactor/composer." Indeed, what this scribe did was to take the book of Deuteronomy as a basis but to interweave it with, on the one hand, material from other parts of the Torah or other parts of the (what was later called) Hebrew Bible and from other sources, and, on the other hand, exegetical comments. Crawford clearly demonstrated that for the members of the community of Qumran, *their present could not be read or interpreted without the book of Deuteronomy.*

Kristin De Troyer worked on the book of Joshua. She noted that the text about erecting the altar and reading the law in Josh 8:30–35 had been moved to different positions in the Greek text of Joshua and 4QJosh$^a$. In her threefold analysis of this section of the story of Joshua (MT Josh 8:30–35; OG Joshua "post 9:2," and 4QJosh$^a$ "post chapter 4") she focused on the figure of Moses, the reinterpretation of Deut 27, and the precise location of the altar. She demonstrated that the text of Josh 8:30–35 was reused in order to fit the experiences of the Qumran community and to interpret their present. De Troyer came to the same conclusion as Stuckenbruck did in his analysis of the Animal Apocalypse, namely, that the members of the Qumran community saw themselves as distinct from the Hasmoneans. Moreover, in their self-description, the members of the Qumran community automatically attached the blessings uttered in Deut 27 to themselves, leaving the curses to the lot of Beliah, their opponents. The members of the community of Qumran no longer allowed themselves to be on Mount Ebal, the mountain of the curses, let alone to build an altar on it.

Beate Ego studied the texts of Ezek 33:23–34; Isa 51:1–3; 63:15–16; and Neh 9:7–8. According to Ego, these texts offer views on how the exile was experienced. Moreover, in her analysis Ego demonstrated how already-existing Abraham traditions were over and over again changed and developed in order to fit the new "presents" of the "narrating communities." In the text of Ezek 33, Abraham is seen as a symbol of the hope for the possession of the land. The figure of Abraham (and Sarah) also plays a crucial role in the context of the problems with the destruction of the temple and the devastating desolation of the land as described in Isa 51. In this text the Abraham tradition is connected with the hope of the restitution of Zion and God's "wonderful might to create new life." Then Ego showed how the Abraham tradition, and especially its element of hope, was rejected in the lament regarding the destruction of the temple in Isa 63. Finally, Ego surprisingly dealt with Neh 9:7–8, a text that postdates the exile. She demonstrated, however, that the text still deals with the exilic experience. In it Abraham again plays a pivotal role. His life is aptly described. In this description, one expression stands out "you found his heart faithful before you." Ego's analysis showed that this expression should be read in the line of Gen 15:6. The addition of this expression can be seen as an attempt to actualize the Abraham tradition, instructing the people how to behave in order to be found worthy to live in the land as free people.

In his analysis of Neh 6:1–14, Lange first showed that prophecy was no longer in high esteem in the Persian period but, to the contrary, was deemed to be for sale and for hire. On top of that, aural prophecy became very sparse in this period, whereas reworking and rewriting of prophetic texts seemed a blooming activity, leading to the conclusion that aural prophecy was seen as a phenomenon of the past. Stronger, Zech 13:2–6 longs for the eschatological removal of prophets and prophecy as part of the eschatological purification.

The author of Jer 23:33–40, which according to Lange dates to the Persian period, then addressed the issue of the decline of prophecy, applying a different perspective and attitude. One was no longer to ask a prophet to inquire an answer from God regarding the present situation but to consider that the answer had already been given in the past (Jer 23:33). Instead of aural prophecy, one needed thus turn to literary prophetic tradition to inquire about one's own present. Literary prophetic tradition thus acquired the role of aural prophecy.

Lange then turned to the hermeneutics applied in the Qumran pesharim and compared them with the hermeneutics of Jer 23:33–40. Like the author of Jer 33:33–40, "the pesharim isolate items out of their biblical lemmata and recontextualize them into the life of the Essene movement."[2] To understand the decline of aural prophecy, the author of Jer 23:33–40 thus applied the same hermeneutics to the Jeremiah tradition as the pesharim do. Therefore, Lange concludes cautiously, "the understanding of pesher hermeneutics might illuminate the mechanisms of literary prophecy."

As the seminar came to its conclusion, the contributors realized that indeed authoritative literature had become the means by which the present was interpreted in texts of the Hebrew Bible and ancient Jewish literature. In conclusion, Qumran texts document a hermeneutics of appropriating the present by way of scriptural interpretation. Comparison with both biblical literature (Ego and Lange) as well as ancient Jewish literature shows that the hermeneutics of reading the present that can be observed in the Qumran pesharim are widespread. They already can be found in texts from the exilic and Persian times and are popular in ancient Jewish literature from Hellenistic and later times as well. The Qumran literature thus helps one better to understand Jewish hermeneutics.

The organizers of the seminar hope to have achieved a double goal. First, we hope that this volume has given insight in how the present of, for instance, the members of the Qumran community was interpreted by means of authoritative literature. Second, we hope that this volume has demonstrated that reading the present can lead to a vital future.

---

2. See the contribution by Armin Lange.

# BIBLIOGRAPHY

Abegg, Martin G., Jr. "Exile and the Dead Sea Scrolls." Pages 111–25 in *Exile: Old Testament, Jewish, and Christian Conceptions*. Edited by James M. Scott. JSJSup 56. Leiden: Brill, 1997.

Abraham, William J. *Canon and Criterion in Christian Theology: From the Fathers to Feminism*. Oxford: Clarendon, 1998.

Albertz, Rainer. *Die Exilszeit (6. Jahrhundert)*. Biblische Enzyklopädie 7. Stuttgart: Kohlhammer, 2001.

———. *Israel in Exile: The History and Literature of the Sixth Century* B.C.E. Translated by David Green. SBLSBL 3. Atlanta: Society of Biblical Literature, 2003.

Allegro, John M. *Qumran Cave 4.I (4Q158–4Q186)*. DJD 5. Oxford: Clarendon, 1968.

Applegate, John. "Jeremiah and the Seventy Years in the Hebrew Bible: Inner-Biblical Reflections on the Prophet and His Prophecy." Pages 91–110 in *The Book of Jeremiah and Its Reception /Le livre de Jérémie et sa réception*. Edited by Adrian H. W. Curtis and Thomas Römer. BETL 128. Leuven: Leuven University Press, 1997.

Baumgarten, Joseph M. *Qumran Cave 4.XIII: The Damascus Document (4Q266–273)*. DJD 18. Oxford: Clarendon, 1996.

———. "Theological Elements in the Formulation of Qumran Law." Pages 33–41 in *Emanuel: Studies in Hebrew Bible, Septuagint, and Dead Sea Scrolls in Honor of Emanuel Tov*. Edited by Shalom M. Paul, Robert A. Kraft, Lawrence H. Schiffman, and Weston W. Fields. VTSup 94. Leiden: Brill, 2003.

———. "Yom Kippur in the Qumran Scrolls and Second Temple Sources." *DSD* 6 (1999): 184–91.

Bayer, Oswald. *Das Leibliche Wort: Reformation und Neuzeit im Konflikt*. Tübingen: Mohr Siebeck, 1992.

Bengtsson, Håkan. *What's in a Name? A Study of Sobriquets in the Pesharim*. Uppsala: Uppsala University Press, 2000.

Berger, Peter L. *The Heretical Imperative*. Garden City, N.Y.: Doubleday, 1979.

Bernstein, Moshe J. "Pseudepigraphy in the Qumran Scrolls: Categories and Functions." Pages 1–26 in *Pseudepigraphic Perspectives: The Apocrypha and Pseudepigrapha in Light of the Dead Sea Scrolls: Proceedings of the International Symposium of the Orion Center for the Study of the Dead Sea Scrolls and Associated Literature, 12–14 January 1997*. Edited by Esther G. Chazon, Michael Stone, and Avital Pinnick. STDJ 31. Leiden: Brill, 1999.

Berrin, Shani L. "Pesharim." Pages 644–47 in vol. 2 of *Encyclopedia of the Dead Sea Scrolls*. Edited by Lawrence H. Schiffman and James C. VanderKam. Oxford: Oxford University Press, 2000.

Bickermann, Elias. *Der Gott der Makkabäer: Untersuchungen über Sinn und Ursprung der makkabäischen Erhebung*. Berlin: Schocken/Jüdischer Buchverlag, 1937.

———. *The Jews in the Greek Age*. Cambridge: Harvard University Press, 1988.

Blenkinsopp, Joseph. *Ezra-Nehemiah: A Commentary*. OTL. Westminster: Philadelphia, 1988.

Blum, Erhard. *Die Komposition der Vätergeschichte*. WMANT 57. Neukirchen-Vluyn: Neukirchener, 1984.

Boda, Mark J. *Praying the Tradition: The Origin and Use of Tradition in Neh 9*. BZAW 277. Berlin: de Gruyter, 1999.

Bogaert, Pierre-Maurice. *Apocalypse de Baruch: Introduction, traduction du syriaque et commentaire*. 2 vols. SC 144–45. Paris: Cerf, 1969.

Brooke, George J. "Deuteronomy 5–6 in the Phylacteries from Qumran Cave 4." Pages 57–70 in *Emanuel: Studies in Hebrew Bible, Septuagint, and Dead Sea Scrolls in Honor of Emanuel Tov*. Edited by Shalom M. Paul, Robert A. Kraft, Lawrence H. Schiffman, and Weston W. Fields. VTSup 94. Leiden: Brill, 2003.

———. "*E pluribus unum:* Textual Variety and Definitive Interpretation in the Qumran Scrolls." Pages 107–19 in *The Dead Sea Scrolls in Their Historical Context*. Edited by Timothy H. Lim with Larry W. Hurtado, A. Graeme Auld and Alison Jack. Edinburgh: T&T Clark, 2000.

———. *Exegesis at Qumran. 4QFlorilegium in Its Jewish Context*. Edited by David J. A. Clines and Philip R. Davies. JSOTSup 29. Sheffield: Sheffield Academic Press, 1985.

———. "Isaiah in the Pesharim and Other Qumran Texts." Pages 609–32 in *Writing and Reading the Scroll of Isaiah: Studies of an Interpretive Tradition*. Edited by Craig C. Broyles and Craig A. Evans. VTSup 70. Leiden: Brill, 1997.

———. "The Kittim in the Qumran Pesharim." Pages 135–59 in *Images of Empire*. Edited by Loveday Alexander. JSOTSup 122. Sheffield: Sheffield Academic Press, 1991.

———. "Miqdash Adam, Eden and the Qumran Community." Pages 285–301 in *Gemeinde ohne Tempel—Community without Temple: Zur Substituierung und Transformation des Jerusalemer Tempels und seines Kultes im Alten Testament, antiken Judentum und frühen Christentum*. Edited by Beate Ego, Armin Lange, and Peter Pilhofer. WUNT 118. Tübingen: Mohr Siebeck, 1999.

———. "The Pesharim and the Origins of the Dead Sea Scrolls." Pages 339–53 in *Methods of Investigation of the Dead Sea Scrolls and the Khirbet Qumran Site: Present Realities and Future Prospects*. Edited by Michael O. Wise et al. New York: New York Academy of Sciences, 1994.

Brooke, George J., et al. *Qumran Cave 4.XVII: Parabiblical Texts, Part 3*. DJD 22. Oxford: Clarendon, 1996.

Brownlee, William H. *The Midrash Pesher of Habakkuk*. SBLMS 24. Missoula, Mont.: Scholars Press, 1979.

Bryan, David J. "Exile and Return from [sic] Jerusalem." Pages 60–80 in *Apocalyptic in History and Tradition*. Edited by Christopher Rowland and John Barton. JSPSup 43. London: Sheffield Academic Press, 2002.

Burrows, Millar ed., with the assistance of John C. Trever and William H. Brownlee. *Isaiah Manuscript and the Habakkuk Commentary*. Vol. 1 of *The Dead Sea Scrolls of St. Mark's Monastery*. New Haven: American Schools of Oriental Research, 1950.

Busto Saiz, José R. "La interpretation del relato de Susanna." *EstEcl* 57 (1982): 421–28.

Callaway, Phillip R. *The History of the Qumran Community: An Investigation*. JSPSup 3. Sheffield: Sheffield Academic Press, 1988.

Campbell, Jonathan G. "Essene-Qumran Origins in the Exile: A Scriptural Basis." *JJS* 46 (1995): 143–56.

Capper, Brian J. "The Palestinian Cultural Context of the Earliest Christian Community of Goods." Pages 323–56 in *The Book of Acts in Its Palestinian Setting*. Edited by Richard J. Bauckham. The Book of Acts in Its First Century Setting 4. Grand Rapids: Eerdmans, 1995.

Carroll, Robert P. *The Book of Jeremiah: A Commentary*. OTL. London: SCM, 1986.

Charlesworth, James H. *The Pesharim and Qumran History: Chaos or Consensus?* Grand Rapids: Eerdmans, 2002.

Chazon, Esther G. "Hymns and Prayers in the Dead Sea Scrolls." Pages 244–70 in vol. 1 of *The Dead Sea Scrolls after Fifty Years: A Comprehensive Assessment*. Edited by Peter W. Flint and James C. VanderKam. 2 vols. Leiden: Brill, 1998.

Childs, Bernard S. *Biblical Theology of the Old and New Testaments: Reflections on the Christian Bible*. Minneapolis: Fortress, 1997.

Churgin, Pinkhos. *Targum Jonathan to the Prophets*. Yale Oriental Series, Researches 14. New Haven: Yale University Press, 1927.

Cohen, Shaye J. D. *The Beginnings of Jewishness: Boundaries, Varieties, Uncertainties*. Hellenistic Culture and Society 31. Berkeley and Los Angeles: University of California Press, 1999.

Collins, John J. *The Apocalyptic Imagination: An Introduction to Jewish Apocalyptic Literature*. 2nd ed. Grand Rapids: Eerdmans, 1998.

———. *Daniel. A Commentary on the Book of Daniel*. Hermeneia. Minneapolis: Fortress, 1993.

———. "Forms of Community in the Dead Sea Scrolls." Pages 97–111 in *Emanuel: Studies in Hebrew Bible, Septuagint, and Dead Sea Scrolls in Honor of Emanuel Tov*. Edited by Shalom M. Paul et al. VTSup 94. Leiden: Brill, 2003.

Crawford, Sidnie White. "4QDeutn." Pages 117–28 in Eugene Ulrich et al., *Qumran Cave 4.IX: Deuteronomy, Joshua, Judges, Kings*. DJD 14. Oxford: Clarendon, 1995.

———. *The Temple Scroll and Related Texts*. Sheffield: Sheffield Academic Press, 2000.

———. "Three Fragments from Qumran Cave 4 and Their Relationship to the 'Temple Scroll.'" *JQR* 85 (1994): 259–73.

Daumas, F. "Littérature prophétique et exégétique égyptienne et commentaires esséniens." Pages 203–21 in *A la rencontre de Dieu: Mémorial Albert Gélin*. Edited by A. Baruq et al. Bibliothèque de la Faculté Catholique de Théologie de Lyon 8. Le Puy: Mappus, 1961.

Davies, Philip R. *Behind the Essenes: History and Ideology in the Dead Sea Scrolls.* BJS 94. Atlanta: Scholars Press, 1987.
Delling, Gerhard. *Jüdische Lehre und Frömmigkeit in den Paralipomena Jeremiae.* BZAW 100. Berlin: de Gruyter, 1967.
De Troyer, Kristin. "Did Joshua Have a Crystal Ball? The Old Greek and the MT of Joshua 10:15, 17 and 23." Pages 571–89 in *Emanuel: Studies in Hebrew Bible, Septuagint, and Dead Sea Scrolls in Honor of Emanuel Tov.* Edited by Shalom M. Paul, Robert A. Kraft, Lawrence H. Schiffman, and Weston W. Fields. VTSup 94. Leiden: Brill, 2003.

———. *Joshua.* Papyri Graece Schøyen. PSchøyen 1; Papyrologica Florentina 35; Manuscripts in the Schøyen Collection 5. Firenze: Edizioni Gonnelli, 2005.

———. "Reconstructing the Old Greek of Joshua." In *The Septuagint in Ancient Judaism and Early Christianity.* Edited by Wolfgang Kraus and Glenn Wooden. SBLSCS 35. Atlanta: Society of Biblical Literature, forthcoming.

———. *Rewriting the Sacred Text: What the Old Greek Texts Tell Us about the Literary Growth of the Bible.* SBLTCS 4. Atlanta: Society of Biblical Literature; Leiden: Brill, 2003.

deSilva, David A. *Introducing the Apocrypha: Message, Content and Significance.* Grand Rapids: Baker, 2002.
Dimant, Devorah. "Pesharim, Qumran." *ABD* 5:244–51.

———. *Qumran Cave 4.XXI: Parabiblical Texts, Part 4: Pseudo-Prophetic Texts.* Partially based on earlier transcriptions by John Strugnell. DJD 30. Oxford: Oxford University Press, 2001.

Doering, Lutz. "Jeremia in Babylonien und Ägypten: Mündliche und schriftliche Toraparänese für Exil und Diaspora nach *4QApocryphon of Jeremiah C.*" Pages 50–79 in *Frühjudentum und Neues Testament im Horizont Biblischer Theologie: Mit einem Anhang zum Corpus Judaeo-Hellenisticum Novi Testamenti.* Edited by Wolfgang Kraus and Karl-Wilhelm Niebuhr. WUNT 162. Tübingen: Mohr Siebeck, 2003.
Doudna, Gregory L. *4Q Pesher Nahum: A Critical Edition.* JSPSup 35. London: Sheffield Academic Press, 2001.
Duhm, Bernhard. *Das Buch Jeremia.* KHC 11. Tübingen: Mohr Siebeck, 1901.
Duncan, Julie. "4QDeut$^j$." Pages 75–83 in Eugene Ulrich et al., *Qumran Cave 4.IX: Deuteronomy, Joshua, Judges, Kings.* DJD 14. Oxford: Clarendon, 1995.

———. "Deuteronomy, Book of." Pages 198–202 in vol. 1 of *The Encyclopedia of the Dead Sea Scrolls.* Edited by Lawrence H. Schiffman and James C. VanderKam. 2 vols. Oxford: Oxford University Press, 2000.

Ego, Beate, and Armin Lange. "Und es ward ihm zur Gerechtigkeit angerechnet" (4QPsJub$^a$ 2 I 8). Gen 15, 6 im Pseudo-Jubiläentext von Qumran und in der antik-jüdischen Literatur." Pages 171–192 in *Der Mensch vor Gott: Forschungen zum Menschenbild in Bibel, antikem Judentum und Koran: Festschrift für Hermann Lichtenberger zum 60.Geburtstag.* Edited by Ulrike Mittman-Richert, Friedrich Avemarie, and Gerbern S. Oegema. Neukirchen-Vluyn: Neukirchener, 2003.
Elliott, John H. *What Is Social-Scientific Criticism?* Minneapolis: Fortress, 1993.

Ellis, E. Earle. "Biblical Interpretation in the New Testament Church." Pages 691–725 in *Mikra: Text, Translation, Reading and Interpretation of the Hebrew Bible in Ancient Judaism and Early Christianity*. Edited by Martin Jan Mulder. CRINT 1. Assen: Van Gorcum; Minneapolis: Fortress, 1990.
Engel, Helmut. *Die Susanna-Erzählung: Einleitung, Übersetzung und Kommentar zum Septuaginta-Text und zur Theodotion-Berarbeitung*. OBO 61. Göttingen. Vandenhoeck & Ruprecht, 1985.
Exler, Francis X. J. *The Form of the Ancient Greek Letter: A Study in Greek Epistolography*. Washington, D.C.: Catholic University of America, 1923.
Finkel, Asher. "The Pesher of Dreams and Scriptures." *RevQ* 4 (1963–64): 357–70.
Fishbane, Michael. *Biblical Interpretation in Ancient Israel*. New York: Oxford University Press, 1985.
———. "The Qumran Pesher and Traits of Ancient Hermeneutics." Pages 97–114 in *Proceedings of the Sixth World Congress of Jewish Studies Held at the Hebrew University of Jerusalem 13–19 August 1973 Under the Auspices of the Israel Academy of Sciences and Humanities*. Vol. 1: Division A. Jerusalem: World Union of Jewish Studies, 1977.
Frei, Hans W. *The Eclipse of Biblical Narrative: A Study of Eighteenth and Nineteenth Century Hermeneutics*. New Haven: Yale University Press, 1974.
Frey, Jörg. *Das johanneische Zeitverständnis*. Vol. 2 of *Die johanneische Eschatologie*. WUNT 110. Tübingen: Mohr Siebeck, 1998.
Gafni, Isaiah M. *Land, Center and Diaspora: Jewish Constructs in Late Antiquity*. JSPSup 21. Sheffield: Sheffield Academic Press, 1997.
García Martínez, Florentino, and Eibert J. C. Tigchelaar, eds. *The Dead Sea Scrolls Study Edition*. 2 vols. Leiden: Brill, 1997.
———. *The Dead Sea Scrolls Translated: The Qumran Texts in English*. Leiden: Brill, 1996.
Gaster, Moses. *The Chronicles of Jerahmeel*. London: Royal Asiatic Society, 1899.
———. "The Unknown Aramaic Original of Theodotion's Additions to the Book of Daniel." *Proceedings of the Society of Biblical Archaeology* 16 (1894): 280–90, 312–17; 17 (1895): 75–94.
Gese, Hartmut. "Die Bedeutung der Krise unter Antiochus IV. Epiphanes für die Apokalyptik des Danielbuches." Pages 202–17 in idem, *Alttestamentliche Studien*. Tübingen: Mohr Siebeck, 1991.
———. "Das Geschichtsbild des Danielbuches und Ägypten." Pages 189–201 in idem, *Alttestamentliche Studien*. Tübingen: Mohr Siebeck, 1991.
———. "Zur Komposition der Abrahamserzählung." Pages 29–51 in *Alttestamentliche Studien*. Tübingen: Mohr Siebeck, 1991.
Gilbert, M. "La prière d'Azarias (Dn 3: 26–45 Théodotion)." *NRTh* 96 (1974): 561–82.
Goldenstein, Johannes. *Das Gebet der Gottesknechte: Jes 63, 7–64, 11 im Jesajabuch*. WMANT 92. Neukirchen-Vluyn: Neukirchener, 2001.
Goldstein, Jonathan A. "The Apocryphal Book of I Baruch," *PAAJR* 46/47 (1979/80): 179–99.

Goode, Erich. *Deviant Behavior: An Interactionist Approach.* Englewood Cliffs, N.J.: Prentice-Hall, 1978.
Gordon, Cyrus H. *Smith College Tablets.* Smith College Studies in History 38. Northampton, Mass: Department of History of Smith College, 1952.
Gosse, Bernard. "Les traditions sur Abraham and sur le jardin d'Éden en rapport avec Is 51,2–3 et avec le livre d'Ézéchiel." Pages 421–428 in *Studies in the Book of Genesis: Literature, Redaction and History.* Edited by André Wénin. BETL 155. Leuven: Leuven University Press/Peeters, 1999.
Griel, Arthur, and David Rudy. "Social Cocoons: Encapsulation and Identity Transformation Organizations." *Sociological Inquiry* 54 (1984): 260–78.
Groß, Heinrich. *Klagelieder;* Josef Schreiner, *Baruch.* NEchtB 14. Würzburg: Echter, 1986.
Grossman, Maxine L. *Reading for History in the Damascus Document: A Methodological Study.* STDJ 45. Leiden: Brill, 2002.
Gruen, Erich S. *Diaspora: Jews amidst Greeks and Romans.* Cambridge: Harvard University Press, 2002.
Gunneweg, Antonius H. J. "Der Brief Jeremias." *JSHRZ* 3/2 (1975): 183–92.
Hacham, Noah. "Communal Fasts in the Judean Desert Scrolls." Pages 127–45 in *Historical Perspectives: From the Hashmoneans to Bar Kokhba in Light of the Dead Sea Scrolls: Proceedings of the Fourth International Symposium of the Orion Center, 27–31. January 1999.* Edited by David Goodblatt, Avital Pinnick, and Daniel R. Schwartz. Leiden: Brill, 2001.
Hamm, Winfried. *Der Septuaginta-text des Buches Daniel (3–4) nach dem Kölner Papyrus 967.* Papyrologische Texte und Abhandlungen 21. Bonn: Habelt, 1977.
Hardmeier, Christof. "Erzählen–Erzählung–Erzählgemeinschaft: Zur Rezeption der Abrahamserzählungen in der Exilsprophetie." *Wort und Dienst* NS 16 (1981): 27–47.
Harnisch, Wolfgang. *Verhängnis und Verheißung der Geschichte: Untersuchungen zum Zeit- und Geschichtsverständnis im 4. Buch Esra und in der syr. Baruchapokalypse.* FRLANT 97. Göttingen: Vandenhoeck & Ruprecht, 1969.
Harris, J. Rendel. *The Rest of the Words of Baruch: A Christian Apocalypse of the Year 136 A.D.: The Text Revised with an Introduction.* London: Clay, 1889.
Hayward, Robert. *The Targum of Jeremiah.* Aramaic Bible 12. Edinburgh: T&T Clark, 1987.
Helbling, Dominik. *Transzendierung der Geschichte: Dan 3:57–90 LXX als hymnische Exegese.* Biblische Notizen Beihefte 14. Munich: Urlaub, 2002.
Helmer, Christine. "Biblical Theology: Bridge over Many Waters." *Currents in Biblical Research* 3 (2005): 169–96.
———. "Novelty and System in Schleiermacher's Thought." Pages 126–27 in *Schleiermacher and Whitehead: Open Systems in Dialogue.* Edited by Christine Helmer in cooperation with Marjorie Suchocki, John Quiring, and Katie Goetz. TBT 125. Berlin: de Gruyter, 2004.
———. "Transhistorical Unity of the New Testament Canon from Philosophical, Exegetical and Systematic-Theological Perspectives." Pages 13–50 in *One Scripture or Many? Canon from Biblical, Theological and Philosophical Perspectives.* Edited by Christine Helmer and Christof Landmesser. Oxford: Oxford University Press, 2004.

Heppe, Heinrich, *Reformed Dogmatics: Set Out and Illustrated from the Sources*. Revised and edited by Ernst Bizer. Translated by G. T. Thomson. London: Allen & Unwin, 1950. Repr., Grand Rapids: Baker, 1978.

Herzer, Jens. *Die Paralipomena Jeremiae: Studien zu Tradition und Redaktion einer Haggada des frühen Judentums*. TSAJ 43. Tübingen: Mohr Siebeck, 1994.

Himbaza, Innocent. "Le Décalogue du Papyrus Nash, Philon, 4Qphyl G, 8Qphyl 3 et 4Qmez A." *RevQ* 20 (2002): 411–28.

Hogg, Michael A., and Dominic Abrams. *Social Identifications: A Social Psychology of Intergroup Relations and Group Processes*. London: Routledge, 1988.

Horgan, Maurya P. *Pesharim: Qumran Interpretations of Biblical Books*. CBQMS 8. Washington, D.C.: Catholic Biblical Association of America, 1979.

Ishida, Tomoo. "The Structure and Historical Implications of the List of Pre-Israelite Nations." *Bib* 60 (1979): 461–90.

Janowski, Bernard. "The One God of the Two Testaments: Basic Questions of a Biblical Theology." Translated by Christine Helmer in *ThTo* 57 (2000): 297–324.

Janzen, J. Gerald. " Rivers in the Desert of Abraham and Sarah and Zion (Isaiah 51:1–3)." *HAR* 10 (1986): 139–55.

Jowett, Benjamin. "On the Interpretation of Scripture." Page 377 in *Essays and Reviews*. Edited by F. Temple et al. London: Parker and Son, 1860.

Kay, David M. "Susanna." *APOT* 1:638–651.

Keown, Gerald L., Pamela J. Scalise, and Thomas G. Smothers. *Jeremiah 26–52*. WBC 27. Dallas: Word, 1995.

Kilpp, Nelson. *Niederreißen und aufbauen: Das Verhältnis von Heilsverheißung und Unheilsverkündigung bei Jeremia und im Jeremiabuch*. Biblisch-Theologische Studien 13. Neukirchen-Vluyn: Neukirchener, 1990.

Klauck Hans-Josef. *Die antike Briefliteratur und das Neue Testament: Ein Lehr- und Arbeitsbuch*. Paderborn: Schöningh, 1998.

Klijn, Albertus Frederik J. "Die syrische Baruch-Apokalypse." *JSHRZ* 5/2 (1976): 103–91.

Knibb, Michael A. "The Exile in the Literature of the Intertestamental Period." *Heythrop Journal* 17 (1976): 253–72.

Koch, Klaus. *Deuterokanonische Zusätze zum Danielbuch: Entstehung und Textgeschichte*. AOAT 38. Kevelaer: Butzon & Bercker; Neukirchen-Vluyn: Neukirchener, 1987.

Köckert, Matthias. *Vätergott und Väterverheißungen: Eine Auseinandersetzung mit Albrecht Alt und seinen Erben*. FRLANT 142. Göttingen: Vandenhoeck & Ruprecht, 1998.

Koskenniemi, Heikki. *Studien zu Idee und Phraseologie des griechischen Briefes bis 400 n. Chr*. Annales Academiae Scientiarum Fennicae Ser. B 102/2. Helsinki: Suomalainen Tiedeakatemia, 1956.

Kottsieper, Ingo. *Zusätze zu Daniel*. ATD, Apokryphen 5. Göttingen: Vandenhoeck & Ruprecht, 1998.

Kraabel, A. Thomas. "Unity and Diversity among Diaspora Synagogues." Pages 49–60 in *The Synagogue in Late Antiquity*. Edited by Lee I. Levine. Philadelphia: American Schools of Oriental Research, 1987.

Kratz, Reinhard G. "Die Rezeption von Jeremia 10 und 29 im pseudepigraphen Brief des Jeremia." *JSJ* 26 (1995): 2–31.

Krüger, Thomas. *Geschichtskonzepte im Ezechielbuch.* BZAW 180. Berlin: de Gruyter, 1989.
Lange, Armin, with Ulrike Mittman-Richert. "Annotated List of the Texts from the Judaean Desert Classified by Content and Genre." Pages 115–64 in *The Text from the Judaean Desert: Indices and an Introduction to the Discoveries in the Judaean Desert Series.* Edited by Emanuel Tov. DJD 39. Oxford: Clarendon, 2002.
―――. "Considerations Concerning the 'Spirit of Impurity' in Zech 13:2." Pages 254–68 in *Die Dämonologie der israelitsch-judischen und früchristlichen Literatur in Kontext iher Umwelt/ The Demonology of Israelite-Jewish and Christian Literature in the Context of Their Environment.* Edited by Armin Lange, Hermann Lichtenberger, and K. F. Diethard Römheld. Tübingen: Mohr Siebeck, 2002.
―――. "Interpretation als Offenbarung: Zum Verhältnis von Schriftauslegung und Offenbarung in apokalyptischer und nichtapokalyptischer Literatur." Pages 17–33 in *Wisdom and Apocalypticism in the Dead Sea Scrolls and in the Biblical Tradition.* Edited by Florentino García Martínez. BETL 168. Leuven: Leuven University Press, 2003.
―――. *Vom prophetischen Wort zur prophetischen Tradition: Studien zur Traditions-und Redaktionsgeschichte innerprophetischer Konflikte in der Hebräischen Bibel.* FAT 34. Tübingen: Mohr Siebeck, 2002.
Larson, Erik, Manfred R. Lehmann, and Lawrence H. Schiffman. "Halakhot." Pages 45–46 in Joseph Baumgarten et al., *Qumran Cave 4.XXV: Halakhic Texts.* DJD 35. Oxford: Clarendon, 1999.
Lauha, A. *Kohelet.* BKAT 19. Neukirchen-Vluyn: Neukirchener, 1978.
Lebram, Jürgen. "Daniel/Danielbuch und Zusätze." TRE 8:325–49.
Leemhuis, F., Albertus Frederik J. Klijn, and G. J. H. van Gelder. *The Arabic Text of the Apocalypse of Baruch.* Leiden: Brill, 1986.
Lessing, Ephraim. "On the Proof of the Spirit and Power." Page 53 in *Lessing's Theological Writings.* Edited by Henry Chadwick. Library of Modern Religious Thought. Stanford, Calif.: Stanford University Press, 1967.
Lim, Timothy H. *Holy Scripture in the Qumran Commentaries and Pauline Letters.* Oxford: Clarendon, 1997.
―――. "Kittim." Pages 469–71 in vol. 1 of *Encyclopedia of the Dead Sea Scrolls.* Edited by Lawrence H. Schiffman and James C. VanderKam. Oxford: Oxford University Press, 2000.
―――. *Pesharim.* London: Sheffield Academic Press, 2002.
Link, Hannelore. *Rezeptionsforschung: Eine Einführung in Methoden und Probleme.* 2nd ed. Stuttgart: Kohlhammer, 1980.
Livingstone, Alasdair. *Mystical and Mythological Explanatory Works of Assyrian and Babylonian Scholars.* Oxford: Clarendon, 1986.
Llewelyn, S. R. *A Review of the Greek Inscriptions and Papyri Published 1984–85.* Vol. 8 of *New Documents Illustrating Early Christianity.* Grand Rapids: Eerdmans, 1997.
Lloyd, Alan B. "Nationalist Propaganda in Ptolemaic Egypt." *Historia* 31 (1982): 33–55.

Lofland, John, and Rodney Stark. "Becoming a World-Saver: A Theory of Conversion to a Deviant Perspective." *American Sociological Review* 30 (1965): 862–75.

Mathias, Dieter. "Nachexilische Geschichtsrezeption am Beispiel von Neh 9, 6–31." *Mitteilungen und Beiträge* 9 (1995): 3–25.

Matza, David. *Becoming Deviant*. Englewood Cliffs, N.J.: Prentice-Hall, 1969.

McKane, William. "משא in Jeremiah 23: 33–40." Pages 35–54 in *Prophecy: Essays Presented to Georg Fohrer on His Sixty-Fifth Birthday, 6 September 1980*. Edited by John A. Emerton. BZAW 150. Berlin: de Gruyter, 1980.

Mein, Andrew. *Ezekiel and the Ethics of Exile*. Oxford Theological Monographs. Oxford: Oxford University Press, 2001.

Milgrom, Jacob. "The Qumran Cult: Its Exegetical Principles." Pages 165–80 in *Temple Scroll Studies*. Edited by George J. Brooke. JSPSup 7. Sheffield: Sheffield Academic Press, 1989.

———. "The Scriptural Foundations and Deviations in the Laws of Purity of the Temple Scroll." Pages 83–99 in *Archaeology and History in the Dead Sea Scrolls: The New York University Conference in Memory of Yigael Yadin*. Edited by Lawrence H. Schiffman. JSOTSup 8; JSOT/ASOR Monographs 2. Sheffield: Sheffield Academic Press, 1990.

Milik, Józef Tadeusz. *The Books of Enoch: Aramaic Fragments from Qumran Cave 4*. Oxford: Clarendon, 1946.

———. "Daniel et Susanne à Qumrân?" Pages 337–359 in *De la Tôrah au Messie: Études d'exégèse et d'herméneutique biblique offertes à Henri Cazelles pour ses 25 années d'enseignement à l'Institut catholique de Paris*. Paris: Desclée, 1981.

———. "II. Tefillin, Mezuzot et Targums (4Q128–4Q157)." Pages 33–91 in Roland de Vaux and Józef Tadeusz Milik, *Qumrân Grotte 4.II*. DJD 6. Oxford: Clarendon, 1977.

Mittman-Richert, Ulrike. "Einführung zu den historischen und legendarischen Erzählungen." *JSHRZ* 6/1 (2000): 114–38.

Moore, Carey A. *Daniel, Esther and Jeremiah: The Additions*. AB 44. New York: Doubleday, 1977.

Myers, Jacob M. *Ezra-Nehemiah*. AB 14. New York: Doubleday, 1979.

Najman, Hindy. *Seconding Sinai: The Development of Mosaic Discourse in Second Temple Judaism*. JSJSup 77. Leiden: Brill, 2003.

Naumann, Weigand. *Untersuchungen über den apokryphen Jeremiasbrief*. BZAW 25. Gießen: Töpelmann, 1913.

Newman, Judith H. *Praying by the Book: The Scripturalization of Prayer in Second Temple Judaism*. SBLEJL 14. Atlanta: Scholars Press, 1999.

Nickelsburg, George W. E. *1 Enoch 1*. Hermeneia. Minneapolis: Fortress, 2001.

———. *Jewish Literature between the Bible and the Mishnah: A Historical and Literary Introduction*. London: SCM, 1981.

Niebuhr, Karl-Wilhelm. "Der Jakobusbrief im Licht frühjüdischer Diasporabriefe." *NTS* 44 (1998): 420–43.

Nir, Rivka. *The Destruction of Jerusalem and the Idea of Redemption in the Syriac Apocalypse of Baruch*. SBLEJL 20. Atlanta: Society of Biblical Literature, 2003.

Nitzan, Bilhah. "The *Pesher* and Other Methods of Instruction." Pages 209–20 in *Mogilany 1989: Papers on the Dead Sea Scrolls offered in Memory of Jean Carmignac, Part II: The Teacher of Righteousness*. Edited by Zdzisław Jan Kapera. Kraków: Enigma, 1991.

O'Regan, Cyril. *The Heterodox Hegel*. SUNY Series in Hegelian Studies. Albany: State University of New York Press, 1994.

Oeming, Manfred. "Der Glaube Abrahams: Zur Rezeptionsgeschichte von Gen 15,6 in der Zeit des zweiten Tempels." *ZAW* 110 (1998): 16–33.

Oppenheim, A. Leo. *The Interpretation of Dreams in the Ancient Near East: With a Translation of an Assyrian Dream-Book*. Transactions of the American Philosophical Society 46/3. Philadelphia: American Philosophical Society, 1956.

Osswald, Eva. "Zur Hermeneutik des Habakuk-Kommentar." *ZAW* 68 (1956): 243–56.

Pardee, Dennis. *Handbook of Ancient Hebrew Letters: A Study Edition*. With a chapter on Tannaitic letter fragments by S. David Sperling. With the collaboration of J. David Whitehead and Paul E. Dion. SBLSBS 15. Chico, Calif.: Scholars Press, 1982.

Pietersen, Lloyd K. "Teaching, Tradition and Thaumaturgy: A Sociological Examination of the Polemic of the Pastorals." Ph.D. diss., University of Sheffield, 2000.

Plöger, Otto. "Zusätze zu Daniel." *JSHRZ* 1/1 (1973): 63–87.

Pohlmann, Karl-Friedrich. "Das 'Heil' des Landes—Erwägungen zu Jer 29,5–7." Pages 144–64 in *Mythos im Alten Testament und seiner Umwelt: Festschrift für Hans-Peter Müller*. Edited by Armin Lange, Hermann Lichtenberger, and Diethard Römheld. BZAW 278. Berlin: de Gruyter, 1999.

Porten, Bezalel, and Ada Yardeni, eds. *Letters*. Vol. 1 of *Textbook of Aramaic Documents from Ancient Egypt*. Jerusalem: Hebrew University, 1986.

Pröbst, Volker. *Nehemia 9, Psalm 106 und Psalm 136 und die Rezeption des Pentetuchs*. Göttingen: Cuvilliers, 1997.

Puech, Émile. "524. 4QRouleau du Temple." Pages 86–114 in idem, *Qumrân Grotte 4.XVIII: Textes hébreux (4Q521–4Q528, 4Q576–4Q579)*. DJD 25. Oxford: Clarendon, 1998.

———. "Identification de Nouveaux Manuscrits Bibliques: *Deutéronome et Proverbes* dans les Débris de la Grotte 4." *RevQ* 20 (2001): 121–28.

———. *Qumrân Grotte 4.XVIII: Textes hébreux (4Q521–4Q528, 4Q576–4Q579)*. DJD 25. Oxford: Clarendon, 1998.

Qimron, Elisha. *The Temple Scroll: A Critical Edition with Extensive Reconstructions*. Jerusalem: Ben-Gurion University of the Negev and Israel Exploration Society, 1996.

———. "The Text of CDC." Pages 9–49 in *The Damascus Document Reconsidered*. Edited by Magen Broshi. Jerusalem: Israel Exploration Society, 1992.

Quast, Udo. *Liber Iosue*. Septuaginta Vetus Testamentum Graecum Auctoritate Academiae Scientiarum Gottingensis editum. Göttingen: Vandenhoeck & Ruprecht, forthcoming.

Rabin, Chaim. *Qumran Studies*. Scripta Judaica 2. London: Oxford University Press, 1957.

Rabinowitz, I. "Pesher/Pittaron: Its Biblical Meaning and Its Significance in the Qumran Literature." *RevQ* 8 (1972–75): 219–232, 230–232.

Rahlfs, Alfred. *Septuaginta: Id est Vetus Testamentum graece iuxta LXX interpretes*. Stuttgart: Deutsche Bibelgesellschaft, 1979.
Rambo, Lewis R. *Understanding Religious Conversion*. New Haven: Yale University Press, 1993.
Rüger, Hans-Peter. "Apokryphen I." *TRE* 3:289–316.
Regev, Eyal. "Abominated Temple and a Holy Community: The Formation of the Notions of Purity and Impurity in Qumran." *DSD* 10 (2003): 243–78.
Römer, Thomas. *Israels Väter: Untersuchungen zur Väterthematik im Deuteronomium und in der Deuteronomistischen Redaktion*. OBO 99. Fribourg: Universitätsverlag; Göttingen: Vandenhoeck & Ruprecht, 1990.
Rudolph, Wilhelm. *Esra und Nehemia samt 3. Esra*. HAT. Tübingen: Mohr Siebeck, 1949.
Ruwe, Andreas. "Die Veränderung tempeltheologischer Konzepte in Ez 8–11." Pages 3–18 in *Gemeinde ohne Tempel—Community without Temple: Zur Substituierung und Transformation des Jerusalemer Tempels und seines Kultes im Alten Testament, antiken Judentum und frühen Christentum*. Edited by Beate Ego, Armin Lange, and Peter Pilhofer. WUNT 118. Tübingen: Mohr Siebeck, 1999.
Sanders, E. P. "The Dead Sea Sect and Other Jews: Commonalities, Overlaps and Differences." Pages 7–43 in *The Dead Sea Scrolls in Their Historical Context*. Edited by Timothy H. Lim et al. Edinburgh: T&T Clark, 2000.
Schaller, Berndt. "Paralipomena Jeremiou." *JSHRZ* 1/8 (1998): 659–777.
Schiffman, Lawrence H. "Architecture and the Law: The Temple and Its Courtyards in the Temple Scroll." Pages 267–84 in vol. 1 of *From Ancient Israel to Modern Judaism: Intellect in Quest of Understanding: Essays in Honor of Marvin Fox*. Edited by Jacob Neusner, Ernest S. Frerichs, and Nahum M. Sarna. 4 vols. BJS 159. Atlanta: Scholars Press, 1989.

———. "Exclusion from the Sanctuary and the City of the Sanctuary in the *Temple Scroll*." *HAR* 9 (1985): 301–20.

———. *The Halakhah at Qumran*. SJLA 16. Leiden: Brill, 1975.

———. "The King, His Guard and the Royal Council in the *Temple Scroll*." *PAAJR* 54 (1987): 237–59.

———. "Phylacteries and Mezuzot." Pages 675–77 in vol. 2 of *Encyclopedia of the Dead Sea Scrolls*. Edited by Lawrence H. Schiffman and James C. VanderKam. Oxford: Oxford University Press, 2000.

———. *Reclaiming the Dead Sea Scrolls: The History of Judaism, the Background of Christianity, the Lost Library of the Qumran*. Jerusalem: Jewish Publication Society, 1994.

———. "Sacred Space: The Land of Israel in the *Temple Scroll*." Pages 398–410 in *Biblical Archaeology Today, 1990: Proceedings of the Second International Congress on Biblical Archaeology*. Edited by Avraham Biran and Joseph Aviram. Jerusalem: Israel Exploration Society, 1993.

———. "The Temple Scroll and the Halakhic Pseudepigrapha of the Second Temple Period." Pages 121–31 in *Pseudepigraphic Perspectives: The Apocrypha and Pseudepigrapha in Light of the Dead Sea Scrolls: Proceedings of the International Symposium of the Orion Center for the Study of the Dead Sea Scrolls and Associated Literature, 12–14*

*January 1997*. Edited by Esther G. Chazon, Michael Stone, and Avital Pinnick. STDJ 31. Leiden: Brill, 1999.

Schleiermacher, Friedrich D. E. *Brief Outline of Theology as a Field of Study.* Translated by Terrence N. Tice. Schleiermacher Studies and Translations 1. Lewiston, N.Y.: Mellen, 1990.

———. *The Christian Faith (1830/31).* Edited by Hugh Ross Mackintosh and J. S. Stewart. Translated by D. M. Baille et al. Edinburgh: T&T Clark, 1999.

———. *Hermeneutics and Criticism and Other Writings.* Translated by Andrew Bowie. Cambridge Texts in the History of Philosophy. Cambridge: Cambridge University Press, 1998.

———. *On Religion: Speeches to Its Cultured Despisers.* Translated by Richard Coulter. Cambridge Texts in the History of Philosophy. Cambridge: Cambridge University Press, 2000.

———. "The Second Letter." Pages 60–62, 65–68 in *On the Glaubenslehre: Two Letters to Dr. Lücke.* Translated by James Duke and Francis Fiorenza. American Academy of Religion Texts and Translations Series 3. Atlanta: Scholars Press, 1981.

———. *Vorlesungen über die Dialektik.* Vols. 2.10/1–2 of *Kritische Gesamtausgabe.* Edited by Andreas Arndt. Berlin: de Gruyter, 2000.

Schmid, Heinrich, ed. *Doctrinal Theology of the Evangelical Lutheran Church.* 3rd ed. Translated by Charles A. Hay and Henry E. Jacobs. Minneapolis: Augsburg, 1961.

Schmid, Konrad. *Buchgestalten des Jeremiabuches: Untersuchungen zur Redaktions- und Rezeptionsgeschichte von Jer 30–33 im Kontext des Buches.* WMANT 72. Neukirchen-Vluyn: Neukirchener, 1996.

Schnider, Franz, and Werner Stenger. *Studien zum neutestamentlichen Briefformular.* New Testament Tools and Studies 11. Leiden: Brill, 1987.

Schottroff, Willy. "ידע." *THAT,* 682–701.

Schürer, Emil. *The History of the Jewish People in the Age of Jesus Christ (175 B.C.–A.D. 135).* Revised and edited by Geza Vermes, Fergus Millar, and Matthew Black. 3 vols. Edinburgh: T&T Clark, 1973–87.

Schwiderski, Dirk. *Handbuch des nordwestsemitischen Briefformulars: Ein Beitrag zur Echtheitsfrage der aramäischen Briefe des Esrabuches.* BZAW 295. Berlin: de Gruyter, 2000.

Scott, James M. "Exile and Self-Understanding of Diaspora Jews in the Greco-Roman Period." Pages 173–218 in *Exile: Old Testament, Jewish, and Christian Conceptions.* Edited by James M. Scott. JSJSup 56. Leiden: Brill, 1997.

Seebass, Horst. *Genesis.* 3 vols. in 4. Neukirchen-Vluyn: Neukirchener, 1997.

Segal, Michael. "4QReworked Pentateuch or 4QPentateuch?" Pages 391–99 in *The Dead Sea Scrolls Fifty Years after their Discovery, 1947–1997.* Edited by Lawrence H. Schiffman, Emanuel Tov, and James C. VanderKam. Jerusalem: Israel Exploration Society, 2000.

Seitz, Christopher. *Theology in Conflict: Reactions to the Exile in the Book of Jeremiah.* BZAW 176. Berlin: de Gruyter, 1989.

Seybold, Klaus. *Nahum, Habakuk, Zephanja.* ZBK.AT 24/2. Zurich: Theologischer Verlag, 1991.

Silberman, Lou H. "Unriddling the Riddle: A Study in the Scripture and Language of the Habakkuk Pesher (1 Q p Hab)." *RevQ* (1961–62): 323–64.
Skehan, Patrick W., and Alexander A. Di Lella. *The Wisdom of Ben Sira: A New Translation with Introduction*. AB 39. New York: Doubleday, 1987.
Sperber, Alexander, ed. *The Latter Prophets According to Targum Jonathan*. Vol. 3 of *The Bible in Aramaic: Based on Old Manuscripts and Printed Texts*. Leiden: Brill, 1962.
Spiegelberg, Wilhelm. *Die sogenannte Demotische Chronik: Pap. 215 der Bibliothèque Nationale zu Paris nebst den auf der Rückseite des Papyrus stehenden Texten*. Leipzig: Hinrichs, 1914.
Steck, Odil Hannes. *Das apokryphe Baruchbuch: Studien zur Rezeption und Konzentration "kanonischer" Überlieferung*. FRLANT 160. Göttingen: Vandenhoeck & Ruprecht, 1993.
———. "Deuterojesaja als theologischer Denker." Pages 202–20 in *Wahrnehmungen Gottes im Alten Testament. Gesammelte Studien*. Theologische Bücherei 70. Munich: Kaiser, 1972.
———. "Die letzte Jesajaredaktion in Tritojesja." Pages 229–265 in idem, *Studien zu Tritojesaja*. BZAW 203. Berlin: de Gruyter, 1991.
———. *Die Prophetenbücher und ihr theologisches Zeugnis: Wege der Nachfrage und Fährten zur Antwort*. Tübingen: Mohr Siebeck, 1996.
———. "Zions Tröstung: Beobachtungen und Fragen zu Jes 51, 1–11." Pages 257–76 in *Die Hebräische Bibel und ihre zweifache Nachgeschichte: Festschrift für Rolf Rendtorff zum 65. Geburtstag*. Edited by Erhard Blum, Christian Macholz, and Ekkehard W. Stegemann. Neukirchen-Vluyn: Neukirchener, 1990.
Steck, Odil Hannes, Reinhard G. Kratz, and Ingo Kottsieper. *Das Buch Baruch, Der Brief des Jeremia, Zusätze zu Ester und Daniel*. ATD, Apokryphen 5. Göttingen: Vandenhoeck & Ruprecht, 1998.
Stegemann, Hartmut. *The Library of Qumran: On the Essenes, Qumran, John the Baptist, and Jesus*. Grand Rapids: Eerdmans, 1998.
———. "The Qumran Essenes—Local Members of the Main Jewish Union in Late Second Temple Times." Pages 83–166 in *The Madrid Qumran Congress: Proceedings of the International Congress on the Dead Sea Scrolls, Madrid 18–21 March, 1991*. Edited by Julio Trebolle Barrera and Luis Vegas Montaner. STDJ 11. Leiden: Brill, 1992.
Steudel, Annette. "אחרית הימים in the Texts from Qumran." *RevQ* 11 (1993): 225–46.
Steussy, Marti Jo. *Narrative and Faith in the Greek Legends of Daniel*. SBLDS 141. Atlanta: Scholars Press, 1993.
Strugnell, John. "Notes en Marge du Volume V des 'Discoveries in the Judaean Desert of Jordan,'" *RevQ* 7 (1969–70): 163–276.
Sussman, Ya'akov. "Šeqer Toldedot ha-Halakhah u-Megillot Midbar Yehudah: Hirhurim Talmudiyim Rishonim le-'Or Megillat Miqṣat Maʿaśe ha-Torah." *Tarbiz* 59 (1989/90): 11–17.
Taatz, Irene. *Frühjüdische Briefe: Die paulinischen Briefe im Rahmen der offiziellen religiösen Briefe des Frühjudentums*. NTOA 16. Fribourg: Universitätsverlag; Göttingen: Vandenhoeck & Ruprecht, 1991.
Talmon, Shemaryahu. "The 'Desert Motif' in the Bible and Qumran Literature." Pages 31–61 in *Biblical Motifs: Origins and Transformations*. Studies and Texts 3. Cam-

bridge: Harvard University Press, 1966. Repr. as pages 216–54 in Shemaryahu Talmon, *Literary Studies in the Hebrew Bible. Form and Content: Collected Studies.* Leiden: Brill, 1993.

———. "The Signification of אחרית and אחרית הימים in the Hebrew Bible." Pages 795–810 in *Emanuel: Studies in Hebrew Bible, Septuagint, and the Dead Sea Scrolls in Honor of Emanuel Tov.* Edited by Shalom M. Paul et al. Leiden: Brill, 2003.

———. *The World of Qumran from Within.* Jerusalem: Magnes, 1989.

Tcherikover, Victor, *Hellenistic Civilization and the Jews.* Peabody, Mass., Hendrickson, 1999.

Thiel, Winfried. *Die deuteronomistische Redaktion von Jeremia 26–45: Mit einer Gesamtbeurteilung der deuteronomistischen Redaktion des Buches Jeremia.* WMANT 52. Neukirchen-Vluyn: Neukirchener, 1981.

Tiller, Patrick A. *A Commentary on the Animal Apocalypse of 1 Enoch.* SBLEJL 4. Atlanta: Scholars Press, 1993.

Topper, Joseph. *Nekromantie: Totenbefragung im Alten Orient und im Alten Testament.* AOAT 223. Neukirchen-Vluyn: Neukirchener, 1989.

Tov, Emanuel. "Rewritten Bible Compositions and Biblical Manuscripts, with Special Attention to the Samaritan Pentateuch." *DSD* 5 (1998): 334–54.

Tov, Emanuel, and Sidnie White. "364–367. 4QReworked Pentateuch[b-e] and 365a. 4QTemple?" Pages 187–351 in Harold Attridge et al., *Qumran Cave 4.VIII: Parabiblical Texts, Part 1.* DJD 13. Oxford: Clarendon, 1994.

Trapp, Michael, ed. *Greek and Latin Letters: An Anthology with Translation.* Cambridge Greek and Latin Classics. Cambridge: Cambridge University Press, 2003.

Tsuji, Manabu. *Glaube zwischen Vollkommenheit und Verweltlichung: Eine Untersuchung zur literarischen Gestalt und zur inhaltlichen Kohärenz des Jakobusbriefes.* WUNT 2/93. Tübingen: Mohr Siebeck, 1997.

Ullman, C. "Cognitive and Emotional Antecedents of Religious Conversion." *Journal of Personality and Social Psychology* 43 (1982): 183–92.

Ulrich, Eugene. "4QJosh[a]." Pages 143–152 in Eugene Ulrich, Frank Moore Cross, Sidnie White Crawford, Julie Ann Duncan, Patrick W. Skehan, Emanuel Tov, and Julio Trebolle Barrera, *Qumran Cave 4.IX: Deuteronomy, Joshua, Judges, Kings.* DJD 14. Oxford: Clarendon, 1995.

———. "The Absence of 'Sectarian Variants' in the Jewish Scriptural Scrolls Found at Qumran." Pages 179–95 in *The Bible as Book: The Hebrew Bible and the Judaean Desert Discoveries.* Edited by Edward D. Herbert and Emanuel Tov. London: The British Library, 2002.

———. "The Qumran Scrolls and the Biblical Text." Pages 51–59 in *The Dead Sea Scrolls Fifty Years after their Discovery, 1947–1997.* Edited by Lawrence H. Schiffman, Emanuel Tov, and James C. VanderKam. Jerusalem: Israel Exploration Society, 2000.

Unnik, Willem C. van. *Das Selbstverständnis der jüdischen Diaspora in der hellenistischrömischen Zeit.* Edited by Pieter W. van der Horst. AGJU 17. Leiden: Brill, 1993.

Van Seters, John. *Abraham in History and Tradition.* New Haven: Yale University Press, 1975.

Van Uchelen, Nico Adriaan. "Abraham als Felsen (Jes 51,1)." *ZAW* 80 (1968): 183–91.

VanderKam, James C. "Sinai Revisited." Pages 44–60 in *Biblical Interpretation at Qumran*. Edited by Matthias Henze. Studies in the Dead Sea Scrolls and Related Literature. Grand Rapids: Eerdmans, 2005.
Vermes, Geza. *The Complete Dead Sea Scrolls in English*. London: Penguin, 1998.
Violet, Bruno. *Die Apokalypsen des Esra und des Baruch in deutscher Gestalt*. Die griechischen christlichen Schriftseller der ersten drei Jahrhunderte 32. Leipzig: Hinrichs, 1924.
Volten, Aksel. *Demotische Traumdeutung (Pap. Carlsberg XIII und XIV verso)*. Analecta Aegyptica 3. Kopenhagen: Munksgaard, 1942.
Walker-Ramisch, Sandra. "Graeco-Roman Voluntary Associations and the Damascus Document: A Sociological Analysis." Pages 128–45 in *Voluntary Associations in the Graeco-Roman World*. Edited by John S. Kloppenborg and Stephen G. Wilson. London: Routledge, 1996.
Wanke, Gunther. *Jeremia 1,1–25,14*. Vol. 1 of *Jeremia*. ZBK.AT 21/1. Zurich: Theologischer Verlag Zurich, 1995.
Weinfeld, Moshe. "Grace after Meals at Qumran." *JBL* 111 (1992): 427–40.
———. "'Megillat Miqdash' 'o 'Torah la-Melekh.'" *Shnaton* 7 (1987/9): 214–37.
Werline, Rodney Alan. *Penitential Prayer in Second Temple Judaism: The Development of a Religious Institution*. SBLEJL 13. Atlanta: Scholars Press, 1998.
Westermann, Claus. *Genesis*. 2nd ed. 3 vols. BKAT 1. Neukirchen-Vluyn: Neukirchener, 1989.
Whitters, Mark F. *The Epistle of Second Baruch: A Study in Form and Message*. JSPSup 42. London: Sheffield Academic Press, 2003.
Williamson, Hugh G. M. *Ezra, Nehemiah*. WBC 16. Waco, Tex.: Word, 1985.
Wise, Michael O. "Dating the Teacher of Righteousness and the *Floruit* of His Movement." *JBL* 122 (2003): 53–87.
Wolff, Christian. *Jeremia im Frühjudentum und Urchristentum*. TUGAL 118. Berlin: Akademie-Verlag, 1976.
Wysny, Andreas. *Die Erzählungen von Bel und dem Drachen, Untersuchungen zu Dan 14*. SBB 33. Stuttgart: Katholisches Bibelwerk, 1996.
Xeravits, Géza G. *King, Priest, Prophet: Positive Eschatological Protagonists of the Qumran Library*. Edited by Florentino García Martínez. STDJ 47. Leiden: Brill, 2003.
Yadin, Yigael. *The Temple Scroll*. Rev. ed. 3 vols. Jerusalem: Israel Exploration Society, 1983.
Zimmerli, Walther. *Ezechiel*. 2nd ed. 2 vols. BK 13. Neukirchen-Vluyn: Neukirchener, 1979.

# Contributors

**Susan Bond** holds a B.A.L.S. degree in Religious Studies from Georgetown University and an M.A.T.S. in New Testament/ Hebrew Bible from Claremont School of Theology. She is a Ph.D. Hebrew Bible candidate at Claremont Graduate University and research assistant to Dr. Kristin De Troyer.

Since 1998, **George J. Brooke** has been Rylands Professor of Biblical Criticism and Exegesis at the University of Manchester, England, where he has taught since 1984. He is best known for his work on biblical interpretation in the Scrolls, and a collection of his essays on *The Dead Sea Scrolls and the New Testament* appeared in 2005 (Fortress/ SPCK).

**Sidnie White Crawford** is Professor of Hebrew Bible and Chair of the Classics and Religious Studies-Department of the University of Nebraska-Lincoln in Lincoln, Nebraska. She also serves as the editor of the Society of Biblical Literature's Text-Critical Studies series.

**Kristin De Troyer** is Professor of Hebrew Bible at the Claremont School of Theology and Professor of Religion at the Claremont Graduate University, Claremont, California. Her most recent publications are *Rewriting the Sacred Text: What the Old Greek Texts Tell Us about the Development of the Hebrew Bible* (Society of Biblical Literature, 2003); *Joshua* (Edizioni Gonnelli, 2005); and the *Twelve Minor Prophets* (fasc. 3B of *Biblia Qumranica;* Brill, 2004; co-edited with Beate Ego and Armin Lange).

**Lutz Doering** studied theology and Jewish Studies at Erlangen, Jerusalem, and Heidelberg, received his doctoral degree from the University of Göttingen with a thesis on ancient Sabbath law and practice (published as *Schabbat: Sabbathalacha und -praxis im antiken Judentum und Urchristentum* [Mohr Siebeck, 1999]), and since 2004 has been Lecturer in New Testament Studies at King's College London, United Kingdom. He is currently working on 1 Peter and ancient Jewish epistolography.

**Beate Ego** is Professor of Old Testament and Ancient Judaism at the Department of Education and Culture at the University of Osnabrueck, Germany. Her main areas of research are the literature and theology of the Second Temple era as well as the interpretation of rabbinic literature and the targums.

**Katie Goetz** completed her Master of Divinity at Claremont School of Theology and is a candidate for ordination in the United Methodist Church. She pastors the UMC of Twentynine Palms and Community UMC in Joshua Tree, California. She also assisted in editing *Truth: Interdisciplinary Dialogues in a Pluralist Age* (Peeters, 2003) and *Schleiermacher and Whitehead: Open Systems in Dialogue* (de Gruyter, 2004).

**Christine Helmer** is Senior Scholar of Theology at Harvard Divinity School (Cambridge, Massachusetts), and before this she was Associate Professor of Theology at the Claremont School of Theology (Claremont, California). She is the author or editor of many books, including the prize-winning *The Trinity and Martin Luther* (von Zabern, 1999). Her most recent edited collection is *Biblical Interpretation: History, Context, and Reality* (Society of Biblical Literature, 2005).

**Jutta Jokirantak** is researcher at the Department of Biblical Studies of the University of Helsinki, Finland. She is currently working in a research project financed by the Academy of Finland and led by Prof. Raija Sollamo. She hopes to finish her dissertation on social identity and sectarianism in the Qumran movement.

**Armin Lange** is Professor for Jewish Studies at the University of Vienna. His most important works are *Weisheit und Prädestination: Weisheitliche Urordnung und Prädestination in den Textfunden von Qumran* (Brill, 1995); *Vom prophetischen Wort zur prophetischen Tradition: Studien zur Traditions- und Redaktionsgeschichte innerprophetischer Konflikte in der Hebräischen Bibel* (Mohr Siebeck, 2002); and the *Twelve Minor Prophets* (fasc. 3B of *Biblia Qumranica;* Brill, 2005; co-edited with Kristin De Troyer and Beate Ego).

**Ulrike Mittmann-Richert** studied in Tübingen, Münster, and St. Paul, Minnesota, earning a Ph.D. in Theology (Tübingen, 1996) and a Habilitation in New Testament (Tübingen, 2005). Since 2002, she has been a researcher at the Institut für antikes Judentum und hellenistische Religionsgeschichte and, since 2005, Privatdozentin. Her areas of research include New Testament, Jewish writings from the Hellenistic-Roman period, and Qumran.

**Lawrence H. Schiffman** is Chair of New York University's Skirball Department of Hebrew and Judaic Studies and serves as Ethel and Irvin A. Edelman Professor of Hebrew and Judaic Studies. His publications include *The Halakhah at Qumran* (Brill, 1975); *Sectarian Law in the Dead Sea Scrolls: Courts, Testimony, and the Penal Code* (Scholars Press, 1983); *Reclaiming the Dead Sea Scrolls* (Jewish Publication Society, 1994); and some 150 articles on the Dead Sea Scrolls and rabbinic Judaism.

**Loren T. Stuckenbruck** is B. F. Westcott Professor in Biblical Studies at the University of Durham, United Kingdom. Known for his publications on the Dead Sea Scrolls, Jewish apocalyptic and wisdom literature, and the New Testament, he is Chief Editor of the Commentaries on Early Jewish Literature series (de Gruyter) and Senior Editor for the *Journal for the Study of the Pseudepigrapha*.

# INDEX OF BIBLICAL AND RELATED LITERATURE

## MASORETIC TEXT

**Genesis**
| | |
|---|---|
| 1:26–31 | 115 |
| 10:15 | 120 |
| 11:28 | 175–77 |
| 11:31 | 176–77 |
| 12:1–3 | 170–71 |
| 12:1–5 | 175–77 |
| 13 | 168 |
| 13:6 | 167 |
| 15:6 | 175 |
| 15:7a | 177 |
| 15:7 | 168 |
| 15:8 | 168 |
| 15:17–21 | 175 |
| 15:19–21 | 175 |
| 17:5 | 175 |
| 17:7 | 175 |
| 18–19 | 168 |
| 22 | 175 |
| 22:1 | 175 |
| 22:17 | 168 |
| 28:4 | 168 |
| 30:36 | 133 |
| 40:5 | 187 |
| 40:8 | 187 |
| 40:12 | 187 |
| 40:16 | 187 |
| 40:18 | 187 |
| 40:22 | 187 |
| 41:8 | 187 |
| 41:11–13 | 187 |
| 41:15 | 187 |

**Exodus**
| | |
|---|---|
| 2:1–8 | 131 |
| 6:8 | 168 |
| 12:43–13:16 | 128, 130 |
| 13:1–10 | 130 |
| 13:11–16 | 130 |
| 19:10–15 | 86 |
| 20:8–11 | 129 |

**Leviticus**
| | |
|---|---|
| 5:3 | 86 |
| 7:21 | 86 |
| 14:33–57 | 36 |
| 18 | 40 |
| 19:19 | 140 |
| 19:31a | 173 |
| 20 | 40 |
| 21:16–24 | 86 |

**Numbers**
| | |
|---|---|
| 18:17 | 182 |
| 20 | 131 |
| 29:14–25 | 136 |
| 29:32–30:1 | 135 |

**Deuteronomy**
| | |
|---|---|
| 1–9 | 131 |
| 1–14 | 133 |
| 1:17 | 138 |
| 2 | 134 |
| 2:7 | 131 |
| 2:8 | 132 |
| 4:20 | 110 |

*Deuteronomy (cont.)*

| | | | |
|---|---|---|---|
| 5 | 128 | 27:9–10 | 146, 150 |
| 5:1–6:1 | 128, 130 | 27:11 | 150 |
| 5:1–6:3 | 128 | 27:12 | 150 |
| 5:12–15 | 129 | 27:13 | 150, 156 |
| 5:28–32 | 128 | 27:14 | 150 |
| 6 | 129 | 27:15 | 150 |
| 6:4–9 | 130 | 27:16–25 | 150 |
| 6:4–5 | 79 | 27:26 | 150 |
| 8:5–10 | 128, 130 | 30:30–31 | 132 |
| 6:4–5 | 79 | 32:1–9 | 128 |
| 8:1–10 | 129 | 32:1–43 | 128–30 |
| 8:5–10 | 128, 130 | 32:17–18 | 128 |
| 9:21 | 133 | 32:22–23 | 128 |
| 9:25 | 133 | 32:25–27 | 128 |
| 10 | 129 | | |
| 10:1–4 | 133 | **Joshua** | |
| 10:12–11:21 | 128, 130 | 2:1–5:15 | 153, 155 |
| 11 | 129 | 3:16 | 159 |
| 11:6–13 | 128 | 4 | 145, 157 |
| 11:13–21 | 130 | 4:1 | 147 |
| 11:29 | 150, 156 | 4:15 | 147 |
| 14:13–21 | 134 | 4:19–20 | 159 |
| 16:18–20 | 138 | 5 | 157, 159 |
| 16:13–14 | 135 | 5:2 | 145, 147, 156 |
| 17:14–20 | 137 | "5:X" | 145, 158 |
| 18:20 | 138 | 6:1–8:35 | 153, 155 |
| 18:22 | 138 | 6:2 | 147 |
| 22:9–11 | 140 | 8 | 145, 156–57 |
| 22:28–29 | 139 | 8:1 | 147 |
| 23:2–4 | 86 | 8:18 | 147 |
| 23:11 | 86 | 8:30–31 | 146 |
| 27 | 146–50, 152–57, 158–59, 161 | 8:30–35 | 141–62 |
| 27:1 | 150 | 8:31 | 155 |
| 27:1–3 | 148, 150 | 8:34–35 | 145–46, 155 |
| 27:1–8 | 152 | 8:35 | 155, 158 |
| 27:2 | 150 | 9 | 145, 156 |
| 27:2–3 | 145, 147, 149, 150 | 9:1–2 | 153–54 |
| 27:2–8 | 142–43, 146, 149–52 | 9:1–12:24 | 153, 155 |
| 27:4 | 146–47, 149, 150, 156 | 9:3 | 148, 153 |
| 27:5–6a | 149–50 | 9:3–27 | 147 |
| 27:5–7 | 150 | 9:6 | 156, 158 |
| 27:5–8 | 150 | 9:27–11:3 | 141–42 |
| 27:6b–7 | 149, 150 | 10:15 | 141 |
| 27:8 | 146, 149, 150 | 10:17 | 141 |
| | | 10:43 | 141 |

| | | | |
|---|---|---|---|
| 13:1–22:34 | 153, 155 | 41:6–7 | 50 |
| 24 | 157 | 41:8 | 173 |
| | | 41:8–9 | 171 |
| **Judges** | | 41:19–20 | 115 |
| 2:1 | 156 | 41:29 | 115 |
| | | 43:3 | 173 |
| **1 Samuel** | | 43:6 | 173 |
| 7:16 | 156 | 43:14 | 173 |
| 9–10 | 182 | 44:6–20 | 115 |
| 10:8 | 156 | 44:9–20 | 50 |
| 11:14–15 | 156 | 45:20 | 50 |
| | | 49:14 | 170 |
| **1 Kings** | | 51:1–3 | 165, 169–71, 178 |
| 1:32–40 | 182 | 51:1–8 | 173 |
| 8:14–53 | 117 | 51:7 | 170 |
| 8:46 | 118 | 56:5–7 | 50 |
| 8:46–47 | 118 | 52:11–12 | 105 |
| 8:47 | 117 | 55:12–13 | 105 |
| 8:51 | 110, 118 | 58:13–14 | 115 |
| 8:60 | 118 | 60:1–22 | 105 |
| | | 63:7–64:11 | 172 |
| **2 Kings** | | 63:15 | 179 |
| 9:1–13 | 182 | 63:15–16 | 165, 172–73 |
| 24:10–18 | 166 | 63:18 | 172 |
| 25:8–9 | 60 | 64 | 10–11, 172 |
| 25:11–12 | 166 | 64:7 | 173 |
| 25:18–21 | 166 | 64:10–11 | 172 |
| | | 64:17 | 172 |
| **Isaiah** | | | |
| 2:10 | 33 | **Jeremiah** | |
| 5 | 24 | 10 | 49–50 |
| 6:9–10 | 172 | 10:1–16 | 50 |
| 8:19 | 173 | 10:11 | 55, 112 |
| 13:1 | 190 | 10:14 | 112 |
| 15:1 | 190 | 11:4 | 110 |
| 17:1 | 190 | 12:11 | 119 |
| 19:1 | 190 | 13:26–27 | 121 |
| 21:1 | 190 | 15:16 | 16 |
| 21:11 | 190 | 16:13 | 50 |
| 21:13 | 190 | 16:13 | 50 |
| 22:1 | 190 | 23:9–32 | 191 |
| 23:1 | 190 | 23:15 | 119, 120 |
| 28:14 | 30 | 23:25–32 | 186 |
| 30:19 | 170 | 23:33–40 | 181, 184–86, 189–91 |
| 40:18–20 | 50 | 25:11–12 | 47, 67 |

*Jeremiah (cont.)*

| | | | |
|---|---|---|---|
| 29 | 43–49, 50, 55, 59, 69, 70, 197 | 3:9 | 17 |
| 29:1 | 120 | 11:15 | 168 |
| 29:1–23 | 45–48, 49–50, 52, 54, 55 | 16:37–39 | 121 |
| 29:5–7 | 16, 69 | 25:4 | 168 |
| 29:8–9 | 69 | 25:10 | 168 |
| 29:10 | 67 | 28:25 | 168 |
| 29:10–14 | 69 | 33:25–29 | 169 |
| 29:12 | 121 | 33:21–23 | 166, 171 |
| 29:15 | 120 | 33:23–28 | 179 |
| 29:24–28 (29) | 43 | 33:23–34 | 165–69, 178 |
| 29:23 | 119 | 34 | 99 |
| 29:30–32 | 49 | 36:2–3 | 168 |
| 29:31 | 43 | 36:5 | 168 |
| 30–31 | 47 | 37:13 | 11 |
| 31:31 | 16 | 37:25 | 168 |
| 40:6 | 167 | 38 | 27 |
| 40:7 | 166 | 47 | 170 |
| 40:8 | 167 | | |
| 40:9–12 | 167 | **Hosea** | |
| 50 | 111–12 | 2:4–5 | 121 |
| 50:2 | 111 | 4:6 | 120 |
| 50:24 | 112 | 4:9–15 | 120 |
| 51 | 50, 111–12 | 4:12–15 | 120 |
| 51:15–16 | 112 | 4:15 | 120 |
| 51:15–19 | 50, 115 | 8:4–5 | 115 |
| 51:17 | 111 | 8:14 | 115 |
| 51:17–18 | 112 | 9:15 | 157 |
| 51:34 | 111 | 11:1 | 172 |
| 51:34–35 | 111 | 12:11 | 157 |
| 51:38–39 | 111 | **Joel** | |
| 51:44 | 111 | 2–4 | 33 |
| 51:45 | 105 | 4:18 | 170 |
| 51:47 | 111 | | |
| 51:48 | 112 | **Amos** | |
| 51:52 | 111 | 4:4 | 157 |
| 51:58 | 113 | 5:5 | 157 |
| 51:60 | 47 | | |
| 52:12 | 60 | **Nahum** | |
| | | 1:1 | 190 |
| **Ezekiel** | | | |
| 2:10 | 16 | **Habakkuk** | |
| 3 | 195 | 1:1 | 190 |
| 3:3 | 16 | 1:7 | 187, 189 |
| 3:7 | 17 | 2 | 24 |

# INDEX OF BIBLICAL AND RELATED LITERATURE 225

| | | | |
|---|---|---|---|
| 2:2–3 | 116 | **Psalms** | |
| 2:15 | 29 | 1:3–4 | 15 |
| 2:18–19 | 116 | 1:6 | 15 |
| 3 | 24, 117 | 2 | 24 |
| 3:6 | 116 | 23 | 16 |
| 3:8–11 | 116 | 27:5 | 170 |
| | | 33:9 | 16 |
| **Zechariah** | | 37 | 24 |
| 9:1 | 190 | 46:5 | 170 |
| 11 | 99 | 61:3 | 170 |
| 12–14 | 184 | 65:110 | 170 |
| 13:2–3 | 183–84 | 87:7 | 170 |
| 13:2–6 | 183–84 | 98:5 | 115 |
| | | 103:19–22 | 118 |
| | | 113:15–17 | 50 |
| **Malachi** | | 115:3–7 | 115 |
| 1:1 | 190 | 115:4–7 | 50 |
| 3:3 | 33 | 135:6–7 | 115 |
| 3:19–21 | 113 | 135:15–17 | 115 |
| | | | |
| **Daniel** | | **Qoheleth** | |
| 1–6 | 123 | 8:1 | 187 |
| 1:1 | 114 | | |
| 2:1 | 114 | **Esther** | |
| 3 | 106 | 9:20–28 | 71 |
| 6 | 115 | | |
| 7–12 | 91, 123 | **Ezra** | |
| 7:1–28 | 91 | 9 | 33 |
| 7:21 | 105 | | |
| 7:25 | 105 | **Nehemiah** | |
| 8:9–12 | 105 | 6:1–14 | 181–83 |
| 8:13 | 105 | 6:6–7 | 181–82 |
| 9 | 52, 117, 120 | 6:10–14 | 182 |
| 9:1–27 | 91 | 9:5–37 | 178 |
| 9:5 | 117 | 9:6–37 | 174, 176 |
| 9:2 | 49, 67 | 9:7–8 | 165, 174–77 |
| 9:12 | 121 | 9:9b–15 | 174 |
| 9:24 | 100 | 9:15a | 177 |
| 9:24–27 | 49, 67 | 9:16–18 | 174 |
| 9:27 | 105 | 9:19–25 | 174 |
| 10:1–12:4 | 91 | 9:22b–24a | 177 |
| 11:31 | 105 | 9:26–27 | 174 |
| 11:32–35 | 33 | 9:29–31 | 174 |
| 11:33–35 | 123 | 9:33–35 | 174 |
| 11:40–45 | 105 | 9:35–36 | 177 |
| 12:11 | 105 | | |

| | | | |
|---|---|---|---|
| 9:36–37 | 174 | **2 Chronicles** | |
| | | 5:11;7:6 | 117 |
| **1 Chronicles** | | 21:12–15 | 43 |
| 16:4 | 117 | | |

### Septuagint

| | | | |
|---|---|---|---|
| **Deuteronomy** | | 14:4–15 | 115 |
| 29:27 (28) | 52 | 14:41 | 190 |
| **Joshua** | | **2 Maccabees** | |
| 4–8 | 148 | 1:1 | 60 |
| 9:2 | 148 | 1:1–10a | 44, 71 |
| "post 9:2" | 142, 144–45, 148, 154–55, 157 | 1:10b–2:18 | 44, 71 |
| | | 2:29–38 | 28 |
| 10 | 148 | 4:26–35 | 95 |
| | | 4:32–35 | 28 |
| **2 Chronicles** | | 4:36–61 | 95 |
| 29:9 | 52 | 5:24–27 | 94 |
| | | 6:1–6 | 95 |
| **1 Esdras** | | 6:11 | 28 |
| 6:7 | 49 | 10:1–8 | 95 |
| | | 10:1–9 | 95 |
| **Tobit** | | 11:1–12 | 95 |
| 14:4–5 | 174 | 11:6 | 95 |
| 14:4–7 | 52 | 11:6–12 | 95 |
| | | 11:22–33 | 99 |
| **1 Maccabees** | | | |
| 1:41–64 | 95 | **Sirach** | |
| 2:1–14 | 160 | 2:1–5 | 33 |
| 2:15–27 | 160 | 24:1–34 | 16 |
| 2:27 | 160 | 38:1–15 | 187 |
| 2:29–38 | 28 | 38:14 | 187 |
| 2:42–43 | 160 | 44:20 | 175 |
| 2:45–47 | 160 | | |
| 2:52 | 175 | **Psalms of Solomon** | 52 |
| 2:61 | 116 | | |
| 2:67–68 | 160 | **Habakuk** | |
| 3:10–12 | 94 | 3:19 | 117 |
| 3:13–26 | 94 | | |
| 4:13 | 160 | **Jeremiah** | |
| 4:30 | 160 | 36 | 43, 70, 197 |
| 4:36–61 | 95 | 36:1–23 | 45–48 |
| 4:46 | 190 | 36:26 | 57 |
| 9:27 | 190 | 36:28 | 49 |

## INDEX OF BIBLICAL AND RELATED LITERATURE

| | | | |
|---|---|---|---|
| 36:32 | 57 | 3:61 | 118 |
| | | 3:83–87 | 118 |
| **Baruch** | 52, 67–69 | 3:85 | 117 |
| | | 3:85–86 | 118 |
| **Ep.Jer** | 48–54, 59, 69 | | |
| | | **Theodotion Daniel** | 108–10, 117–20, 122 |
| **Susanna** | | 3:26–45 | 118 |
| 5 | 119 | 3:28 | 122 |
| 22 | 121 | 3:34 | 122 |
| 29 | 122 | 3:41 | 122 |
| 32 | 121 | | |
| 34 | 122 | **Bel and the Dragon** | |
| 35–36 | 121 | 1 | 117–18 |
| 45 | 110 | 4–7 | 50 |
| 60–62 | 122 | 5–7 | 111 |
| 63 | 123 | 6 | 115 |
| | | 7 | 112 |
| **LXX Daniel** | 108–23 | 13–22 | 112 |
| 1–12 | 110, 116 | 19 | 112 |
| 3 | 116–17 | 24 | 115 |
| 3:29 | 118 | 24–25 | 111 |
| 3:32–33 | 108 | 25 | 112 |
| 3:38 | 108 | 27 | 112 |
| 3:40 | 116 | 27 | 111–12 |
| 3:41–43 | 118 | 31–42 | 116 |
| 3:45 | 118 | 32 | 115 |
| 3:53–55 | 118 | 33–39 | 114 |
| 3:57–58 | 118 | | |

### Pseudepigrapha

| | | | |
|---|---|---|---|
| *Assumption of Moses* | 52 | 83:1–2 | 93 |
| | | 84–90 | 67 |
| *2 Baruch* | 52, 55–65 | 85:1–2 | 93 |
| 78–86 | 5–62, 70 | 85–90 | 91–102 |
| | | 89–90 | 52 |
| *1 Enoch* | | 90:6–19 | 198 |
| 1–36 | 100 | 91:1–3 | 93 |
| 1:2 | 93 | 91:11–17 | 52 |
| 15:1–16:4 | 100 | 92–105 | 93 |
| 15:8 | 100 | 93:1–10 | 52, 67 |
| 37–71 | 100 | 106–107 | 93 |
| 81:5–82:3 | 93 | 108 | 93 |
| 82:1–2 | 93 | | |
| 83–84 | 94 | *4 Esdras* | 52 |

| | | | |
|---|---|---|---|
| ***Jubilees*** | 52, 67 | 4:11 | 62 |
| 1:9–18 | 52 | 5:1–6:10 | 62 |
| 10 | 100 | 6:1 | 62 |
| 23:8–32 | 91 | 6:11–13 | 62 |
| 32:21 | 91 | 6:13–14 | 62 |
| 36:1–11 | 91 | 6:17–23 | 62–65, 70 |
| | | 7:1 | 62 |
| ***Paralipomena Jeremiae (4 Baruch)*** | 59 | 7:9 | 59 |
| 3:9–10 | 62 | 7:23–29 | 62–65, 70 |
| 3:15–16 | 62 | | |

## Dead Sea Scrolls

| | | | |
|---|---|---|---|
| **1QpHab** | 24, 27, 30–33 | 4QDeut<sup>g</sup> (= 4Q34) | 128 |
| 2:5–10 | 35 | | |
| 2:7–10 | 189 | 4QDeut<sup>h</sup> (= 4Q35) | 128 |
| 3:2–6 | 187, 189 | | |
| 5:4 | 81 | 4QDeut<sup>j</sup> (= 4Q37) | 128–29 |
| 7:1–5 | 35 | | |
| 7:4 | 189 | 4QDeut<sup>k</sup> (= 4Q38) | 128 |
| 11:2–8 | 28 | | |
| | | 4QDeut<sup>n</sup> (= 4Q41) | 128–29, 131–32 |
| **1QH** | | | |
| 12 | 28, 29 | 4QDeut<sup>q</sup> (= 4Q44) | 128 |
| 15:13–19 | 81 | | |
| 12:7–9 | 85 | 4QJosh<sup>a</sup> (= 4Q47) | 141–43, 145–49, 155, 157–59, 162 |
| **1QS** | 79, 86–87 | | |
| 1:21–2:18 | 84 | 4QPhyl G (= 4Q134) | 130–31 |
| 5:1 | 74 | | |
| 5:7–12 | 81 | 4QPhyl N (= 4Q141) | 130 |
| 5:8–9 | 74 | | |
| 6:7–8 | 85 | 4QRP<sup>a</sup> (= 4Q158) | 132 |
| 8:15–16 | 81, 85 | | |
| 9:13 | 41 | 4QpIsa<sup>b</sup> (= 4Q162) | 24, 30 |
| 9:13–14 | 81 | 2:1 | 25 |
| 9:18–20 | 81 | | |
| | | 4Qpap pIsa<sup>c</sup> (= 4Q163) | 23 |
| **1QS<sup>a</sup> (=1Q28a)** | | | |
| 2:4 | 161 | 4QpHos<sup>a</sup> (= 4Q166) | |
| 2:1–2 | 161 | 2:1–7 | 33 |
| 2:4–9 | 86 | | |
| | | 4QpNah (= 4Q169) | 27, 34 |
| **1QM (=1Q33)** | 28, 36 | 2:10 | 25 |

# INDEX OF BIBLICAL AND RELATED LITERATURE

| | | | |
|---|---|---|---|
| 4QpPs$^a$ (= 4Q171) | 24 | 4QZodiology and Brontology ar | |
| 2:2–12 | 33 | (= 4Q318) | 80 |
| 3:11–13 | 33 | | |
| | | 4QReworked Pentateuch$^b$ | |
| 4QMidrEschat$^a$ (= 4Q174, 4QFlor) | 24, 86 | (= 4Q364) | 131–34, 136 |
| 2:3 | 122 | 4QReworked Pentateuch$^c$ | |
| 4:1ff. | 33 | (= 4Q365) | 132, 134, 136–37 |
| 9:9ff. | 33 | | |
| | | 4QTemple? (= 4Q365a) | 137 |
| 4QMidrEschat$^a$? (= 4Q178 1:1) | 122 | | |
| | | 4QReworked Pentateuch$^d$ | |
| 4QEnoch$^e$ ar (= 4Q206) | | (= 4Q366) | 132, 134–37 |
| 4 III:15–89:27 | 97 | | |
| | | 4QRP$^e$ (= 4Q367) | 132 |
| 4QpsDan$^a$ ar (= 4Q243) | 91, 110 | | |
| | | 4QApocrJerC$^a$ (= 4Q385a) | 65–66, 69 |
| 4QpsDan$^{b-c}$ ar (= 4Q244–245) | 91, 110 | | |
| | | 4QapocrJerC$^b$ (= 4Q387) | 67 |
| 4QapocrDan ar (= 4Q246) | 110 | | |
| | | 4QApocrJerC$^d$ (= 4Q389) | 65–67, 68 |
| 4QHalakha A (= 4Q251) | | | |
| 2–3:17 | 40 | 4QT$^b$ (= 4Q524) | 137 |
| | | 15–22:4 | 40 |
| *Damascus Document* (CD) | 28, 39, 52, 67, 79 (*see also* 4Q270–271) | 4QDanSuz?ar (= 4Q551) | 100 |
| 3:12–16 | 81 | | |
| 4:2–3 | 74 | 4QFour Kingdoms$^{a-b}$ar | |
| 4:12–17 | 39, 197 | (= 4Q552–553) | 110 |
| 4:17–5:11 | 39, 41 | | |
| 5:1 | 39 | 4QMMT | 38, 86, 140 |
| 5:8 | 40 | | |
| 5:9–10 | 40 | *Song of the Sabbath Sacrifice* | 79 |
| 12:21 | 41 | | |
| | | 11Q13 (=11QMelch) | |
| 4QD$^e$ (= 4Q270) 7 1:13–14 | 84 | 2:18 | 122 |
| 5:16 | 139 | | |
| | | 11QT$^a$ | 37–38, 136–40 |
| 4QD$^f$ (= 4Q271) | | 50:12 | 36 |
| 3:9–10 | 139 | 60:16–17 | 40 |

## Ancient Jewish and Rabbinic Literature

**Aristobulus** 181

**Babylonian Talmud**
'Arak. 61
B. Roš. Haš. 31a 129
Giṭ. 83a 40
Ḥag. 13b 59
Meg. 14b–15a 57
Sanh. 11 44
Sanh. 76b 40
Ta'an. 29a 61
Yebam. 13:2, 13c 40
Yebam. 62b 40
Zev. 116b 38

**Jerusalem Talmud**
Ḥag. 2:2 44
Ma'aś. Š. 5:6 44
Meg. 3:6, 74b 129
Sanh. 1:2 44
Sanh. 6:9 44

**Josephus, *Jewish Antiquities***
12.6.6 40, 49, 51
12.138–144 51
12.145–146 51
12.147–153 51
17.149–167 59

**Josephus, *War***
1.648–655 59
3.123 59
5.48 59
6.249–250 60
6.316 59

**Maimonides, *H. Bet ha-Beḥirah***
7:14 38

*Mekilta*
1 57

*Midrash Tanḥuma* (*MHG*)
Deut 26:13 44

**Mishnah**
Tamid 5:1 129

***Numbers Rabbah***
7:8 38

**Passover Papyrus** 44, 60, 71

**Philo** 49, 52

**Pseudo-Philo**
106 98

***Seder 'Olam Rabbah***
20 57

***Sifre Numbers***
78 57

***Sifre Numbers Naso***
1 38

***Targum Jonathan***
(Jer 10:11) 54–55

**Tosefta**
Kelim B. Qam. 1:12 38
Sanh. 2:6 44, 57
Ta'an. 29a 61

## New Testament

**Luke**
24:31 — 11

**John**
1:3 — 16
1:14 — 16
6:68 — 11

**Acts**
15:23–29 — 60

**Romans**
1:1 — 64
7:24–25 — 11

**Hebrews**
1:1 — 14

**1 Thessalonians**
1:1 — 58

**Titus**
1:1 — 64

**2 Peter**
1:1 — 64

**Revelation**
10:10 — 16

## Classical Literature

**Aeschylus,** *Agamemnon*
113 — 59

***Anthologia palatina***
9.223 — 59
9.265 — 59

**Callimachus,** *Hymns*
1:68 — 59

**Homer,** *Iliad*
8.245–252 — 59
24.292–298 — 59
24.310–312 — 59

**Pindar,** *Pythionikai*
1:13 — 59

**Pindar,** *Isthmionikai*
6:50 — 59

# INDEX OF AUTHORS

| | | | |
|---|---|---|---|
| Abegg, Martin G., Jr. | 67, 143 | Carroll, Robert P. | 46 |
| Abraham, William J. | 16 | Charlesworth, James | 26–28, 34 |
| Abrams, Dominic | 32 | Chazon, Esther | 161–62 |
| Africanus, Julius | 109 | Childs, Brevard S. | 10 |
| Albertz, Rainer | 167–72 | Churgin, Pinkhos | 54 |
| Allegro, John M. | 24 | Cohen, Shaye J. D. | 44 |
| Applegate, John | 47 | Collins, John J. | 30, 58–59, 115 |
| Augustine | 11 | Crawford, *see* White Crawford | |
| Barth, Karl | 11 | Daumas, François | 188 |
| Bauckham, Richard | 56 | Deissmann, Adolf | 63 |
| Baumgarten, Joseph M. | 28–29, 39 | Delling, Gerhard | 56 |
| Bayer, Oswald | 17 | DeSilva, David A. | 109 |
| Bengtsson, Håkan | 28 | De Troyer, Kristin | 141, 152, 157, 160, 199–200 |
| Berger, Peter | 78 | | |
| Bernstein, Moshe | 37 | DiLella, Alexander A. | 187 |
| Berrin, Shani L. | 24 | Dimant, Devorah | 24, 65–67 |
| Bickerman, Elias | 51, 160 | Doering, Lutz | 65–66, 197 |
| Blenkinsopp, Joseph | 183 | Dorival, Gilles | 45 |
| Blum, Erhard | 168–69, 171 | Doudna, Gregory | 27 |
| Boda, Mark J. | 174, 176 | Downing, F. Gerald | 52, 75 |
| Bogaert, Pierre-Maurice | 55–62, 64 | Duhm, Bernhard | 184 |
| Brenton, Charles Lee | 144 | Duncan, Julie A. | 128, 130 |
| Brooke, George J. | 25–27, 30, 33–34, 77, 84, 110, 130, 197–98 | | |
| | | Ego, Beate | 176, 200 |
| Brownlee, William H. | 24, 31, 33 | Elliot, John H. | 27 |
| Bryan, David J. | 52 | Ellis, E. Earle | 35 |
| Burke, David G. | 68 | Engel, Helmut | 109, 119–20 |
| Burrows, Millar | 24 | Exler, Francis X. J. | 63 |
| Busto Saiz, José | 120 | | |
| | | Fabry, Heinz-Josef | 146, 149, 151–53, 157 |
| Callaway, Phillip R. | 27 | | |
| Calvin, John | 11 | Finkel, Asher | 187 |
| Campbell, Jonathan G. | 67 | Fischer, Irmtraut | 168, 171 |
| Capper, Brian J. | 73 | Fishbane, Michael | 150–52, 165, 186–87 |

| | | | |
|---|---|---|---|
| Frei, Hans | 6 | Kaiser, Otto | 68 |
| Frey, Jörg | 61 | Kant, Immanuel | 13 |
| | | Karrer, Martin | 54, 58, 64 |
| Gafni, Isaiah M. | 53 | Kay, David M. | 108 |
| Gangert, Jörg-Dieter | 51 | Killp, Nelson | 46 |
| García Martínez, Florentino | 24, 85, 161 | Klauck, Hans-Josef | 56, 83 |
| Gaster, Moses | 109 | Klijn, Albertus Frederik J. | 56, 58 |
| Gese, Hartmut | 106, 171, 177 | Knibb, Michael | 52, 60, 69 |
| Gilbert, Maurice | 118 | Koch, Klaus | 108–9, 118 |
| Goldenstein, Johannes | 172–73 | Köckert, Matthias | 171 |
| Goldstein, Jonathan A. | 68 | Koskenniemi, Heikki | 63 |
| Goode, Erich | 73 | Kottsieper, Ingo | 108, 115, 118 |
| Gordon, Cyrus H. | 188 | Kraabel, A. Thomas | 52 |
| Gosse, Bernard | 167–68 | Kratz, Reinhard Gregor | 48–54 |
| Griel, Arthur | 83 | Krüger, Thomas | 166 |
| Grossman, Maxine L. | 28 | Kuhrt, Amélie | 51 |
| Gruen, Erich S. | 52 | | |
| Gunneweg, Antonius H. J. | 48, 68 | Lange, Armin | 11, 67, 110, 176, 184–86, 189, 200–201 |
| Hacham, Noah | 29 | Larson, Erik | 40 |
| Hamann, Johan Georg | 13 | Lauha, Aarre | 187 |
| Hamm, Winnfried | 109 | Lebram, Jürgen | 109 |
| Hardmeier, Christoph | 165, 171, 178 | Leemhuis, Fred | 56 |
| Harl, Marguerite | 45 | Lehmann, Manfred R. | 40 |
| Harnish, Wolfgang | 60–61 | Lessing, Gotthold Ephraim | 7 |
| Harris, J. Rendel | 62 | Levinson, Bernard M. | 151 |
| Hayward, Robert | 54–55 | Lieu, Judith M. | 58 |
| Hegel, Wilhelm Friedrich | 12 | Lim, Timothy H. | 28–29, 34, 82, 187 |
| Helbling, Dominik | 109, 112–13 | Link, Hannelore | 50 |
| Helmer, Christine | 8–10, 17, 195, 198 | Livingstone, Alasdaire | 188 |
| Heppe, Heinrich | 6 | Llewellyn, S. R. | 43 |
| Herder, Johannes Gottfried | 13 | Lloyd, Alan B. | 188 |
| Herzer, Jens | 62–64 | Lofland, John | 74–76, 78, 80, 86, 198 |
| Hieronymus | 108 | Lombard, Peter | 11 |
| Himbaza, Innocent | 130 | Lücke, Friedrich | 6 |
| Hogg, Michael A. | 32 | | |
| Horgan, Maurya P. | 24–27, 35 | McKane, William | 185 |
| | | Martínez, see García Martínez | |
| Ishida, Tomoo | 175 | Mathias, Dieter | 174, 176 |
| | | Matza, David | 75 |
| Janzen, J. Gerald | 170 | Mein, Andrew | 169 |
| Janowski, Bernd | 8 | Milgrom, Jacob | 37 |
| Jokiranta, Jutta | 196 | Milik, Józef Tadeusz | 94, 109, 130 |
| Jowett, Benjamin | 4 | Mittmann-Richert, Ulrike | 25, 67, 104, 108–10, 117–18, 121, 198–99 |

# INDEX OF AUTHORS

Moore, Carey A.  50, 53, 68, 108–9, 111, 118
Munnich, Olivier  45
Myers, Jacob M.  176

Najman, Hindi  37
Naumann, Wiegand  51
Newman, Judith H.  175–78
Nickelsburg, George W. E.  48–49, 51, 93–94, 99
Niebuhr, Karl-Wilhelm  43, 49–50, 53, 60
Nir, Rivka  56
Nitzan, Bilhah  26

Oeming, Manfred  175
Oetinger, Christoph  17
Oppenheim, A. Leo  188
O'Regan, Cyril  12
Origen  109
Osswald, Eva  186

Plöger, Otto  109
Porten, Bezalel  44
Pröbstl, Volker  174–76
Puech, Émile  40, 137

Qimron, Elisha  36, 39
Quast, Udo  148

Rabin, Chaim  40
Rabinowitz, Isaac  187
Rahlfs, Alfred  144, 148
Rambo, Lewis R.  74–75, 77–78, 82–83
Ramisch, *see* Walker-Ramisch
Regev, Eyal  139
Richert, *see* Mittmann-Richert
Römer, Thomas  167–68
Rudolph, Wilhelm  175
Rudy, David  83
Ruwe, Andreas  166
Rüger, Hans-Peter  108

Saiz, *see* Busto Saiz
Sanders, E. P.  82
Scalise, Pamela  46–47
Schalit, Abraham  51
Schaller, Bernd  62–64
Schiffman, Lawrence H.  35–37, 39–41, 81, 130, 196–97
Schleiermacher, Friedrich  6–9, 13–14, 18, 196
Schmid, Heinrich  6
Schmid, Konrad  46
Schnider, Franz  43–44
Schottroff, Willy  173
Schreiner, Joseph  51, 68
Schürer, Emil  54, 104
Schwiderski, Dirk  45, 48
Scott, James  52
Seebass, Horst  171
Segal, Michael  132, 134
Seitz, Christopher  46
Seybold, Klaus  30
Sherwin-White, Susan  51
Siegert, Folkert  46
Silbermann, Lou H.  187
Skehan, Patrick W.  187
Sollamo, Raija  23
Sperber, Alexander  54
Sperling, S. David  44
Spiegelberg, Wilhelm  188
Stark, Rodney  74–76, 78, 80, 86, 198
Steck, Odil Hannes  68–69, 169–70, 173, 190
Stegemann, Hartmut  73, 83
Steudel, Annette  25
Stenger, Werner  43–44
Steussy, Marti Jo  108, 114, 119–20
Strugnell, John  132
Stuckenbruck, Loren  198, 200
Styers, Randall  181
Sussman, Ya'acov  38

Taatz, Irene  43–44, 56, 58, 63–64
Talmon, Shemaryahu  25, 28–29, 39
Tcherikover, Victor  160
Thiel, Winfried  43, 46
Tigchelaar, Eibert J. C.  24, 161
Tiller, Patrick A.  94–95, 98

| | | | |
|---|---|---|---|
| Tov, Emanuel | 68, 131–32, 136, 151 | Weinfeld, Moshe | 37, 129 |
| Trapp, Michael | 48 | Werline, Rodney Alan | 174 |
| Trevor, John C. | 24 | Westermann, Claus | 171 |
| Tropper, Joseph | 173 | White, *see* Sherwin-White | |
| Troyer, *see* De Troyer | | White Crawford, Sidnie | 130, 133–34, 136–37, 199 |
| Tsuji, Manabu | 43, 57 | Whitters, Mark F. | 43–44, 55–56, 59–60, 62 |
| Uchelen, Nico Adriaan van | 170 | Williamson, Hugh G. M. | 183 |
| Ullman, Chana | 83 | Wise, Michael O. | 27 |
| Ulrich, Eugene | 77, 136, 141, 143, 145–48, 155–56, 158 | Wolff, Christian | 44, 47, 57–58, 60, 62 |
| Unnik, Willem C. van | 53 | Wright, Nicholas T. | 52 |
| | | Wysny, Andreas | 108–9, 114–15 |
| VanderKam, James | 84 | | |
| Van Seters, John | 171 | Xeravits, Géza | 25, 34 |
| van Uchelen, *see* Uchelen | | | |
| Vermes, Geza | 74, 81, 84 | Yadin, Yigael | 36–37, 138–39 |
| Volten, Aksel | 188 | Yardeni, Ada | 44 |
| Walker-Ramisch, Sandra | 30 | Ziegler, Josef | 48 |
| Wanke, Günther | 185 | Zimmerli, Walther | 166 |

www.ingramcontent.com/pod-product-compliance
Lightning Source LLC
Chambersburg PA
CBHW030341240426
43661CB00052B/1708